W9-APY-949

THE REGIONS OF THE WORLD

EDITED BY

H. J. MACKINDER, M. A.

Reader in Geography in the
University of Oxford

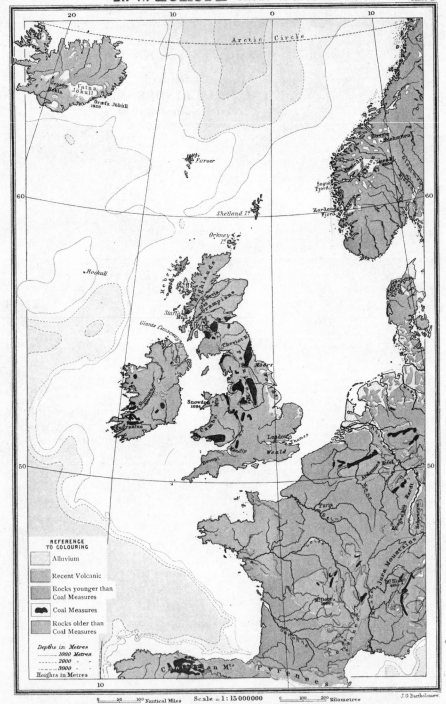

N.W. EUROPE BATHY-GEOLOGICAL

Plate 1.

Arctic Circle

Geyser
Hekla
Vatna Jökull
Oræfa Jökull 1959

Faroer

Shetland Iˢ

Orkney Iˢ

Rockall

Hebrides
Highlands
Staffa
Ben Nevis
Grampians
Giants Causeway
Cheviot Hˢ
Moors

Snowdon 1094
Connemara
Cambrian Mtˢ
London
Thames
Macgillicuddy
Mendip
Weald
Devon

Dovre
Trondhjem
Jostedal
Sogne Fjord
Hardanger Fjord
Glommen

Ardennes
Eifel
Moselle
Vosges
Schwarzwald

Paris

Puy de Dôme
M. Dore
Jura Mountains
Mt Blanc 4810
Rhone
Garonne
Cevennes
Cantabrian Mtˢ
Pyrenees

REFERENCE TO COLOURING

Alluvium

Recent Volcanic

Rocks younger than Coal Measures

Coal Measures

Rocks older than Coal Measures

Depths in Metres
.... 1000 Metres
--------- 2000 -
········· 3000 -
Heights in Metres

0 50 100 Nautical Miles
Scale = 1 : 15 000 000
0 100 200 Kilometres

J.G.Bartholomew

BRITAIN

AND THE

BRITISH SEAS

BY

H. J. MACKINDER, M.A.

STUDENT OF CHRIST CHURCH
READER IN GEOGRAPHY IN THE UNIVERSITY OF OXFORD
PRINCIPAL OF READING COLLEGE

With Maps and Diagrams

GREENWOOD PRESS, PUBLISHERS
WESTPORT, CONNECTICUT

Originally published in 1902
by D. Appleton and Company

First Greenwood Reprinting 1969

SBN 8371-2754-8

PRINTED IN UNITED STATES OF AMERICA

PREFACE

THE idea of this book was first suggested to me by the needs of some foreign students visiting Britain, but when my publishers proposed a description of the world, my scheme was expanded to twelve volumes by different authors. The aim of each is to present a picture of the physical features and condition of a great natural region, and to trace their influence upon human societies.

Of the twelve selected divisions, Britain is the smallest, and is known in such detail that it has been possible to attempt a complete geographical synthesis. The phenomena of topographical distribution relating to many classes of fact have been treated, but from a single standpoint and on a uniform method.

It is obvious that in a work involving the accurate statement of data so various, some amount of help from students in kindred subjects is essential. Two of my colleagues at Oxford and Reading, Mr. H. N. Dickson and Dr. T. T. Groom, have very kindly read the proof, the one of Chapters III., IV., X., and XI., the other of Chapters VI., VII., and VIII. They have made several important contributions, but have no responsibility whatever for any errors into which I may have fallen. To Mr. J. L. Myres and to Major P. G. Craigie I am indebted for sources of information pertinent to Chapters XII. and XIX. respectively. My gratitude is also due to my Wife and to my friend, Mr. W. M. Childs, for correcting portions of the proof.

Most of the diagrams in the text have been executed

by the Diagram Company—some by Mr. B. B. Dickinson, but a majority by Mr. A. W. Andrews. A few, however, were designed by Mr. B. V. Darbishire. The coloured maps have been drawn specially for this book by Mr. G. J. Bartholomew. I wish to thank all of these gentlemen for the pains they have taken.

The notes on authorities at the ends of the chapters are intended merely to remind students of some accessible books dealing at large with topics here touched upon. Only in the case of a few statements has it been felt necessary to refer to original papers.

H. J. M.

October 1901.

CONTENTS

LIST OF ILLUSTRATIONS

COLOURED MAPS

MAPS AND DIAGRAMS

The figures marked with the initials B.B.D. are by Mr. Dickinson, and those with the initials B.V.D. by Mr. Darbishire. The remainder are by Mr. Andrews. The outlines of ancient land and sea in figs. 55, 56, 57 follow the suggestions of Jukes-Browne in his *Building of the British Isles*, but with certain changes and the addition of names.

LIST OF ILLUSTRATIONS XV

BRITAIN AND THE
BRITISH SEAS

CHAPTER I

THE POSITION OF BRITAIN

"England . . . that utmost corner of the West."—*King John*, ii. 1.

BEFORE the great geographical discoveries of the fifteenth and sixteenth centuries, the known lands lay almost wholly in the Northern Hemisphere and spread in a single continent from the shores of Spain to those of Cathay. Britain was then at the end of the world—almost out of the world. At one point her white cliffs might be seen from the mainland, and from this she stretched, northward and westward, away from the life of Europe, to the dark rocks and bird-haunted skerries where the Celt listened to the waves rolling in from the unknown. No philosophy of British history can be entirely true which does not take account of this fact. During two thousand years Britain was at the margin, not in the centre, of the theatre of politics, and for most practical purposes her position was accurately shown in the maps of the Greek geographers (Figs. 2, 8) and in the fantastic charts of the mediæval monks (Figs. 1, 8a).

The historical meaning of the Columbian discoveries can best be realised by turning a terrestrial globe so that Britain may be at the point nearest to the eye (Fig. 3). Europe, Asia, Africa, and the two Americas are thus included within the visible hemisphere; but the chief feature even of the land-half of the globe is a great arm of mediterranean ocean, Atlantic and Arctic, winding northward through the midst of the lands to encircle the pole, and to end beyond on the shores of Alaska and Siberia. There, across the narrow and shallow Bering Strait, the

FIG. 1.—Thirteenth Century Map preserved in Hereford Cathedral, showing the terminal position of Britain in the then known world. A key to the map is given on p. 13. The names Africa and Europe are transposed in the original, but have been corrected in the key.

mountains of America are visible from the Asiatic coast and the ocean-end is almost land-girt. The southern entry, from the water hemisphere, is an ocean-bay between Cape Horn and the Cape of Good Hope, which narrows

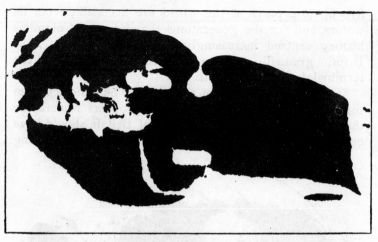

FIG. 2.—The World according to Eratosthenes, showing the terminal
position of Britain.—*After* BUNBURY.

somewhat towards the Equator, and is there half-closed
by the western wing of Africa. A wide passage is left,
some fifteen hundred miles in breadth, which leads into
the triangular basin of the North Atlantic, essentially only
the vastest of lakes. Two of the sides are the coasts of
South and North America, where they recede into the
West Indian Gulf; the third is the edge of Europe and
Africa northward and southward of the Strait of Gibraltar.
No flat chart can give a correct impression of the form of
the North Atlantic. Only a globe can suggest its vast
bulging centre, and the relative insignificance of its Arctic,
Mediterranean, and Caribbean recesses (Fig 4). A broad
channel, with parallel shores trending north-eastward,
connects the North Atlantic with the Polar Sea. Iceland
stands in the midst of this entry; Greenland defines it
on the one hand, and Britain and Scandinavia on the
other. Practically, however, this, like Davis Strait, is a
mere gulf of the North Atlantic, extending only to the
edge of the ice-pack. For most purposes, therefore, the
North Atlantic is a rounded basin, with eastward, northward, and westward gulfs, and a southern exit. But the

five historic parts of the world are accessible from its waters, and for the generations that followed Columbus history centred increasingly round its shores. Thus Britain gradually became the central, rather than the terminal, land of the world.

Two natural ways seem, therefore, to be indicated from the Old World to the New, and it appears remarkable that the change in the relations of Britain should have been so long deferred. On the one hand, by following

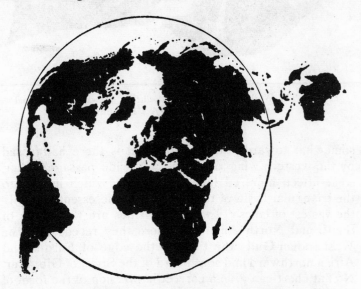

FIG. 3.—The Land Hemisphere, showing the Mediterranean Ocean and the central position of Britain.

the coasts of Europe and Africa southward, a way appears to open diagonally across the Equator to the eastern angle of South America—a way actually followed in the second Portuguese voyage round the Cape to the Indies. On the other hand, a course is marked out from Britain to Greenland, by the Faroe Islands and Iceland, and thence by Labrador to the eastern angle of North America: a course, as the Icelandic Sagas tell us, followed nine hundred years ago by the Norse Vikings. The map alone,

the mere lie of the coasts, cannot explain why the southern road was not found until after the longer westward
voyage of Columbus; and why the Norsemen so far failed
to utilise their discovery of the northern road, that the
very record of it was almost forgotten. The causes
which limited human enterprise were, in the main, climatic.

In the ninth century the Viking Othere, as he told

FIG. 4.—Photograph of a globe showing the true form
of the North Atlantic.

King Alfred,[1] had already found the open waterway past
the mouths of the Norwegian fiords into the region of the
midnight sun, and round the North Cape into the seas of
the walrus. Even in the depth of the mid-winter night
no iceberg approaches the Scandinavian coasts; for a
great bay of relatively warm air and water passes by Britain from the North Atlantic, between Iceland and Norway,

[1] For a convenient translation of Othere's narrative, together with notes,
see Nordenskiöld, "The Voyage of the *Vega*," chap. i.

to the coasts of Spitsbergen and Nova Zembla (Fig. 5).
Between these islands is the edge of the northern pack,
advancing in some seasons southward, and in others receding, but always leaving a broad lane of open water
off Norway and Lapland.   To the west of Spitsbergen
there is a narrower lane by which the steam yachts of
to-day occasionally penetrate to within ten degrees of the
pole ; but to westward of this again is the edge of the pack,

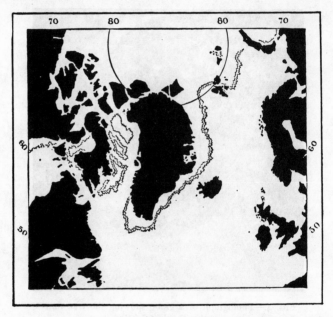

FIG. 5.—The entry to the Arctic Sea, showing the minimum extent
of ice-impeded water off Greenland.

spreading without break to the front of ice-clad Greenland.
Here is the outflow from the Arctic Basin, through which,
as was shown by the voyage of Nansen, an endless supply of convergent floes is drawn, even from the far coasts
of America and Asia. In slow procession they pass southward along the East Greenland coast, reinforced by great
bergs from the neighbouring glaciers, through Denmark
Strait, across twenty degrees of latitude, to turn Cape

Farewell under the parallel of the Shetland Islands. Two facts give some indication of the character and efficacy of the ice-barrier which shielded America from Europe precisely where the passage from the one to the other is shortest. In 1869 a German exploring ship, the *Hansa*, was caught in the ice under north latitude 74° and sunk. Her crew took refuge on a floe, and in eight months were carried southward eight hundred miles, and finally made their way to the Danish settlements on the west coast. On the 11th of June, 1888, Nansen sighted the highlands of Greenland under latitude 65°, at a distance of about sixty miles. He battled with the ice for seven weeks, effecting a landing only on the 29th of July, under latitude 62°, having been within sight of land the whole time —often not more than ten or twelve miles away—while he was carried to leeward, down the stream, nearly two hundred miles.[1] The ice-stream pours on for some distance along the west coast of Greenland, then bends southward and, having received a tributary from Baffin Bay, passes by the Labrador coast, across the entry to the Strait of Belle Isle, and leaves its stranded bergs on the shores of Newfoundland. The cold water mingles finally with the warm amid the fogs of the Great Bank, and in the spring and early summer—when the ice burden is heaviest and stray bergs reach their most southern latitude—the great liners which work the ferry between Liverpool and New York deflect their course southward to avoid the risks of collision. It was this ice-stream which was the physical boundary of mediæval Europe.

The passage south-westward from Africa to South America was closed to the early coasters by very different causes. In the sub-tropical regions, which lie south of the Mediterranean latitudes, there is a belt of some twenty degrees where the trade-winds blow steadily from the northeast (Fig. 6). This belt swings somewhat northward and southward in harmony with the seasons; but there is a breadth of ten degrees, known as the "heart of the trades,"

[1] For an account of the long series of efforts to penetrate the ice off East Greenland, see Nansen, "The First Crossing of Greenland," chap. x.

within which the north-east winds never fail.   The trade-winds are dry, and the moisture they drink from the land is only sparingly returned in rare storms.   Beneath them the great desert of Sahara stretches from shore to shore of Northern Africa, and divides the black men from the white.   Spreading almost to America, to the westward, is an invisible extension of the Sahara—a belt within

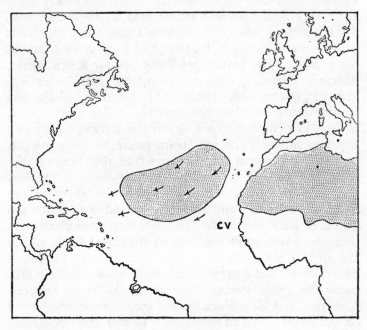

Fig. 6.—Diagram of the North Atlantic and Northern Africa.

C V=Cape Verde.
⤡ =Trade Wind.

{ On Land=Desert.
{ On Sea=Exceptionally salt surface.

which the surface of the sea is a little salter than else-where—an oceanic desert, where the trade-winds take fresh water from the salt sea, and shed no compensating rain.   Three months were needed to cross the Sahara on camel-back; the high seas were counted impassable; while the clumsy coaster, incapable of sailing near the wind, could not venture southward on a current which would never veer to bring her home.   For a thousand miles the brown edge of the desert offered neither water nor food, and the name "Cape Verde" stands for all time to mark the joy of the Portuguese explorers when they first saw the vegetation of the south.   The trade-wind and its deserts were the true southern boundary of mediæval Europe. Columbus, by brilliant inspiration, committed himself to the trade-wind on his outward voyage, but shaped his return on the prevalent westerly breezes of a more northern latitude, thus breaking the secular spell which had closed the ocean-path.

In pre-Columbian times, then, Britain lay off the western shore of the world, almost precisely midway between the North Cape and the coast of Barbary, the northern and southern limits of the known.   Northward and westward was the ice; south-westward lay a waste of waters; southward, beyond the Mediterranean, was the great desert.   Only eastward and south-eastward did the world of men spread far through the known into the half-known, and only in those directions was Britain related to opposing coasts.   But, as though in compensation, those very coasts had an almost unique character, facilitating to a remarkable degree intercourse between the continent and the island.   The fiords of Norway, the Baltic gulfs, the great series of navigable rivers from the Neva to the Tagus, and all the intricacy of the Mediterranean— extending almost to Indian seas—gave inevitably a maritime aspect to European civilisation; and though Britain was insular, yet Europe was at least peninsular, and the English belonged naturally to the European group of nations. Madagascar, on the other hand, off the unbroken coast of Bantu Africa, was controlled—until France intervened—by Malayan Hovas, and belonged, for many purposes, rather to remote Australasia than to the neighbouring continent.

How important for Britain was the coastal intricacy of Europe is indicated by the fact that the shipping of the Middle Ages belonged for the most part not to the English, despite their immigrant history, but to the inhabitants

of the mainland. For many centuries the English were
a race of shepherds rather than mariners, and the most
significant feature of British geography was not the
limitless ocean, but the approach of the south-eastern
corner of the islands to within sight of the continent.
Kent was the window by which England looked into the
great world, and the foreground of that world, visible
from Dover Castle, had no ordinary character. Immedi-

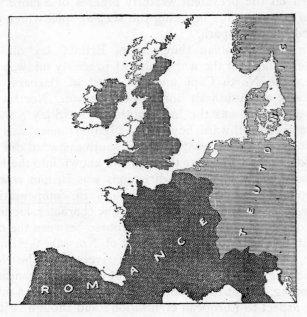

FIG. 7.—Western Europe, showing the Linguistic Frontier
between the Teutonic and Romance Peoples.

ately to the east of Calais is the end of the linguistic frontier which, crossing Europe from south to north, divides
the two great races, Romance and Teutonic, whose interaction has made European history (Fig. 7). From Calais
eastward, in succession, were nations of Germanic sea-
men,—Flemings, Hollanders, Frieslanders, Hansards, and
Vikings. Westward was the Frenchman, and behind him
the Spaniard and the Italian. To the Teutons—" Easter-

lings" and "Norsemen"—England owes her civil institutions and her language; to the peoples of the west and
south, her Christianity and her scholarship. Two distinct
streams of ethical and artistic influence converged upon
the island from the Rhine delta and from the estuary of
the Seine; and the balanced English character has therefore a physical counterpart in the symmetry of the eastern
and southern shores pivoted on the Kentish forelands.

Behind Europe, and seen through Europe as through
a coloured glass, lay the imagined wealth of the Indies;
and it is not without significance that the lie of the
physical features—gulfs, rivers, and peninsulas—drew the
great roads from the Indies north-westward through
Persia, Mesopotamia, and Egypt—by the Danube, the
Adriatic, and the Rhone—to Flanders and Paris, and so
to Kent and to London.

Seen thus in relation to earlier and to later history,
Britain is possessed of two geographical qualities, complementary rather than antagonistic: insularity and universality. Before Columbus, the insularity was more
evident than the universality. Within closed coasts,
impregnable when valiantly held, but in sight of the world
and open to stimulus—Teutonic, Romantic, and Oriental
—her people were able to advance with Europe, and
yet, protected from military necessities, to avoid tyranny
and to retain the legacy of freedom bequeathed in the
German forests. Ordered liberty, fitted to the complex
conditions of modern civilisation, needed centuries of
slow experimental growth, and was naturally cradled in
a land insulated yet not isolated.

After Columbus, value began to attach to the ocean-
highway, which is in its nature universal. Even the great
continents are only vast islands and discontinuous; but
every part of the ocean is accessible from every other
part. In the second century of the Christian era Ptolemy,
an Alexandrine Greek, wrote a book which was the
classic of geography a thousand years later. He pictured
the land as continuous and the sea as divided into vast
but separate lakes, Atlantic and Indian (Fig. 8). In such a

world general maritime empire would have been impossible. The unity of the ocean is the simple physical fact underlying the dominant value of sea-power in the modern globe-wide world. Britain—*of* Europe, yet not *in* Europe —was free to devote resources, drawn ultimately from the continent, to the expansion of civilisation beyond the ocean. The sea preserved liberty, and allowed of a fertility of private initiative which was incompatible with supreme military organisation. The same sea, by reducing the reserve of men and material needed for the protection

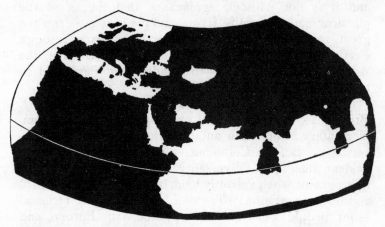

FIG. 8.—The World according to Ptolemy, showing separate Eastern and Western Oceans.—*After* BUNBURY.

of the island home, has permitted the devotion of British initiative and energy to trade and rule abroad. Great consequences lie in the simple statements that Britain is an island group, set in the ocean, but off the shores of the great continent ; that the opposing shores are indented ; and that the domains of two historic races come down to the sea precisely at the narrowest strait between the mainland and the island.

Note on the word "world."—The word "world" has been used throughout this chapter in a more or less technical sense, as equivalent to the Greek "Œcumene" and the Latin "Mundus." Five centuries before the Christian Era, Greek philosophers were aware of the globular form of the earth; they none the less confined the "Habitable World" to a definite area, situated wholly in the Northern Hemisphere and limited eastward and westward by the ocean. It was, in fact, the known continent with its off-set islands. Whether or not there were other "worlds" on the globe, amid the western waters or in the Southern Hemisphere, was a matter of speculation. Christian Fathers denounced the idea of the Antipodes as heretical, but Dante put his Purgatory within the Southern Ocean. The *new* world of America was not, therefore, a chance expression descriptive of mere vastness, but a definite reference to a controversy of long standing.

From another point of view, discoveries have constantly extended the limits of *the* world, until it has become nearly equivalent to the surface of the globe; hence the popular confusion of the terms "world" and "globe." The map of the "world" according to Eratosthenes (Fig. 2) simply ignored the globe, although, as a fact, its author measured the size of the globe by sound methods and, considering his lack of instruments, with remarkable accuracy. Very naturally, therefore, ignorant people, using such charts or others still more conventional (Fig. 1), concluded that the world was flat.

It is necessary to bear these facts in mind in order to appreciate the contrast between "Britain at the end of the world" and "Britain in the midst of the (globe-wide) world." For a discussion of the word and concept "Œcumene," see Bunbury, "History of Ancient Geography," vol. i. chap. xvi., also Ratzel, "Anthropogeographie," vol. ii. chap. i.

FIG. 8A.—Key to Fig. 1.

CHAPTER II

THE BRITISH SEAS

THE clue to many contrasts in British geography is to be found in the opposition of the south-eastern and north-western—the inner and outer faces of the land. Eastward and southward, between the islands and the continent, are the waters known to history as the Narrow Seas [1]; northward and westward is the Ocean. From the forelands of Kent the coasts which face the mainland run with few breaks, and fewer islets, on the one hand northward and somewhat westward for nearly six hundred miles to Caithness, Pentland Firth, and the Orkneys, on the other hand westward and somewhat southward for more than three hundred to Cornwall, the Lizard and Land's End, and the Scilly Isles. Beyond, on the oceanic side, between the Scilly Isles and the Orkneys, is a great curve of jagged coastline, broken into promontories and islands. More than five thousand out of the five thousand five hundred islets said to be contained in the British archipelago are set along its north-western border. The contrast suggests that presented by the islandless, merely embayed Atlantic coast of Patagonia and the fiorded Pacific coast, guarded by innumerable islands.

The south-eastern coasts of Britain are relatively flat, and the occasional cliffs are for the most part merely the cut edges of low table-lands, such as constitute the chalk Wolds and Downs. Lofty cliffs predominate on the oceanic border—cliffs, moreover, which are the scarped ends of slopes rising inland to mountain summits. There is a similar contrast even below the level of the sea,

[1] See note on the Narrow Seas at p. 24.

14

for on the continental side the sea-bed merely undulates, whereas among the islets of the west are deep pits and sudden slopes, in some degree negative equivalents of the mountains on the neighbouring land.

Two of the larger channels which penetrate the oceanic edge of Britain bend inward and join, detaching the great fragment of land which constitutes Ireland. The seas dividing Ireland from Great Britain not only break the continuity of what would otherwise be a single compact British land, but also reduce the greater island to a long, comparatively narrow strip, whose farthest points were so remote in days when travel was costly and slow, that two nations—Scottish and English—arose in the two ends of the land, of like mixture of blood, but of distinct characteristics and often hostile. The British peoples owe much to the narrow seas which have divided them from the continent ; it is, however, not infrequently suggested that they have lost by the seas which have held them apart from one another and impeded fusion. But as liberty is the natural privilege of an island people, so wealth of initiative is characteristic of a divided people. Provinces which are insular or peninsular breed an obstinate provincialism unknown in the merely historical or administrative divisions of a great plain ; and this rooted provincialism, rather than finished cosmopolitanism, is a source of the varied initiative without which liberty would lose half its significance.

The Narrow Seas are the North Sea and the English Channel connected by the Strait of Dover ; but a more important distinction might be drawn between the Narrow and the Narrower Seas (Fig. 9). On either side of the strait, for a distance of more than a hundred miles, the British and the continental coasts are relatively near to each other ; but beyond Holland on the one side, and beyond Normandy on the other, the continent retreats abruptly, leaving space for broader waters, more particularly on the east.

The North Sea is a great rectangle set into the land south-south-eastward between the roughly parallel shores of

Britain and Scandinavia (Plate I.). Midway along its eastern edge the Skager Rak gives entry to the series of inland waters known as the Baltic. Along the southern border, formed by East Anglia in Britain and by Friesland on the Continent, is a second entry, as large as the Skager Rak, but without distinctive name, which curves southward and westward between England and the Netherlands, ending

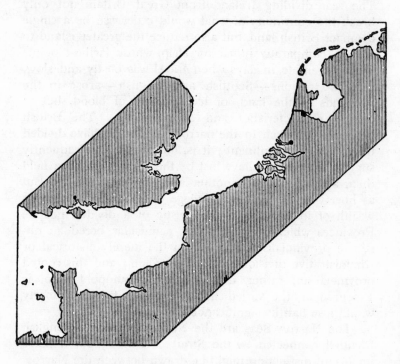

FIG. 9.—The Narrower Seas and the Ferry-towns.

funnel-like in the Strait of Dover. The wide estuary of the Thames imparts to this arm a bifurcate appearance on the chart, while the mouths of the far greater Rhine hardly break its eastern outline.

From Dover Strait the continental coast sweeps again southward and then westward to the estuary of the Seine, giving to the eastern portion of the English Channel a form complementary to that of the nameless arm of the North Sea, and a nearly similar area (Fig. 9). Beyond the Seine the coast of France projects abruptly in the Cotentin peninsula, west of which the outer Channel, with a double breadth, merges with the ocean where the promontories of Cornwall and Brittany stand out, pierlike, into the wider waters.

The Narrow Seas are the strong natural frontier of Britain, but at all times they have been freely traversed, and the islanders have been neighboured by the peoples

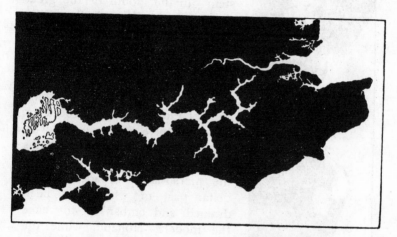

FIG. 10.—South Eastern England and the Sogne Fiord of Norway, drawn to the same scale.

of the opposite shores. For some purposes, at any rate, those opposite shores are the true frontiers of Britain, and no account of the island realm would be complete which ignored their characteristics.

To the north-east is the high table-land of Norway, snow-capped, though washed by an iceless sea (Plate I.). Narrow fiords penetrate far up the valleys, which are deeply scored into the surface of the plateau (Fig. 10). Here and there a sill gives space for a meadow and the home of a Norseman—half farmer, half fisherman—whose only road is by boat on the fiord. He is a Vik-ing, a son of the fiord or wick—in earlier times a restless and piratic neighbour for the tenants of Britain.

South of Norway, across the Skager Rak, the land is low and sandy, clothed with heath and forest, and beset with marshes and intricate tidal channels (Fig. 11). It

is fronted for nearly a thousand miles by a belt of dunes, which range from the northern point of Jutland southward past the old Anglia—now Schleswig and Holstein—to the mouth of the great river Elbe. Beyond the Elbe they are continued westward past the old Saxony—now Hanover—and past Friesland, Holland, Zeeland, and Flanders, to end only west of Calais, where the chalk cliffs of Picardy leave no room for dunes and give a new character to the coastline. Where the mouths of the Rhine break the dune-belt, the marsh-lands broaden into a delta, part of which has been drained and embanked to make the modern Holland, while the remainder has become a lagoon, the so-called Zuider Zee or South Sea of the Hollanders. Elsewhere a tidal passage, parallel to the coast, detaches the dunes from the mainland, converting them into a chain of islands. Though the land behind the dunes is the beginning of the great plain of

FIG. 11.—The Dune Coasts of the North Sea.

Northern and Eastern Europe, and differs, therefore, markedly from the highlands of Norway, yet it has produced similar amphibious races—Jutes, Angles, Saxons, Frieslanders, Hollanders, and Zeelanders—herdsmen who under stress of circumstance could put to sea and found new homes, as did the Anglo-Saxons in Britain, and as the Hollanders threatened to do in Java when pressed by Louis the Fourteenth.

Just westward of Calais, Europe stands forward in a great shoulder, whose substance is a chalk table-land—cliff-edged, the counterpart in structure of the smaller and more slender promontory of Kent. Here the Teutonic Fleming yields to the Latinised Gaul of Picardy, essentially a landsman, and the firm soil is notched only by a few small harbours and has no border of marsh and tidal lagoon. Britain has had to suffer no serious invasion from Picardy and Flanders.

Picardy is followed by Normandy, where the mouth of the Seine, corresponding to Southampton Water on the English side, offered to the wandering Vikings a way leading far inland towards Paris, and where the Cotentin peninsula and the Channel Islands—counterparts in some sort of the Isle of Wight and the so-called Isles of Purbeck and Portland—gave to them a secure and sea-girt basis for attack upon Britain.

Last of all is Brittany, a pastoral land, with rocks which form a broken, dangerous coast, though one full of harbours. It is a peninsula analogous to the opposite Cornwall, but more massive in outline, and is peopled by the same Celtic race, driven to bay at the land's end. Alike physically and ethnographically, it has merited its name of Little Britain.

Brittany, Cornwall, the south of Ireland, the southern peninsula of Wales, even the northern and smaller Welsh peninsula, form a group of promontories thrust ocean-ward—westward and southward—along somewhat convergent lines (Fig. 12). Between them the ocean penetrates on the one hand through the English Channel into the Narrow Seas, on the other hand, in rear of Ireland, through the St. George's Channel into the Irish Sea. Just as the Thames estuary branches from the nameless arm of the North Sea, giving to it a bifurcate character and defining Kent, so the Bristol Channel branches from the St. George's Channel, dividing Wales from Cornwall, or, as it used to be called, West Wales. The ocean-ways from all the world, except North-eastern Europe, converge from west and south upon the sea-area off the mouths of the Channels. Here, therefore, to south of Ireland and to

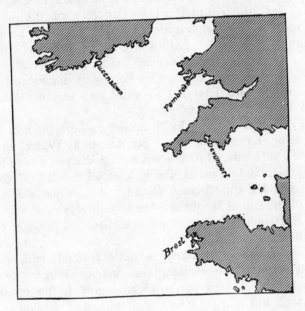

FIG. 12.—The Channel Entries.

west of Cornwall and Brittany, is the marine antechamber of Britain.[1]

The seas which divide Ireland from Great Britain are truly inland waters (Fig. 13). They penetrate through the mountainous oceanic border of Britain to the plains of the interior, and in certain parts present long stretches of flat shore, as in Lancashire and to the north of Dublin. The Irish Sea is a British Mediterranean, a land-girt quadrilateral, wholly British, whose four sides are England, Scotland, Ireland, and Wales. The mountains of all four are visible from Snae Fell—the peak which rises from

[1] Spithead and certain other partially enclosed sea-areas off the British coasts were formerly known to international lawyers as the Queen's Chambers.

the midst of the Irish Sea to a height of two thousand
feet, forming the summit of the Isle of Man, a fifth part
of Britain, neither English, Scottish, Irish, nor Welsh, but
Manx. It is not unimportant to note that the second
entry from the ocean to the Irish Sea, the North or St.
Patrick's Channel, which completes the insulation of
Ireland, is not merely British on both sides, but also
remote from all foreign shores. It is set midway along

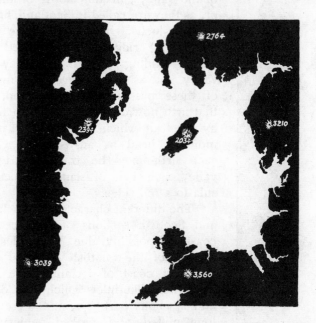

FIG. 13.—The Inland Sea of Britain. (Mountain-heights in feet)

the "back of Britain," a private entry, as it were, to Liverpool and Glasgow. Liverpool, at the south-eastern corner
of the Irish Sea, is almost exactly in the centre of the
British Isles.

From Cape Clear by the west coasts of Ireland and
Scotland to the Orkneys is the oceanic border of Britain
—a maze of channels, like the fiords of Norway, with a
climate mild and moist like that of Brittany, and wind-

swept treeless islands bearing green pasture (Fig. 14).
There is system, however, in the apparent disorder of this
coastline, a system made clear by the reflection that this
is a half-drowned shore. The oceanic border of Britain —
a hill region abundantly watered and deeply trenched by

powerful torrents — has sunk somewhat below its former level, and the
salt-water has filled the lower reaches
of the valleys, making fiords of them,
or, as they are called in Scotland, firths
and sea-lochs. Here and there the
intervening ridges were notched by
passes leading over from valley to
valley, and as the sea-level rose many
of these passes were submerged, so
that firth now communicates with firth
by a strait which detaches the promontory head as an island. Thus
each firth may be traced up to a
valley, each chain of islands and peninsula to a hill ridge.

The different character of the Irish
and Scottish sections of the oceanic
coast is possibly due to a deeper
sinking of the Scottish section. On
the west coast of Ireland there are
many fiord-like inlets which form deep
and spacious harbours, and there are
long cliffed and peaked peninsulas,
but few important islands. To the
west of Scotland there is a whole
archipelago of islands known as the
Hebrides or Western Isles, ranged
for the most part in chains, and

FIG 14.—The Oceanic
Border of Britain.

alternating with peninsulas. Two such feature-lines
stretch from Scotland almost to Ireland : the peninsula
of Kintyre and the island chain of Jura and Islay.
These and the considerable islands of Mull and Skye,
with a multitude of smaller islands, are severed from

the mainland only by narrow kyles, through which the tourist steamer finds calm ways; but outside, beyond the relatively broad channel of the Minch, is a mountain ridge striking north-north-eastward and south-south-westward, and rising steeply from the sea like a great breakwater (Fig. 27). Being pierced by several straits it forms a chain of islands, the Outer Hebrides; yet is so obviously a single feature, that the whole is known to the inhabitants simply as Long Island, and the northernmost and largest island has no single name, but is the Lewis in its northern —wider and lower—portion, and Harris in its southern and loftier part.

There are thus four natural parts of the sea round Britain. To the east and south are the narrow seas between the islands and the continent. To the southwest is the marine antechamber dividing into channels at the Land's End. Spreading four square in the midst of the British Kingdoms is the inland Irish Sea; while for six hundred miles off the north-western shores is the border of the ocean. It is noteworthy that, whereas in the south-west the peninsulas and channels, having the same general lie, alternate longitudinally, in the north-west the St. Patrick's Channel, between Ireland and Scotland, breaches the oceanic margin of the land transversely. On a greater scale, the North Sea appears to be of the same transverse nature, for the general direction and the mountainous and fiorded character of the oceanic coasts of Britain suggest a former continuity with the long stretch of similar Norwegian coast which lies between the North Cape and the blunt angle of the peninsula near Bergen at the entry to the North Sea. The Outer Hebrides also, divided from the Scottish mainland by the channel of the Minch, are closely analogous to the Lofoten Islands, cleft from Norway by the West Fiord. Moreover, the Shetland Islands, which rise like a stepping-stone in the mouth of the North Sea, may be a remnant of the land which has vanished. But the mere plan and type of the coastlines can only suggest analogies; to prove an underlying unity it is necessary to consider the form of the intervening sea-bed and the rock structure of the divided lands.

Note on the " Narrow Seas."—England formerly claimed sovereignty over the Narrow Seas as far as the continental coasts, and sent out ships to keep the peace upon them.   Her men-of-war exacted a salute from all other flags while in the British Seas.   The right was recognised by international action as early as the year 1299.   It was maintained by Selden in his " Mare Clausum," published in 1635, and, by the Treaty of Westminster made between England and Holland in 1674, the British Seas were expressly defined as extending from Cape Finisterre, in Spain, to Stadland, in Norway, thus including the Bay of Biscay as well as the North Sea.   The exercise of the dominion fell gradually into desuetude, but as late as 1805 the Admiralty regulations directed officers of British men-of-war to require a salute from foreign ships "within His Majesty's seas, which extend to Cape Finisterre."   At the present time the territory of Britain spreads by international law to no more than three miles from the shore, although under certain circumstances sovereignty might no doubt be asserted over estuaries and firths.   Indeed, it has apparently been decided by the King's Bench that the whole of the Bristol Channel between Somerset and Glamorgan is British territory.   The subject is discussed in Hall's " International Law," Part II., Chap. II.

The English names of the Narrow Seas lack symmetry.   In Denmark the Baltic is called the East Sea, and the German Ocean is the West Sea.   The ancient geographers spoke of the North Sea as Oceanus Germanicus, and of the English Channel as Oceanus Britannicus, the German and British portions, that is to say, of the ocean.   The North Sea has been so called by the Dutch fishermen, who contrasted it with the Zuider Zee, or South Sea, of their own country, and the expression was probably adopted in England from the great Flemish geographers of the sixteenth century.   See Egli, " Nomina Geographica," art. " Nordsee."

CHAPTER III

THE SUBMARINE PLATFORM

THE Strait of Dover is so shallow, that were 'St. Paul's Cathedral sunk in it, the dome would rise above the water even in the deepest part. It is seven hundred times broader than it is deep. In section it is a cliff-edged trough, whose nearly flat bottom is little more than covered with water (Fig. 15). Northward and westward of Dover the Narrow Seas increase in depth, but it is not until beyond the Shetland Islands on the one hand, and far to the west of Cornwall and Brittany on the other, that there are a hundred fathoms of water (Figs. 17, 18). All the sea-beds between the Continent and Great Britain, between Great Britain and Ireland, and off the west coasts of Scotland and Ireland would, if dry, present the aspect of a plain occasionally varied by an undulation visible to the eye. The general tilt northward and westward would be indicated only by the flow of the rivers.

Beyond the hundred-fathom line the sea-bed slopes suddenly downward, with the steepness of a visible hill, to a depth of a thousand and more fathoms (Fig. 16). This slope, which is the true, though submerged, edge of the Continent, follows the coast of Norway a short distance seaward from the North Cape until off Bergen ; then, crossing the mouth of the North Sea, it passes outside the Shetland Islands and the Hebrides to a point some distance westward of Ireland. Here it makes an inward bend and strikes through the centre of the Bay of Biscay almost to its head, in such manner as to divide the bay into two halves, the one, towards France, relatively shallow, the other, on the Spanish side, very deep. All the shallow seas within the hundred-fathom line are a portion of the continental plain dipped just beneath the ocean surface. The submarine platform thus defined is known as the continental shelf, and Britain, merely an emergent area of the platform, is spoken of as a group of continental islands. If we consider only the configuration of the rock globe—the form, that is to say, of the solid earth, whether covered by air or continued beneath the sea —Britain is a part of the Continent of Europe, and its insular character is an accident of the present level of the sea relatively to the land. Were the sea surface to fall a thousand fathoms, an explorer on the Atlantic would see

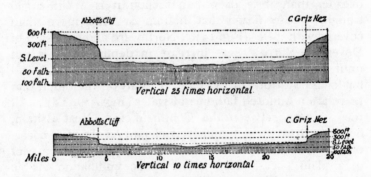

FIG. 15.—Section across the Strait of Dover.

before him what would, to all appearance, be a long mountain range rising by stream-furrowed and forest-clad slopes to a height of more than five thousand feet.[1] Were he to land and to push forty miles inland up some winding valley, through the forests and over the moors, possibly to the snow, he would find himself on a vast plateau flush with the summits of the mountains that were visible from his deck. On this high plain, in the course of his journey, he would come across long lines of terraced slope, the edges of slightly higher plains representing the shore-lines and lands of to-day; and occasionally, at wide intervals,

[1] It must not be assumed that such a change of sea-level has actually taken place.

he would see mountain groups rising above the plain,
much as they do to-day above our British, French,
and German lowlands. Very small changes in the sea-
level would indeed suffice to join Britain to the Continent, or, on the other hand, to flood South-eastern
England and the Flemish plain and to put a wide sea
between Britain and the mainland. Many facts show that
at different times in the prehistoric past both of these conditions have been realised.

A study of the map contoured below the hundred-

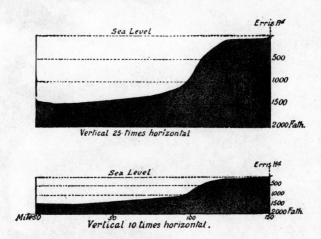

FIG. 16.—Section of the Continental Edge, North-westward from
Erris Head, County Donegal.

fathom line reveals two noticeable features. Spain is a
plateau raised on the average some two or three thousand
feet above the sea. Along its northern edge it is lifted
still further into a mountain rim, Pyrenean and Cantabrian, from whose summits, rising at highest to eleven
thousand feet, the slopes descend, in the east to the plains
of Southern France, in the west into the Biscayan abyss,
more than fifteen thousand feet below the sea surface
(Fig. 17). Unlike Norway, Spain has therefore no submerged connection with Britain. The Bay of Biscay is a
fundamental feature of the map of Europe.

Away to the north-west, on the other hand, between
Cape Wrath and Iceland, is a remarkable rise in the ocean-
bed, which comes to within three hundred fathoms of the
surface and divides the abyss of the Atlantic from that of
the Arctic Basin (Fig. 18).   The Faroe Islands are borne
upon a branch of this rise, and between them and the continental slope is the Faroe Deep, a submarine gulf which,

FIG. 17.—The Biscayan Deep.

but for the Wyville Thomson Ridge, the narrow proximal
end of the Scoto-Icelandic Rise, would give abysmal
access from Arctic to Atlantic waters.   It is clear that the
Arctic entry must formerly have been barred to an even
greater extent than at present, for Iceland and the Faroe
Islands are but the cliff-edged and eroded remnants of
much wider plateaux.

The Scoto-Icelandic Rise is probably one of the most ancient features of the British area,[1] but it is now subordinate to the great slope which, continuously from the head of the Bay of Biscay to the North Cape of Norway, forms the seaward limit of the submerged continental platform. The continental shallow is everywhere covered with débris of gravel, sand, and silt, whereas the floor

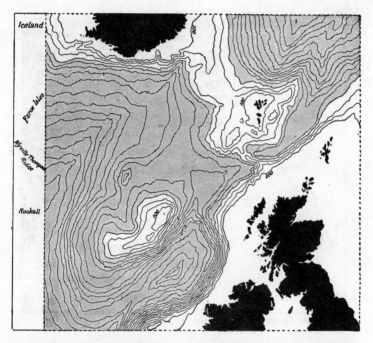

FIG. 18.—The Scoto-Icelandic Rise. The Deep between Ireland and Rockall measures 1600 fathoms, the contour lines being drawn at intervals of 100 fathoms.

of the abyss is laid with a grey ooze made by the secular accumulation of the shells of minute foraminifera, chiefly of the form known as globigerina.

Upon the surface of the submarine platform the largest and most marked feature, apart from Britain itself, is the Norway Deep, a broad submerged channel which follows

[1] Compare Chapter VIII. and especially Fig. 57 at p. 105.

the outline of Norway from the head of the Skager Rak
to the continental edge, where it breaks the continuity of
the hundred-fathom sill by an entry some two hundred
fathoms deep (Fig. 19).   Southward of this entry the
hollow grows deeper as it penetrates the continental area,
until, after rounding the southern point of Norway, it
attains a maximum of four hundred fathoms, and then

Depths.- 100-200 Fath.☐ 200 - 300 Fath.▒ over 300 Fath.▨

FIG. 19.—The Norway Deep.

ends bluntly against the coast of Sweden between Gothen-
burg and Christiania.   No adequate explanation can as yet
be given of the origin and meaning of the Norway Deep,
but two facts are suggestive: the deepening of the channel
inland is analogous to the similar deepening of the fiords
of Norway and Scotland in their upper reaches; and the
position of the Deep, off the plateau edge of Norway, is
analogous, although the contrasts are less emphatic, to the

position of the Biscayan abyss along the foot of the Cantabrian front of the Spanish table-land.   Nor is the interest
of the Norway Deep wholly scientific.   In foggy weather
the mariner bound for Copenhagen and the Baltic finds
his way into the Skager Rak by the use of the sounding-
lead.   Groping northward, in fear of the Danish coast,
he reaches a position where the depths increase quickly
from seventy to two hundred and more fathoms, and

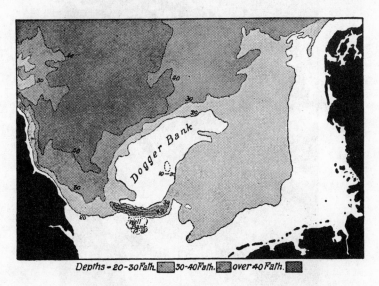

Depths - 20-30 Fath. ▨ 30-40 Fath. ▨ over 40 Fath. ▨

FIG. 20.—The Dogger Bank, the Well Bank, and, between them,
the Great Silver Pits.

he knows that he may then steer boldly north-eastward
clear of the Jutish promontory.

Rather more than half-way across from Denmark to
England, spreading between the latitudes of Newcastle and
Scarborough, is a great shoal known as the Dogger Bank,
whose north-western margin is a submerged escarpment
sinking for a distance of nearly a hundred miles to deeper
waters than those which lie south of the bank (Fig. 20).
From its lie, the edge of the Dogger would seem to be
connected in some way with the Cleveland shoulder of

Yorkshire and the north-western coast of Jutland. South
of the Dogger is a second but smaller patch of shallow,
known as the Wells Banks.

Minor features of a similar character are a marked

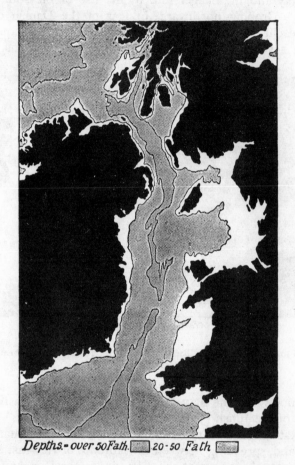

Depths.- over 50Fath. [   ] *20-50 Fath* [   ]

Fig. 21.—The Seas between Great Britain and Ireland.

deep along the northern edge of the Buchan shoulder
of Scotland ; a straight furrow, known as the Hurd,
in the bed of the English Channel, off the Cotentin and

the Channel Islands ; and certain lake-like pans (Fig. 27) in the bed of the straits which divide the Western Isles from Scotland. But it is a remarkable fact that, except in the depression along the Norwegian coast, the deepest point on the British continental platform occurs in the fresh-water Loch Morar, in the county of Inverness. The surface of that loch is only about thirty feet above the sea, and its deepest sounding measures one hundred and eighty fathoms.

Away to the west of Brittany and to the south of Ireland the edge of the continental shelf is notched in a manner suggestive of a group of submerged estuaries (Fig. 17), and here, perhaps, may once have been the mouths of rivers which traversed the plains now replaced by the English, the Bristol, and the St. George's Channels. There is a long furrow to the east of Ireland, which penetrates northward through the St. Patrick's Channel and then fails between Islay and Donegal, leaving the shallow sill off western Ireland continuous with that off western Scotland (Figs. 21, 29). A river rising between Islay and Donegal, flowing southward through this furrow, and bending westward into one of the submerged estuaries, would follow a course longer than that of the river Shannon, but part for part precisely similar. It is possible that the submerged valley of such a greater Shannon may have been one of the proximate causes of the separation of Ireland from Great Britain. But remoter causes must have determined the continuity of the shallows off Ireland and Scotland, and the opening of the broad gap between the mountains of Wales and Wicklow.

Thus the study of the configuration of the sea-bed emphasises the conclusions drawn from the coastal outlines. The Oceanic Border, the Narrow Seas and the Channel Entries appear to have a fundamental significance. The eastern half of the Irish Sea is shallow (Fig. 21), and the Isle of Man belongs therefore to Great Britain rather than to Ireland, but the western half is a northward extension of the relatively deep St. George's Channel.

3

Note on the hypothetical valleys of the submarine platform.—It is assumed as beyond doubt that the features of the platform surface have been shaped by atmospheric and glacial agencies. Yet there is much difficulty in giving a precise interpretation to many of the facts. The form of the notches, for instance, in the continental slope south-west of Ireland has not been determined by soundings numerous enough to reveal their nature with certainty. The submerged valley, again, along the east of Ireland appears to be broken into a succession of hollows by transverse bars which would preclude the flow of a river, unless through a chain of lakes as in the case of the Shannon (Figs. 21, 68). Innumerable soundings taken and recorded with extreme care, and some method of investigating the superficial geology of the sea-bed, will be needed for the sure solution of such problems. Valuable discussions upon these subjects are associated with the names of Professor E. Hull in the *Geographical Journal,* vol. xiii., and Mr. W. H. Huddleston in the *Geological Magazine,* 1899. The chief general authorities on the British Seas are the *Admiralty Charts,* and the *North Sea* and *Channel Pilots.*

Note on the submerged continental edge.—This feature has long been known, in part at any rate, to the North Sea fishermen. It is inserted in a map published at Leyden, about A.D. 1700, by *Van der Aa,* and the following note is placed against it :—" Le Borneur nommé par les Hollandois De Kimmen est un espece de Coteau dans le fond de la mer qui s'étend depuis le Banc de Jutlande par le Nord des Isles de Schetland jusques a la partie Occidentale des Isles Hebrides."

CHAPTER IV

THE MOVEMENT OF THE WATERS

A SHALLOW marginal sea, wherein the oceanic waters superficially invade the continental area,[1] is necessarily the scene of more vigorous movements than is the deep ocean or a land-girt mediterranean. In no small degree Britain owes to the submarine platform the currents and tidal fluctuations which have shaped the detail of her coast-lines, increased the value of her estuarine harbours, contributed to the motive power of her shipping, and determined the position and seasons of her fisheries.

The most general and important of these movements is the rhythmical rise and fall of the surface, with the resultant ebb and flow across the shallows, which constitutes the tide. Although generated in the abysmal waters by lunar and solar influence, the tides are not a striking phenomenon as exhibited on the shores of small islands in mid-ocean. The rise and fall, at a distance from continental shallows, is limited to three or four feet, and there are no appreciable alternating currents. At intervals of rather more than twelve hours the crest of a vast, though imperceptible wave passes each point of the deep ocean with a speed of several hundred miles an hour. From trough to trough the wave measures several thousand miles; from trough to crest it has a vertical altitude of only a few feet. The wave form is carried rapidly forward, but there is no measurable transference of water in a horizontal direction, each successive particle being moved, slowly and rhythmically, merely upward

[1] "A transgressing sea" (Transgressionsmeer)—Penck, "Morphologie der Erdoberfläche," Buch. I, cap. 4.

35

and downward. The astronomical causes of the tide have been subjected to accurate mathematical analysis, but tidal geography—the places of origin and subsequent movement of the tidal waves—being affected in the most intricate manner by coastal obstruction and the varying depth of the sea, is still inexactly known. It suffices here to state that the oceanic tides approach Britain from the south-west (Fig. 22).

On the edge of the British submarine platform, the tidal wave passes suddenly into shallow water, and is sharply checked. Its speed is reduced to less than a hundred miles an hour. At the same time the crest, moving over slightly deeper water and being therefore less impeded, tends to overtake the preceding trough. The shape of the wave is, consequently, changed: the amplitude, or vertical height, is increased, while the length, from trough to trough, is diminished, with the result that along the coasts of Britain the tide often exhibits a rise and fall many times greater than on the abysmal ocean. Moreover, where the depth of the sea becomes comparable with the altitude of the tide, it is obvious that to allow of the rise of the surface, large bodies of water must be drawn on to the shallows. The so-called ebb and flow of the tide—the tidal current, or bodily transference of water from one part of the sea to another—is therefore a purely local phenomenon, characteristic of the continental shelf and imperceptible on the high seas. Through Pentland Firth, between the Orkneys and Caithness, the ebb and flow to and from the great shallow of the North Sea produces an alternating tidal race, running with a speed of from six to ten knots an hour.

Striking the coast of Ireland the tide wraps round the British Islands, penetrating on the one side up the English and St. George's Channels, and on the other through the North Channel and through Pentland Firth. As a consequence, the water is high simultaneously a little to the east of Pentland Firth, at Liverpool, and at Dover. In the North Sea the retardation of the tidal advance and the accumulation of tidal altitude reach their maximum (Fig. 23). The whole surface of the sea is heaving to and fro under the influence of tides which have entered both from the north and from the south. The Dogger and Well Banks in the centre appear to control the movement. As a result of their opposition, the northern tide, which

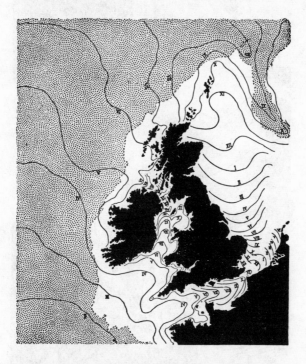

FIG. 22.—The hours of high water in the British Seas, when noon is the hour of high water at Liverpool.

has entered not only through Pentland Firth but also to eastward of the Shetland Isles, is split into two : on the one hand it runs along the coast of Norway into the Skager Rak, and on the other it follows the east coast of Britain to the Thames. Off Britain it brings high water later and later to each successive port, reaching the Thames in the space of about twelve hours from Pentland Firth.

The rate of advance has thus been reduced to some fifty
miles an hour : in other words, high water comes to Scarborough about an hour later than to Shields, which lies
fifty miles to northward.   Midway between East Anglia

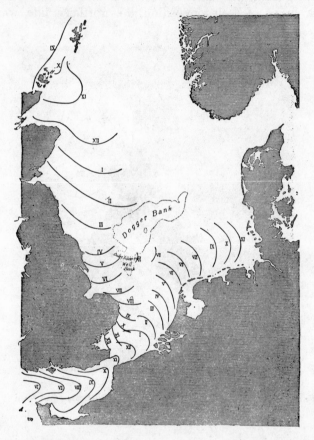

FIG. 23.—The hours of high water in the Narrow Seas, when noon is
the hour of high water at Liverpool.

and Holland is the Well Bank, separated from the Dogger
by a deep channel known as the great or outer Silver Pits,
through which, between the dead waters on the two Banks,
the east-coast tide sends an offshoot in the direction of

Hamburg. The southern tide, moving eastward through
the Strait of Dover, advances along the coast of Holland
to the east of the Well Bank, so that along the Dutch
coast the hour of high tide grows later northward. In
the direction of Hamburg the Dover and Silver Pit tides
coalesce, bringing high water to Heligoland when the
next tide has already reached Dover. At a point midway
between Holland and England the northern and southern
waves neutralise one another, and here, in consequence,
there is no perceptible rise or fall ; but the tides which
thus interfere are, of course, of unequal age, the Dover
tide being at least twelve hours younger than that which
has rounded Scotland.

Phenomena similar to those produced by the division
of the tide round the British Isles are to be found on a
smaller scale, causing all manner of complexities, wherever
the coast is beset with islands. A classical instance of
this, recorded nearly twelve hundred years ago by the
Venerable Bede, who wrote at Jarrow on the remote
Tyne, occurs at Southampton.[1] Here, by reason of the
interference of the Isle of Wight, there are four tides a day,
high water through Spithead being two hours later than
high water from the Solent. The advantages incident to
the Port of Southampton have long been appreciated by
mariners.

More important, however, than the hour of high water,
and perhaps than the amount of rise and fall, are the
alternating tidal currents which, to the great advantage of
commerce, affect all the British Seas (Figs. 24, 25). While
the water is rising at Liverpool and at Dover, currents
set inward up the North, the St. George's, and the English
Channels, running with a speed of from one to three
miles an hour, occasionally racing at six miles an hour
round such promontories as Holyhead and Portland Bill,
but nowhere approaching the rapidity of the inset through
Pentland Firth. When the water is falling at Liverpool
and Dover the currents are generally outward, but owing
to local interferences, the inward and outward sets are not

[1] See note on the Southampton tides at p. 44.

precisely converse, nor does the hour of current reversal always coincide exactly with that of high water. In the North Sea, to the south of the latitude of Edinburgh, the tidal currents appear to set at an average speed of about two miles an hour alternately to and from a point off the mouth of the Tees, between the Dogger Bank and the coast of England. At this point low water is

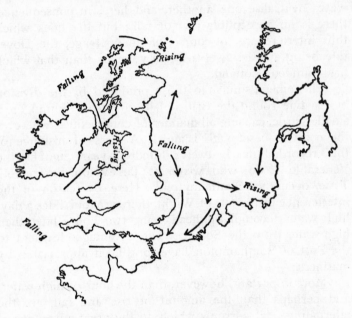

FIG. 24.—The approximate set of the tidal currents, when the water is rising at Liverpool.

simultaneous with high water at Dover, at Heligoland, and off Caithness. When the tide is falling off the Tees the currents set northward past Scotland, southward past England, and eastward, over the Silver Pits, towards Texel and Heligoland. With the turn of the tide the currents flow inward from the north, the east, and the south.

Twice a day the tides convert the lower reaches of most British rivers into arms of the sea. The estuaries are

generally so shaped as to concentrate the tidal energy on
a steadily narrowing front, with the effect of magnifying
the tidal rise and fall for some distance inland.   In the
Severn, for instance, at the mouth of the Bristol Avon,
there is a difference of forty feet between the levels of
high and low water at the time of spring tides.   In some
instances this action is so marked as to produce a crest-

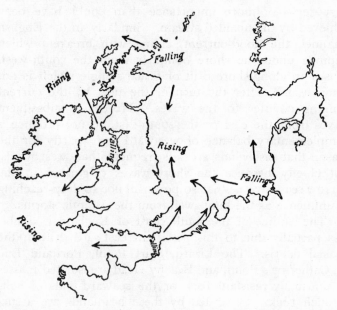

Fig. 25.—The approximate set of the tidal currents, when the water
is falling at Liverpool.

fronted wave, known as the bore on the Severn and as the
aegir on the Trent.[1]   At Liverpool is a reverse condition :
the estuary of the Mersey is bottle-shaped, with the consequence that strong currents flow through the entry,
conveying the large quantity of water needed to fill the
upper basin.   These currents scour the channel between
Liverpool and Birkenhead, keeping it relatively deep.   The
conditions at Portsmouth are somewhat similar.

[1] See note on the word Aegir at p. 44.

The tidal currents, being periodically reversed, have little effect upon the shores when acting alone : it is only when reinforcing or neutralising other currents, or the drift of breaking waves, that they accumulate great changes. When the flood runs up a river channel, it is partially counteracted by the out-flowing stream, but the ebb acts with the stream, producing results which are not effaced by the flood, and—owing to the greater head of water — of more importance than could have been achieved by the unaided stream. Similarly, in the English Channel, the flood-current, acting with breakers which impinge upon the shore obliquely from the south-west, causes an along-shore drift of beach-shingle which is not compensated, after the turn of the tide, by the current running counter to the waves. Moreover, subsequent waves from the east or the south-east, do not produce a complementary balance of westward drift, partly for the reason that east winds are less frequent than west winds, but chiefly because the short waves originated in the narrow seas have neither so powerful nor so deep-reaching an influence as the long swell from the Atlantic storms.[1]

The outline of the south coast of England is doubtless partially due to this persistent eastward drift of the coastal débris. The Lizard, Start Point, Portland Bill, St. Catherine's Point, and Beachy Head are isolated masses of unusually resistant rock or the seaward ends of belts of such rock. Separated by these headlands are a succession of wide, more or less symmetrical bays, shaped— so far as local accidents have permitted—by the scour of the dominating current and surf. While the points have been abraded from the salient portions of the coast, shingle bars—such as the Chesil Beach, west of Portland Bill—have closed the minor inlets, and thus contributed to the even sweep of the shore-lines. Dungeness is a shingle spit, the material of which has been drifted eastward from the cliffs at Hastings, and guided into a seaward cusp by local eddies, possibly connected with the meeting of the North Sea and Channel tides. In early Roman

[1] See note on the coastal changes due to waves at p. 44.

times Dungeness appears not to have existed, but a shingle bar extended with slightly re-entering curve from Winchelsea to Hythe, defining a lagoon now silted up by the little river Rother. The diversion of the Rother mouth for the purpose of reclaiming Romney Marsh seems to have so altered the conditions as to have induced the formation of Dungeness. Along the east coast, similar effects are produced by a combination of the southward tidal current with storm waves from the north-east. The débris travels steadily southward along the coast of Holderness, and is in part driven into the Humber, where it forms shifting banks.

In addition to the tidal movements, there is a complicated circulation of the waters round Britain, due chiefly to the pressure of the prevalent winds and to the inflow of fresh water from the rivers. To the west and north-west of Ireland and Scotland the whole surface of the ocean is driven slowly north-eastward, over the Wyville Thomson Ridge, towards the Arctic basin. At times, after a spell of east wind, this drift is brought to a standstill, and on rare occasions it is even reversed.

A portion of the Atlantic drift enters the North Sea, and flows as a surface current, with a speed of two or three miles a day, along the east coast of Britain as far as the neighbourhood of the Wash, and then towards the coast of Denmark. The principal cause of this current is no doubt the prevalence of winds tending to heap the water up towards the Scandinavian shores. But there are causes in action producing other results of considerable importance. In the spring time cold water from the Baltic and North German rivers reduces the salinity of the water along the southern and eastern margins of the North Sea, and as the season advances a great volume of warmer but still relatively fresh water extends across the surface from these sources. At the same time dense, cooler, and salter oceanic water appears to creep over the sea bed down the east coast of Britain, here and there welling up to the surface when the superficial layer is driven seaward by winds blowing off shore.

The migrations of fish seem to be governed by the fluctuation of the currents.   Herring, perhaps seeking the oxygenated water drawn from the Atlantic, forsake the Norwegian coasts in the spring time, when the cold river water begins to mingle with the sea beyond the Skager Rak.   On the·other hand, they appear in great shoals off the Scottish coast precisely when the oceanic water, bearing supplies of food, creeps southward from the entry between the Orkney and Shetland Islands.   Flat fish have a still more notable relation to the currents.   Myriads of their eggs, floating upon the surface, are carried, while slowly hatching, from the British coast into the great bight off the Elbe mouth.   There, as a consequence, young flat fish abound, which, growing larger, migrate along the bottom in the direction of the spawning grounds east of Scotland.   The occasional deviation of the currents from their normal regime, which may result from spells of unusual winds, is thus productive of sterility upon the fishing grounds.   A systematic observation of the ever changing equilibrium of the sea waters might therefore prove of great economic value by enabling a forecast of the fishing seasons.

Note on the Southampton tides.—See Bede's "Ecclesiastical History," Bk. IV., Cap. xiv. (trans. Giles):—"This island (Wight) is seated opposite to the middle part of the South Saxons and the Gevissae, being separated from it by a sea, three miles over, which is called Solvente.   In this narrow sea, the two tides of the ocean, which flow round Britain from the immense northern ocean, daily meet and oppose one another beyond the mouth of the river Homelea, which runs into that narrow sea ; . . . after this meeting and struggling together of the two seas, they return into the ocean from whence they come."

Note on the word Aegir.—See Carlyle, Hero-Worship, Lecture I. "Of the other Gods or Jötuns I will mention only for etymology's sake, that sea-tempest is the Jötun Aegir, a very dangerous Jötun ; and now to this day, on our river Trent, as I learn, the Nottingham bargemen cry out, ' Have a care, there is the Eager coming !'"

In Wigtown Bay, in a district much visited by the Vikings, a point round which the tides enter vehemently is known as Eggerness.

Note on the coastal changes due to waves and tidal currents.—The effects of waves striking a coast obliquely, and of long as opposed to short waves, together with other kindred subjects, have been carefully discussed by Mr. Vaughan Cornish in a paper on "Sea-Beaches and Sandbanks" in the *Geographical Journal*, vol. xi. The most thorough study of Dungeness, with references to authorities, is by Dr. F. P. Gulliver in the *Geographical Journal*, vol. ix.

Note on the currents in the British seas.—Our knowledge of the circulation in the North Sea is due chiefly to the international survey commenced in 1892, an account of which will be found in a paper by Mr. H. N. Dickson on "The Movements of the Surface Waters of the North Sea," published in the *Geographical Journal*, vol. vii. Reference may also be made to papers on "The Surface Currents of the North Sea," by Dr. T. W. Fulton, in the *Scottish Geographical Magazine*, vol. xiii., and on "The Distribution of Food-fishes in Relation to their Physical Surroundings," by Mr. Dickson, in *Natural Science*, vol. vi.

CHAPTER V

THE UPLANDS AND LOWLANDS

THE rough moulding of the land-surface resembles that of the sea-bed, and is continuous with it. As the sea-bed presents shallows and deeps, so the land has its lowlands and uplands ; and as the deeps are broad basins with gradual slopes sinking to wide undulating bottoms, so the uplands rise from the lowlands in bas-relief, like the sovereign's head on a coin, with slightly-rounded surfaces—broad out of all proportion to their height. But in harmony with the weathering properties of the air, as contrasted with the preservative influence of the deeper waters, the detail of the land-surface differs from that of the sea-bed. In the depths the currents run slowly, and there are neither frosts, nor streams, nor breaking waves, while the deposits from the land settle gradually over wide areas, mantling, like a snowstorm, all detail and replacing angles by curves. Along the bed of the air-ocean, on the other hand, the winds blow with force, driving waves to erode the coasts, and carrying moisture to the hilltops. Streams descend from the heights, scoring the slopes with intricate valleys ; while the frosts, expanding water in the crevasses, break great rocks from the summits, scarp the cliffs, and, on the lowlands, pulverise the surface, so that slow waters carry the reduced particles of soil and wear undulating basins into the plains. Sea-bed and land-surface have the same rock structure underlying them, the same outward features expressive of their common skeleton ; but the one is preserved by the waters and even buried by deposits, while the other is seared and ruined by the weather. The abrupt and sculptured features of the land must be lost, as it were, in the distance, the hills must blend into massive groups, and smaller elevations be confused with the plains, before the broad facts of upland and lowland appear, which are the true analogues of the shallows and deeps of the ocean. The ordinary map with hill-shading is inadequate for the presentation of these greater contrasts; contoured maps and cross-sections are needed for their appreciation.[1]

To grasp the lie of the British uplands, it should be remembered that Scotland, the Irish Sea, Wales, and the Devonian peninsula constitute the central — northward and southward—belt of the land; and that Ireland lies wholly to the west of this belt, and England, with the exception of Devon and Cornwall, wholly to the east of it. The chief uplands rise in great masses disposed along and about the central belt (Fig. 26). In the north are the Northern and the Grampian Highlands of Scotland; in the centre are the Southern Uplands of Scotland, the Cumbrian *massif*, the Pennine Moorland, and the Peak; in Wales is the Cambrian Upland; while Devon contains the lesser uplands of Exmoor and Dartmoor. Cape Wrath and the Lizard lie almost precisely north and south of one another, upon the fifth meridian west of Greenwich, and may be connected by a line with slightly sigmoid curves, convex along the western margin of Scotland, concave where it touches the four successive promontories of the more southern uplands—Man, Carnarvon, Pembroke, and Cornwall (Scilly). That the little Manx upland belongs to the main series is evident from the fact that it is attached by shallows to England and not to Ireland (Fig. 21). A second sigmoid line, curving sympathetically with the first and placed only a few miles to westward of it, would mark the axis of the Hebridean and Irish Seas.

In hilly districts the clouds, as seen from the peaks, often simulate the horizontal sea. A great plain of cloud may roof in the lowlands and extend, fiord-like, up the valleys, while distant mountains rise like islands above the

---

[1] See note on contoured maps at p. 62.

white expanse.   Such a sheet of cloud may be imagined
to surround and penetrate the uplands of Britain at a
level of six hundred feet.   In the far north would emerge
the Northern Scottish Highlands spreading eastward and
southward from Cape Wrath, and divided diagonally from
the still more elevated Grampian Highlands by a straight,

FIG. 26.—The Uplands of Britain.   The black areas are of greater
elevation than 1000 feet.

narrow belt of cloud, a hundred miles in length from
Moray Firth in the north-east to the Firth of Lorne in
the south-west, and not more than about five miles broad
(Fig. 28).   Beneath this cloud streak would be hidden the
Great Glen—in Gaelic, Glenmore—almost like a modern
street in directness, and a chain of lakes, and woods, and

the Caledonian Canal connecting sea with sea across
the island. Many summits in the Northern Highlands

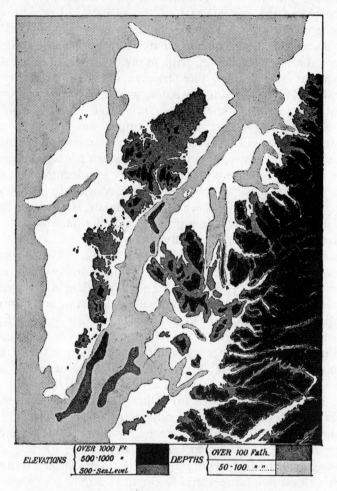

ELEVATIONS { OVER 1000 Ft / 500 - 1000 " / 500 - Sea Level }   DEPTHS { OVER 100 Fath. / 50 - 100 " " }

FIG. 27.—The Outer Hebrides and the Western Margin of the
Northern Highlands.

rise to a little more or less than 3000 feet. As observed
in clear weather from the Western Isles they combine to
form a plateau dipping gently northward; but seen from

4

above, in bird's-eye perspective, when clouds filled the
valleys, their most striking characteristic would be discon-
tinuity, for the high grounds of this district, although
occupying the greater part of the surface and advancing
close to the western shores, are intersected by so intricate
a system of deep valleys, that their horizontal outline
resembles that of a rag, with many rents, held brokenly
together by a seam. The Orkneys and the north-eastern
half of Caithness, being lowlands, would be cloud-covered ;
but one remote Orkney hill, in the island of Hoy, would
rise nearly 1000 feet into the upper air. Groups of
lofty peaks would represent the green islands of Skye and
Mull, and far away, down on the western horizon, would
be the naked summits of Harris, the prominent centre of
the Outer Hebridean ridge, elsewhere comparatively low.

Beyond Glenmore are the Grampian Highlands, the
highest of the British uplands, and by far the most
massive in outline, especially towards the east. Southward they end abruptly in a steep brink, which strikes
diagonally across Scotland, on a line nearly but not
quite parallel to Glenmore. For more than a hundred
miles this edge overlooks the central lowland, and forms
the most conspicuous feature in Scottish geography.
Seen from the plain, it has the appearance of a mountain chain, for it rises from little more than sea-level to
heights of 3000 feet : it was hence formerly described as
the Grampian Range. But the Grampian Highlands are,
in fact, a dissected plateau, with an original tilt from the
north-west, cut short by a relatively steep south-eastern
edge. This tilt is still evidenced by the arrangement of
the chief summits. Ben Lomond and Ben Vorlich, each
rising to 3200 feet, stand close to the south-eastern brink ;
Ben More, Ben Lawers, and Lochnagar, with heads between
3800 and 4000 feet, are set in a line parallel to the edge,
but nearly twenty miles within ; while Ben Nevis and Ben
Macdui, respectively 4400 and 4300 feet high, are on the
crest of the long slope, forty miles from the Midland
plain, and immediately above the steep north-westward
fall to Glenmore and Strathspey. Woodland valleys

trench the heathery uplands and breach their dark south-
eastern front, the most deeply cut being that of the
Garry-Tay, descending from the pass of Drumochter, a
col in the Ben Nevis-Macdui line. It is by this valley

FIG. 28.—The Breaks in the Scottish Uplands.

and pass that the great north road and the Highland
Railway are carried, over a summit level of 1500 feet,
from Perth to Inverness. Eastward and westward of the
Tay the surface of the Highlands presents markedly

different features. To westward, in Western Perthshire and
Argyll, the summits are peaked, the glens are deep and
set with lochs, the heights project seaward, leaving little
or no coastal plain, and firths invade the lower reaches
of the valleys, often insulating the uplands (Fig. 29).

FIG. 29.—The North Channel.

Three important ridges of rocky island and peninsula
are thrust from Argyll towards Ireland—Jura and Islay,
Kintyre, Bute and Arran—and it is worthy of note that
Kintyre and Arran advance to southward of the Highland
edge, in such manner as to give the impression of a
slight bend in that feature, where it is broken by the head

of the Firth of Clyde.   Eastward of the Tay the hill-tops are rounded, the valleys are relatively few and lie high, lakes, with the exception of occasional tarns, are wanting, and the uplands do not approach the sea except at Stonehaven.   The great promontory of Buchan (Fig. 30) to northward of the Stonehaven defile, is a detached

FIG. 30.—The Lowland Sill along the North-east Coast.

lowland of triangular outline, with the sea on its salient eastern and northern limits, and the uplands—here more gradually sloped than elsewhere—along its south-western base, between Stonehaven and Elgin.   From Buchan, a sill of coastal plain ten miles broad, forming the district of Moray, runs along the northern foot of the upland to

Inverness and the entry to Glenmore. Bending sharply north-eastward, where it is intersected by the group of inlets which branch from the head of Moray Firth, this sill ends abruptly in Tarbat Ness, just failing to give a continuous lowland pathway from Stonehaven by Aberdeen and Inverness to the terminal lowland of Caithness. Buchan and the sills of Moray and Cromarty bear corn and many cattle, and support the greater part of the population of the Highland counties.

More than half of Scotland lies to the north of the Highland edge. The remainder consists of the Midland Plain and the Southern Uplands, two belts of country which cross the island obliquely from north-east to south-west, each with a breadth of forty or fifty miles. The area of the plain (Fig. 28) is much reduced by re-entering coast-lines, a fact accentuated by the three great estuaries known as the Firths of Tay, Forth, and Clyde. At one point the eastern and western seas are only forty miles apart, whereas the Southern Uplands range through thrice that distance, from the towering cliffs of St. Abb's Head to the hammer-shaped peninsula called the Rhinns of Galloway. Considerable although isolated hill-masses trench still further upon the space available for agriculture, so that in effect the midland plain is a mere reticulation of lowland tracts, bounded northward and southward by upland walls, invaded eastward and westward by arms of the sea and set at intervals with high sterile moorlands. The remainder of its surface bears two-thirds of the Scottish population. Its features exhibit the same intersection of longitudinal and transverse axes as do those of the Highlands and of the Southern Uplands. Longitudinal—striking, that is to say, in a direction parallel to the Highland edge—are the Pentland Hills in the south, the peninsula of Fife from Dunfermline to St. Andrews, the long belt of hills known in successive parts as Sidlaw, Ochil, and Campsie, and the great flat-floored valley of Strathmore, along the foot of the Highland edge. Transverse, on the other hand, are the courses of the Tay and Forth, with the deep gaps in the line of the Sidlaw-Ochils at Perth and Stirling, the valley of the Clyde, and a belt of moorland dividing the Clyde basin from the fertile coastal plain of Ayr. The broken character of the midland plain is clearly indicated by the facts that a submergence of only a hundred feet would suffice to connect the Clyde and the Forth by two sea straits, the one to the north, the other to the south of the Campsie Fells; whereas a submergence of a hundred fathoms would still leave the insular summits of Sidlaw, Ochil, Campsie, and Pentland more than 1000 feet above the water.

The Central Uplands of Great Britain (Figs. 31, 122) occupy a triangular space spreading from St. Abb's Head for 120 miles south-westward towards Ireland, and for 200 miles southward to the Peak of Derbyshire. They are penetrated from the south-west by Solway Firth and divided into three blocks by deeply-cut gaps, the one near the head of the river Tyne, the other near that of the Aire (Fig. 31). The northern block is composed of the Southern Uplands of Scotland, and the parallel, but shorter, range of the Cheviots, on the border between Scotland and England. The mid block consists of the Lake Mountains and the main area of the Pennine Moorlands, while the southern block culminates in the Peak, and includes the lower, southern portion of the Pennines. Although the Tyne and Aire gaps offer passages from east to west at levels lower than 500 feet, yet these are so narrow as not to break the essential unity of the central upland tract. Three other river valleys are significant features in this region. (1) The Nith, corresponding to the Highland Tay, cuts a dale, from north-west to south-east, completely through the Southern Uplands, dividing them into a more tabular portion in the north-east, and a more dissected portion in the south-west. This is the depression made use of by the Glasgow and South-Western Railway between Kilmarnock and Dumfries. (2) The Teviot-Tweed, comparable perhaps to the Spey, occupies the hollow between the Cheviots and the Lammermuir extremity of the Southern Uplands. A bar of hills round the head of Teviotdale, 1000 feet high, connects the south-western end of the Cheviots with the Southern Uplands, and over this is carried the "Waverley" line of the North British Railway, from Carlisle to Melrose. (3) The Eden makes a deep trench between the Lake Mountains and the principal mass of the Pennines. These are connected round the head of Edendale by a south - eastward ridge of 1000 feet, known as Shapfell. The London and North Western "West Coast" line runs over this pass from Lancaster and the south to Carlisle and the north. Thus the Central Uplands twice come down to the western coast —in the Lake group and in Galloway—

Above 600 Ft.

Fig. 31.—Mid-Britain.

whereas they touch the eastern sea only once, in the cliffs of the Lammermuirs. The great dome of the Cheviot end, which marks the Border for coastwise shipping, stands ten miles inland, leaving a broad passage, occupied as far as the Lower Tweed by a northward tongue of English territory. Like the Northern and the Grampian Highlands, the Central Uplands appear to be the remainder of a table-land, for even the Pennine Range has a breadth of forty miles, and there are certain obvious relations in the heights of the major summits. Mount Merrick, in the Southern Uplands, measures 2750 feet ; Broadlaw, forty miles to north-eastward, is only a few feet lower ; and Cheviot Hill is more than 2650 feet. Southward the heights rise a little, to over 3000 feet in the peaks of the Lake district—Scawfell, Helvellyn, and Skiddaw, and to nearly 2900 feet in Cross Fell, the highest of the Pennines. Thence south-ward there is a fall to Whernside, Ingleborough, and Pen-y-gent, whose summits are between 2200 and 2400 feet. It would thus seem that the axis of the tableland may have run from Cross Fell to the Lake group and per-haps to the Isle of Man, which is placed on the same line. The Peak measures only 1900 feet, and the high ground drops abruptly into the English plain with acute salients in its outline towards Nottingham and towards Stoke.

The Welsh upland has a simpler outline than that of the peninsula, of which it forms the basis, for the hills sink to relative insignificance in the two secondary pen-insulas of Carnarvon and Pembroke, and Anglesea is a lowland (Fig. 32). This upland is, in fact, a roughly-rectangular block, whose length is from the north nearly to the south coast of Wales, the eastern margin running parallel to the direction of the Pennine Range, and coin-ciding approximately with the historic boundary of the Principality. Except where the valleys open to the plain, the political border nearly follows the thousand-foot contour-line, but midway along the margin a group of lower ridges is thrust north-eastward through Southern Shropshire, as though to meet the salient south-western angle of the Peak upland. A stratum of cloud spread uniformly at the thousand-foot level would mask indis-tinguishably the Irish Sea and the Cheshire plain ; and would extend unbroken, but for the islets of Clee, Malvern,

and Cotswold, from Wales to London and the Netherlands. Over Shropshire and South Staffordshire, however,
the cloud would be narrowed to a strait, from which the
Wrekin would emerge, the mark of a line of somewhat
higher ground connecting Wales with the Peak beneath
the surface of the cloud. From a historical point of view,
this lowland passage north-westward, defined by the Welsh

FIG. 32.—The Welsh Upland.

and the Peak uplands, is one of the most significant facts
in British geography. Geologically it may be related with
the ancient Hebridean Gulf (Fig. 56).

As in the case of the Northern Uplands, the general
uniformity of the more considerable mountain-heights is
evidence of an original Welsh plateau, reduced to the
present inequalities by long denudation. Cader Idris in
the north, and Brecknock Beacon in the south, each have

an elevation of 2900 feet, although Plynlimmon, between them, falls to 2450 feet. Ramsay long ago pointed out that a plain, inclined very gently seaward, would touch many of the hill-tops of Carmarthenshire and Cardiganshire, and that not one would rise above it. The only approach to a mountain-ridge runs from the Great Orme's Head south-westward towards the Lleyn peninsula, and culminates in the peak of Snowdon at a height of nearly 3600 feet. In rear of this bulwark the fertile shores of the Menai Strait constitute the only extensive fastness of Wales : in the Middle Ages this was the last refuge of her independence. On a smaller scale the Menai line has had the same function in history as Glenmore, to which feature it is very nearly parallel. Elsewhere, Wales lies relatively open to the invader, for the lowland sill of Glamorgan connects the peninsula of Pembroke to England, and the wide valleys of the Dee, Severn, Wye, and Usk, seaming all the centre of the upland, descend eastward to the plain, not directly to the sea.

South of Wales, in the Devonian peninsula, are two broken belts of upland, lying eastward and westward, parallel to one another and to the Bristol Channel. The more northern commences in the Quantocks of Western Somerset, is continued in Exmoor, and may once have extended twenty miles beyond the cliffs of Ilfracombe to the islet of Lundy. The other consists of two separate hill-masses, Dartmoor and the Bodmin Moors, divided by the deep valley of the Tamar. Between these uplands—rising to 2000 feet in Dartmoor and to 1700 feet in Exmoor—spreads a broad belt of fertile lowland occupying most of Northern Devon. Beyond Bodmin, Cornwall is not elevated, but is edged with cliffs. The Cornish axis is continued in the Scilly Isles.

Westward of the belt of the greater British uplands, were the land to sink a hundred fathoms, would be an archipelago of mountainous islands representing Ireland, for the configuration of Ireland is in sharp contrast to that of Great Britain, not because it has few or low mountains, but because there are no wide uplands similar to

those of the greater island (Fig. 33).   There are **heights
of two or more thousand feet** in nearly half of the thirty-
three counties of Ireland—in Wicklow of three thousand,
and in Kerry of three thousand four hundred feet—and
yet plain is the characteristic formation of the island, as it
is of Central Scotland—the Scotland of Edinburgh and

OVER 600 FT

MIDLAND PLAIN

FIG. 33.—The High Grounds of Ireland.

Glasgow.   Both regions would be described as **mountainous** by an inhabitant of the centre or south of
England ; for the Scottish and Irish plains, although continuous, are set with isolated mountain groups, between
which the larger areas of lowland are connected by lowland
straits.   Only in one part of Ireland is there a stretch of

plain without sight of the mountains. For fifty miles to the north of Dublin the coasts of the Irish Sea are low, and a tract of plain commencing here spreads westward for 150 miles to where the mountains of Connaught rise like a rim along the Atlantic border. At Galway, at Ballina, and at one or two other points only does the central Irish plain come through to the oceanic coast. Strips of lowland penetrate the northern and southern groups of uplands to the coasts of Ulster and Munster, so that it has been easy to put Belfast and Waterford into canal communication with the water-ways of the central plain. The more considerable of the divided hill-groups are in Donegal—opposite to the Scottish Highlands, in Down—in prolongation of the Southern Scottish Uplands, in Wicklow—over against the Welsh Upland, in Tipperary —by the Lower Shannon, in the Atlantic border of Connaught, and in Munster—where the parallel ridges project seaward, forming the characteristic fringe of promontories to north-west of Cape Clear.

East of the Devonian and Cambrian Uplands, and south and east of the Pennine Upland, is the lowland plain of England, occupying about one-third of the area of all Britain. In the neighbourhood of the defining uplands, its surface is diversified by a few isolated hills of considerable elevation: the North York Moors have tops of nearly 1500 feet, and the Wrekin one of nearly 1350 ; the Malvern Ridge has a peak of nearly 1700 feet and a single point in the Cotswold reaches 1100 feet. Elsewhere the rises on the plain vary from 600 to 1000 feet, except in a district based on the North Sea coast and bounded inland by a curve from Flamborough Head, by Nottingham, Leicester, and Bedford, to Harwich, within which no point touches 300 feet. The plain comes down to the western seas only at two points, through the Cheshire gap, and at the head of the Bristol Channel. It is important, however, to note that the open shore of Ireland north of Dublin —the only considerable stretch of low-lying coast in that island—lies precisely opposite to the Cheshire gap.

Thus Britain is seen to contain three important

uplands and three extensive lowlands. The Scottish Highlands are placed terminally, but the Central Uplands divide the Scottish from the English lowland, and the Welsh upland intervenes between the English lowland and Ireland. In other words, the relief of the surface accentuates the triple division indicated by the coastal outlines. Moreover, the English plain fills the continental angle of Britain to the shores of the narrow seas, whereas the Scottish and Irish plains are isolated among the uplands of the oceanic border. It is noteworthy, however, that the belt of most massive uplands does not lie parallel to the oceanic edge, but northward and southward through the centre of Britain, and that the belt of seas dividing Long Island and Ireland from Great Britain has a similar trend.

Note on contoured maps.—An account of the gradual evolution of the methods of depicting terrain-forms upon maps will be found in an address read by Mr. H. J. Mackinder at the British Association, and printed in the *Geographical Journal,* vol. vi., under the title, " Modern Geography, German and English." An excellent means of studying the land relief of Great Britain is now available in Bartholomew's coloured contour maps, on a scale of two miles to the inch, reduced from the Ordnance Survey. Unfortunately, there is as yet no such publication in Ireland. The new edition of the one-inch Ordnance map with brown hill-shading is for these purposes a great improvement on the old.

Note on Drumalban and the Mounth.—Although the Grampian Highlands constitute merely a dissected tableland and no true mountain-range, yet they contain two dividing lines, which demand special notice, by reason of their historical importance. Drumalban and the Mounth define Perthshire respectively to the west and the north. The former, although not a conspicuous ridge, is a portion of the chief water-parting of Scotland. The latter is a coherent ridge extending from Stonehaven to Drumochter.

CHAPTER VI

THE STRUCTURE OF BRITAIN

THE contrast between the south-east and the north-west of Britain, between the plains and low coasts towards the continent, and the cliff-edged uplands of the oceanic border, with all the resultant differences—agricultural, industrial, racial, and historical—depends on a fundamental distinction in rock structure. In the south-east are sands, clays, friable sandstones, chalk, and soft limestones. In the north and west the sandstones are for the most part hard and gritty, often so hard and compact as to become quartzite; the clays have been pressed into slates; the limestones are crystalline, sometimes becoming marble, and igneous rocks abound, which, together with the sediments, have often been crushed into schists and gneisses. In Britain, but not in all parts of the world, the harder rocks are the more ancient, and despite the lapse of time, they still rise into uplands and into peaks, while the newer softer deposits of the south-east have been reduced to lowlands in a comparatively short geological time (Figs. 26, 34). Wherever borings, whether for water or coal, have been carried to sufficient depth through the clays and chalk of the south-east, these deposits have been found to rest upon a floor of older rocks which, alike in texture and contained fossils, are identical with those exposed in the northern and western hills. The material of the lowlands has been derived, in the process of ages, mainly from the decay of the north-western uplands, but to some extent from old upland districts now denuded and partly buried beneath the newer rocks.

Nowhere is the relation between rock structure and surface-form more simple than in the Pennine Chain, the moorland range which occupies the central belt of the isthmus connecting North to South Britain (Fig. 35). It consists of three series of strata : first and lowest is the Mountain Limestone ; covering the limestone, and there-

FIG. 34.—The Older and the Newer Rocks of Britain.

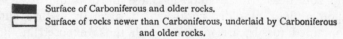

Surface of Carboniferous and older rocks.
Surface of rocks newer than Carboniferous, underlaid by Carboniferous and older rocks.

fore deposited later, is the Millstone Grit ; uppermost, and therefore most recent, is the great series of clays and flag-stones, with occasional seams of coal, which are known as the Coal Measures. The whole carboniferous[1] series—

[1] Note, p. 81.

Limestone, Grit, and Coal Measures—is many thousand feet in vertical thickness, and must have been laid down during long centuries in nearly horizontal strata. Subsequently, irresistible forces acting from east and west, caused the rock-layers to arch upward into a great fold, striking north and south for two hundred miles. As the ground rose into the rains and frosts of the upper air, the crest of the fold was planed down, so that the older rocks, forming the core, came to be exposed along the central line of the denuded arch ; while on either hand, to east and to west, the flanks were formed by the cut edges of the upper strata. Thus the beds of coal which were once continuous across most of the north of England

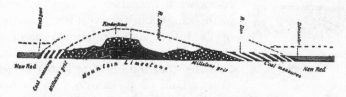

FIG. 35.—East and West Section through the Pennine Chain.

have been removed from the top of the Pennine upfold, and divided into Yorkshire and Lancashire coalfields. Even the mountain limestone has been laid bare along parts of the axis.

At the close of the epoch of rock movement came a fresh series of deposits : the first of the newer, softer rocks of the south-east, as the carboniferous deposits were the last of the older, harder rocks of the north-west. Alike on the Lancashire and the Yorkshire sides of the Pennine Range, clays and sandstones of the series known as the New Red were thrown down in nearly horizontal strata upon the upturned worn edges of the outer, and therefore upper Coal Measures (Fig. 35). These later deposits have suffered little subsequent change. They lie in almost horizontal sheets in the position in which they were originally formed, although somewhat lifted from the level of

5

the shallow seas or lakes in which they accumulated. The occurrence of newer horizontal beds, resting upon the upturned edges of older strata, constitutes the striking geological phenomenon known as unconformability (Fig. 36). Where it is observed, four successive periods of geological history may be enumerated: first, the deposit in nearly horizontal layers of the older rocks; secondly, the crumpling of these rocks, however massive, by giant lateral forces in the earth's crust; thirdly, the denudation of the upper parts of the folds, leaving the cut edges of the tilted strata exposed in a land-surface or shallow sea-bed; and fourthly, the horizontal deposit of newer rocks upon the denuded surface. In the case of the Pennine upland we have no evidence that the New Red rocks were deposited across the crest of the range, but they rest horizontally, or at a low angle, upon the uptilted strata on its flanks. It is, therefore, probable that the Pennine Range stood as an island or promontory above the surface of the New Red waters. To-day, the green and fertile plains of Yorkshire, Lancashire, and Cheshire are underlaid by the soft sandstones and marls of the New Red series, and through these the sterile moorlands emerge from their hidden foundations.

FIG. 36.—Unconformable Strata.

Occasionally the rocks break under the bending stresses, and an upward and downward movement is effected, not by a bend but by the sliding of two rock faces upon one another, the one upward and the other downward. Such fracture of too rigid strata may take place deep under the land-surface, producing an earthquake. When examined in a geological section the result is described as a fault. It may be simulated if a block of grained wood be sawn through and the divided faces be made to slide upon one another for a short distance; though the grain of the two surfaces corresponds with exactness, no point in the one block will remain opposite to its fellow in the other. Such a fault occurs along the north-west of the Pennine Range, where the Eden Valley of Cumberland has been let down and partly filled with newer, softer deposits (Fig. 37), above which, for a distance north and south of some forty miles, the broken edge of the Pennine upland rises cliff-like into Cold and Cross Fells. The dip of the Pennine strata is, in this part, wholly.eastward ; the western front of the upland being formed by a fault-scarp overlooking the Cumbrian lowland. In the district of Craven, where the

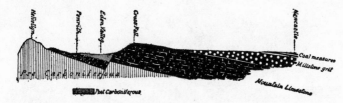

FIG. 37.—East and West Section through the Eden Valley and the Northern Pennine Moors.

Aire breaks through the Pennine upfold, are other great faults, determinative of the surface-forms.

The structure of Scotland is almost precisely the converse of that of England, for whereas the Pennine Range stands as an upland, with coal on its flanks, and is girt and partly overlaid by the softer, more recent deposits of New Red age, in Scotland the coal and other rocks of Pennine age lie low, let down below the general level. Moreover, the greater part of England is a plain composed of rocks of newer than Pennine (or carboniferous) date, while the greater part of Scotland consists of uplands whose rocks are older than the carboniferous. The Scottish Highlands and Southern Uplands are made of hard and very ancient rock. Between them, defined by two long lines of parallel hill-face stretched diagonally across the island from the Firths of Tay and Forth to the Firth of Clyde, is the broad lowland known, for lack of a better name, as the Midland Valley of Scotland (Fig. 38). The surface of this valley

or plain consists of rocks of Old Red and Carboniferous
age, but beneath these is a floor of more ancient date,
contemporary with the surface rocks of the Highlands
and Southern Uplands.   This buried floor was once
flush with the uplands to north and south of it, but
two parallel cracks or faults ran diagonally across the

FIG. 38.—The Structure of Scotland.

once united surface, and the intervening block was let
down to a lower level.   The downward slip was renewed
again and again, and the block itself was crumpled into
troughs and crests, for the most part parallel with the
boundary faults.   The whole process was probably
spread over a considerable period, during which the

district was subjected to violent earthquakes, each caused by a fresh slip of a few feet, the result of a few inches of greater crushing and bending. The facts are somewhat masked in Scotland by antiquity and the accidents of later geological history. In Central Europe, however, there is a district, in Alsace and Baden, where a similar block has been let down, and buried under the fertile alluvium of the Middle Rhine between Basle and Mainz : the Black Forest and the Vosges, once a continuous boss of ancient rocky upland, have been riven by parallel faults, and separated by the collapse of the intervening mass. But the formation of fault-bounded valleys is probably still in active progress in the western United States and in the newly-discovered heart of Africa. Upon the ancient gneissic tableland which constitutes the east of tropical Africa are two lakes of remarkable shape, Tanganyika and Nyasa, each three or four hundred miles long and thirty or forty broad. They are deep, yet a hundred times broader than deep. Their edges, eastern and western, are the scarped fronts of the surrounding tableland visible from shore to shore across the water. The still greater Victoria Nyanza is of quite another formation, rounded and relatively shallow, a mere pan on the surface of the plateau ; but further to eastward is the Great Rift Valley, similar in character to Tanganyika and Nyasa, although dry. It runs from north to south, broad and flat-bottomed, defined by facing cliffs—a slip of the plateau let down below the general level. The Red Sea and the Jordan Valley are of like nature. Thus the Midland Valley of Scotland belongs to a class of phenomena, and is an example of the Rift Valley type of land-structure.

The deposits which have been preserved in the Scottish Rift are of three kinds. Lying upon the ancient floor are Old Red Sandstones ; above these are vast sheets of volcanic rock of a highly resistant character ; uppermost are the Coal Measures, which, like the sandstones, have relatively small power of resisting denudation. The chain of the Ochil and Sidlaw Hills is due to the upfolding of

the volcanic layers in a line parallel to the northern
boundary fault. Owing to the crumpling of the rock
crust along this and other axes, the strata have been
thrown into basin-shaped curves, within which denudation
has spared the Coal Measures, although they have been
removed, as in the case of the Pennine Range, from the
upfolds around. The Scottish coalfields occupy three
such basins (Fig. 39). One underlies the plain between
Ayr and Kilmarnock, to westward
of the hilly belt,
due to an upfold
of the volcanic
beds, which forms
the boundary of
Ayrshire towards
Renfrew and Lanark. The second
and most important extends
south - eastward
along the Clyde
for twenty miles
above Glasgow,
and north - eastward, beneath the
Forth, to Clackmannan. The
third, divided
from the second

FIG. 39.—The Coal-basins of the Scottish Rift Valley.

by the Pentland ridge of volcanic and older rocks, underlies the lower valley of the Midlothian Esk, and spreads
beneath the Firth of Forth into the county of Fife, eastward of Kirkcaldy. The long depression of Strathmore
between the Highland edge and the Ochil-Sidlaw range
has been worn from the Old Red Sandstone, where it
crops out on the surface along the edge of the Rift. In
the other plains of the Rift Valley are many isolated crags,
due to the hard cores which finally cooled in the tubes

of the Carboniferous volcanoes ; such are Edinburgh Castle Rock, the Bass Rock, and North Berwick Law.

Between the Pennine Range and the Carboniferous area of the Scottish Midland Valley is the belt of Ordovician and Silurian rocks which constitutes the Southern Scottish Upland. The rock layers have here been contorted into a great series of folds striking south-westward in harmony with the general trend of the range. The structure is admirably exposed at either end of the system, where it is cut short in the sea cliffs of St. Abb's Head and of the Rhinns of Galloway. Especially in the latter section, the strata are seen to be overfolded (Fig. 40) in an outward direction towards the northern and southern margins of the range. In this respect the rocks of Southern Scotland exhibit the build of a true mountain range (Fig. 41),

but the existing hills and valleys have small relation to that structure. The original range appears to have been planed away, and the present features to have been chiselled afresh from the resulting plateau. Cheviot Hill is a

FIG. 40.—Overfolded Strata.

mass of volcanic rock laid bare by denudation, and the open valley of the Lower Tweed has been worn from a district of less resistant deposits dating from the Old Red and Carboniferous epochs.

The Highlands resemble the Southern Uplands in the south-westerly trend of their rock-folds, and in the fact that the surface features cannot have been directly caused by the crumpling of the strata. No clearer proof can be imagined of the vast denudation which must have preceded the origin of the present features than is supplied by the lie of the rocks in such a mountain as Ben Lawers. To the very top it consists of down-folded beds (Fig. 42), so that the existing summit must be a wedge remaining from the trough of the bend, and great upfolds must once have risen from either flank of the mountain, high above the level of the present peak. In the midst of the Grampian Highlands masses of granite, crystallised in the depths, have been exposed by the removal of overlying rocks, and now stand above the surrounding less resistant schists and slates, as the chief summits of Britain. Ben Macdhui and its great neighbours, Cairn Toul and Cairn Gorm, Lochnagar, Ben Cruachan, Ben Alder, and the greater part of Ben Nevis are granitic, as is also Buchan Ness, the easternmost point of Scotland, which still withstands the scour of the North Sea storms. Glenmore follows the line of a south-westerly fault, and occasional disturbances in the water of Loch Ness, especially at the time of earthquakes in other parts of the world, suggest that a state

FIG. 41.—Cross section through rock-folding in a true mountain range, with subsequent plateau-surface.

of equilibrium may not even yet have been established. The origin of this great fracture must have been in the remote past, for on either bank of Loch Ness the Old Red Sandstones rest nearly horizontally on the upturned edges of the Highland schists. Sandstones of similar date form the plain of Caithness and the coastal sills round Moray Firth. Still further proof of secular denudation is to be found in Glen Avon, at the northern foot of the Cairn Gorm group, in the position of undisturbed sandstones of Old Red age at an elevation of 1700 feet. Similar deposits occur up to the summits of Mealfourvonie and Morven, respectively 2000 and 2200 feet high. The Old Red Sandstones may once, in fact, have filled Moray Firth and have buried the greater part of Buchan.

The western edge of the Northern Highlands, from Cape Wrath to the southern point of Sleat, presents another contrast to the usually schistose structure of the Highlands; this is due, however, not to overlying and newer

FIG. 42.—Down-folded strata in a mountain-summit.

deposits, but to the emergence of Archæan rocks of the remotest antiquity from under the general mass of the upland (Fig. 38). Upon a worn floor of granitoid gneiss are piled great isolated stacks of the most ancient sandstone, rising in the pyramid of Suilven to nearly 2400 feet. These sandstones must once have spread continuously over much of the district, and no more striking evidence is to be found in all Britain of the vast effects wrought by the weather. Long Island, across the Minch, is also composed of granitoid gneiss.

Among the Inner Hebrides are the two important islands of Skye and Mull, whose appearance as seen from the sea betokens a quite other structure and substance from those of the mainland and of most of the islands. From vertical cliffs, towering in places to 1000 feet, their surfaces rise, terrace above terrace, like a giant staircase, to table-topped heights. The scarps are a rich brown, and the sloping treeless terraces covered with green pasture. Here and there are walls of cliff which a close inspection shows to consist of innumerable columns of basalt, caverned at intervals into cathedral-like recesses. Seaward are Staffa and other islets of the same unmistakable structure, indicating the former wider extension of the layers of brown columnar rock. Away to the south, in the county of Antrim, where are the well-known columnar terraces of the Giant's Causeway, occur even greater accumulations of basalt, covering most of the north-eastern corner of Ireland. Each basaltic layer was once a flood of liquid lava welled up from below. As the lava cooled and solidified, intersecting cracks opened its substance, giving to it a columnar structure, precisely as the mud exposed along a tidal river will crack and become columnar when dried by the sun. In the Sound of Mull, where the basalt has invaded the mainland, the deposits on either hand, though separated by the breadth of the channel, correspond with one another, terrace for terrace, to a height of 2000 feet. The Sound has been cut through what were originally continuous beds, and vast quantities of the rock have been removed. It was once a valley, opened by streams, and has been converted into a strait by the partial submergence of the whole region. At four points—in Mull, at Ardnamurchan Point, in the island of Rum, and in the Coolin Hills of Skye—the basaltic beds have been pierced by the intrusive lava of subsequent eruptions, and four great volcanoes (Fig. 43) appear to have rested upon the basaltic plateaux, much as Kenya and Kilimanjaro now stand upon the basaltic plateaux of Eastern Africa. The volcanic rocks of the Western Isles are of early Tertiary date, and, therefore, even younger than the deposits which form the English plain. Here and there along the cliffs, the basalt may be seen to rest on an underlying formation (Fig. 44). Alike in Skye, in Mull, and in Antrim thin layers of soft rock, contemporary with the chalk and clays of South-eastern England, are often sandwiched between the overlying basalt and the ancient floor of

Stumps of Volcanoes
Lavas......

FIG. 43.—The recent volcanic areas of Western Scotland.

gneiss or schists. Such recent rocks are unknown elsewhere in Scotland or Ireland.

If the island of Skye—with the exception of the Sleat peninsula at its eastern end, which is not volcanic—be removed from the map, and the land outline be restored to what it doubtless was before the volcanic outburst, a broad channel, the Minch, will be seen to separate the whole length of Long Island from the mainland of

Scotland. Entering from the north, between the Butt of Lewis and Cape Wrath, it would extend south-south-westward for nearly 150 miles with an average breadth of about 30 miles. At the southern end, a half-drowned ridge, consisting of Sleat, Coll, Tyree, and the storm-beaten rock of Skerryvore, converges somewhat towards the end of Long Island, where this tapers to Barra Head. Eigg, Rum, and Canna are detached portions of the volcanic deposits of Skye, but Sleat, Coll, and Tyree belong to the same rock system as the mainland. Along its

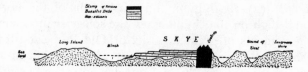

FIG. 44.—Section through the Island of Skye.

clean-cut eastern face, Long Island descends steeply into some of the deepest water within the continental plateau, a line of pits, like submerged lakes, some of them more than a hundred fathoms deep. The suggestion is irresistible that the Minch is a submerged Rift Valley with collapsed floor, fault bounded, like the Rift Valley of Central Scotland. Within the trough, at a time when Long Island and the Scottish Highlands stood above the water much as they do now, were laid the deposits contemporary with those of the plain of England, and a great plain of soft and doubtless fertile rock subsequently extended from Cape Wrath to the site of Belfast. This plain was finally desolated by volcanic eruptions on the scale of those which have formed the island of Java in the Malay Archipelago. Even since that relatively late epoch there has been time enough for the rains and frosts to degrade the new volcanic plateau, and for the Atlantic storms to erode it marginally, with the result that the basalt has been removed, save in Skye, Mull, and Antrim, and at a few other points, and all trace of the lowland deposits which preceded the volcanoes has been lost, except here and there where they crop out along the foot of the basaltic cliffs. Borings would doubtless reveal complete sheets of these softer rocks under Antrim, for white chalk underlying dark basalt is a characteristic feature of the cliffs of that county.

The Scottish Highlands thus consist of four great rock systems, each with a different type of topographical detail and scenery. (1) The central mass, extending through both the Grampian and the Northern Highlands, is mainly of schists and slates with included granite, and occasionally quartzite. (2) Resting on the coastal sills of the north-east, and high on the shoulders of the schistose mountains, are the remains of great deposits of Old Red Sandstone. (3) Emergent along the western rim of the mainland and through the whole length of Long Island is the basement of Archæan gneiss, loaded here and there with pyramids of the most ancient sandstone. (4) Skye and Mull, and some of their lesser neighbours, are of late volcanic make, though founded upon the schists and gneiss. And there are two great structural features, (i.) the fracture marked by Glenmore and the connected Firths of Lorne and Moray, and (ii.) the Rift Valley of the Minch, partly submerged under the sea and partly under the tertiary lavas.

The essential elements of the structure of Ireland become apparent if the basalt and chalk be removed from the map, and the county Antrim be thus reduced to a lowland (Fig. 45). In the north-west, Lough Foyle and Donegal Bay define the peninsula of Donegal, which stretches for sixty miles south-westward from Malin Head and Inishowen to the cliffs of Slieve League. Its valleys and ridges also strike in a south-westerly direction, and its rocks have the same ancient schistose character as the mountains of Islay and of the Grampian Highlands, from which Donegal has obviously been detached. Away to the south-east, opposite to the Isle of Man, are the Mourne Mountains, the most conspicuous group of an upland tract which extends from the North Channel south-westward, and sinks gradually into the central plain on the borders of Leinster. By direction and rock structure this tract is a continuation of the Southern Uplands of Scotland. It is divided from the mountains of Donegal, Tyrone, and Londonderry by a belt of lowland, whose true character is revealed by the imaginary

Precarboniferous	
Carboniferous	
Post Carboniferous	

FIG. 45.—The Structure of Ireland, as related to that of Great Britain.

removal of the recently-formed plateau of Antrim. The Central Valley of Scotland is continued through the Clyde Sea and across the North Channel, beneath Antrim and Lough Neagh, and, far into the heart of Ireland, between the ancient uplands of Donegal on the one hand, and the Mourne Mountains on the other. South-west of Lough Neagh is the little coalfield of Tyrone in the midst of the same Rift Valley as has preserved the coal of Ayr and Lanark.

In the west of Connaught, dividing the central plain from the Atlantic shore, is a belt of ancient upland extended northward and southward through Mayo and Connemara, and defined inland by the chain of Loughs Corrib, Mask, and Conn. This upland rim strikes southward from Donegal, much as the ancient peninsula of Kintyre projects southward of the Highland edge.

Eastward of the Mourne Mountains are two isolated bosses of lofty and ancient rock—the Isle of Man, and the lake mountains of Cumberland and Westmorland. The Lake upland, though markedly different in structure and built of far more ancient rocks, is connected with the Pennine Chain by the neck of high ground known as Shap Fell. The central uplands of Great Britain, while coherent in outline, are thus a group of four separate structural elements. (1) The Southern Scottish Uplands consist of Ordovician and Silurian rocks striking south-westward. (2) The Cheviot Hills are in the main due to the superior resistance of a mass of volcanic rock of Old Red age. (3) The Lake Mountains are due to a similar but much older volcanic mass of Ordovician date. (4) The Pennine Range is an upfold of Carboniferous rocks striking southward.

South of the Irish Sea is the Welsh upland, and opposite to this, in Ireland, the smaller upland of Wicklow or Leinster. Alike in geological age, in structure, and in landscape, Wales and Wicklow present so striking a resemblance that we must think of them as severed portions of a single mass in parts even more ancient than Cumbria, Man, and the Mourne Mountains. On both sides of the St. George's Channel, the lie of the rock-folds is south-westward. The axis of the combined uplands seems to have traversed Anglesey and the corner of Ireland at Carnsore Point. Considerable areas of the basal Archæan rock are exposed in Anglesey, and that island has a position, relatively to the Welsh Upland, which is comparable to that of the Archæan rim of North-western Scotland relatively to the Highlands. It is, moreover, noteworthy that Anglesey has been worn to a lowland, just as has the Archæan Lewis in the north of Long Island. The dominance of the Snowdon Range is due to a series of highly-resistant volcanic beds of Ordovician age, which have been laid bare by vast denudation. Conclusive evidence of such denudation is the fact that the highest peak in Wales is composed of rocks exhibiting a down-folded structure similar to that of Ben Lawers (Fig. 42).

The centre of Ireland is occupied by a plain of almost horizontal and undisturbed carboniferous lime-

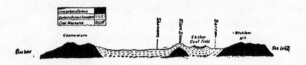

FIG. 46.—West and East Section through Ireland.

stone, usually hidden by surface deposits of marsh and bog. Coal Measures once covered the limestone, and probably spread across the Irish Sea to join the coalfield of Lancashire, but they were guarded by no cross-folding of the strata productive of rock-basins. Their relics, however, still remain, usually on higher grounds, as in the coalfield of Leinster (Fig. 46). Round the margin of the limestone plain, the pre-carboniferous rocks emerge in bordering uplands—the Mourne Mountains, and the mountains of Donegal, Connaught, and Wicklow—but between the Wicklow and the Mourne Mountains there is an interval of nearly fifty miles in which the limestone comes down to the Irish Sea.

Ireland everywhere consists of the detached ends of the features of Great Britain, and the structure of Southern Ireland is intimately connected with that of South Wales and South-western England. The predominant lie of the rock-folds of Southern Britain is from west to east, tending sometimes to south-east and sometimes to south-west. The Mendip Range of Somerset is a complete

upfold of carboniferous limestone, whose axis extends
for twenty miles from south-east to north-west, between
the basin of the Bristol Avon and the marshes round
Glastonbury. At its south-eastern end it dips under the
edge of the newer rocks which constitute the English
plain. To the north-west, beyond Weston-super-Mare,
it has been breached by the mouth of the Severn ; but
the Steep Holme, an islet of carboniferous limestone,
prolongs the axis and indicates the connection with
the coast of Glamorgan. The coalfields of Bristol, the
Forest of Dean, South Wales, and Pembroke lie in basins,
defined by upfolds extended eastward and westward,
which are crossed by other upfolds directed northward
and southward. The peninsula of Gower and the inlets
of Milford Haven and St. Bride's Bay give coastal indications of the east and west lie of the structure-lines. The
Bristol Channel itself belongs to the same system, as does
Exmoor, whose axis is prolonged into the isle of Lundy.
In the south of Ireland the upper valleys of the Blackwater, Lee, and Bandon, with their connected ridges
of Galty More and Knockmealdown, exhibit the same
persistent east and west trend ; while the Ria[1] inlets
which give so characteristic an appearance to the map
of Western Munster—Bantry Bay, Kenmare River, and
Dingle Bay—are bent somewhat to the south of west.
The ridge crests in the south of Ireland are formed of
upfolded sandstone of Old Red date, while the valleys are
floored with strips of carboniferous limestone still preserved in the Old Red downfolds. Geographical valley
and geological downfold here coincide with a precision
that is rare.

Devonshire and Cornwall consist of rocks contemporary with those of Wales. The folding crosses the land
diagonally from east to west, and the south-westerly lie of
the peninsula appears to be due to a series of granitic
bosses similar to those of the Grampian Highlands. The
Land's End and the Scilly Isles represent the most outlying
of these resistant masses.

[1] Note, p. 82.

The most general statements which can be made regarding the structure of Britain appear, therefore, to be
(1) that in Scotland, in two-thirds of Ireland, and in North
Wales, the rock-folds and some of the greater faults have
a south-westerly direction, roughly parallel to the oceanic
border ; (2) that in the Pennine Range the axis of the
folding is southward, parallel to the belt of Hebridean
and Irish Seas and to the chain of the greater British
uplands ; and (3) that in the peninsulas between the
Channel-entries the folds run eastward and westward,
and are broken more or less obliquely by the mouths
of the channels. The immensity of denudation, proved
by the structure of such mountains as Snowdon and Ben
Lawers, may be correlated with the general equivalence
of altitude presented by the higher summits.[1] These facts
lead to the conclusion, that the existing uplands are
essentially dissected plateaux, whose features have only a
subordinate dependence on the folding of the rock beds.
But the discussion of this subject cannot be completed
until after the analysis of the river-systems.

Note on geological terminology and on the successive geological ages.
—Technical terms have been avoided as far as possible in this chapter.
The words " upfold" and "downfold" have been substituted for anticline
and syncline as being more suggestive, and as leading on to the idea of
"overfold," which again is analogous to "overthrust." A concise treat-
ment of the geological ideas involved may be found in such a book as
Marr's " Stratigraphical Geology" in the Cambridge Science Series.

From the point of view here taken the geological epoch of greatest
significance is the carboniferous, shortly before and after whose close
took place the great " Hercynian" rock movements, which have so radi-
cally affected British geography. Deposits are, therefore, counted as
older or newer with reference to this horizon. The terms employed to
indicate the successive ages are as follows :—

Older.	*Newer.*		
Archæan.	Triassic or New Red.		
Cambrian.	Jurassic.		
Ordovician.	Cretaceous.		
Silurian.			Earlier.
Devonian, or Old Red.	Tertiary—		Later.
Carboniferous.			Glacial.
			Post Glacial.

---

[1] See Chap. V.

Note on the difference between fiords and rias.—As pointed out by von Richthofen, a fundamental distinction should be drawn between such inlets as have deeps, like submerged lakes, in their upper reaches, and such as shallow continuously from their mouths. The former are true fiords ; for the latter von Richthofen has proposed the term *Ria*, a name given locally to the inlets of Galicia in Spain. Although differing in physical history, their horizontal outlines are often similar, as may be seen by comparing Scottish fiords like Loch Linnhe and Loch Fyne with such South British Rias as Bantry Bay, Kenmare River, Dingle Bay, Falmouth Sound, and Plymouth Sound. Western Brittany, also, is a Ria-coast.

Note on authorities.—The control exercised by the geological structure on the land-relief is perhaps the only aspect of British geography which has been adequately presented in works generally accessible. Of such it suffices here to enumerate " The Physical Geology and Geography of Great Britain," by Sir A. C. Ramsay (edit. Woodward) ; " The Physical Geology and Geography of Ireland," by E. Hull ; and " The Scenery of Scotland," by Sir A. Geikie. Reference should also be made to Sir A. Geikie's work on " The Ancient Volcanoes of Great Britain." For the purposes of geography the cheap and admirably coloured index maps of the Geological Survey are invaluable. They are on the scale of four miles to the inch, which admits of the insertion of almost every geological fact of sufficient importance to influence the geographical forms and activities.

CHAPTER VII

THE ENGLISH PLAIN

IN few equal areas on the globe is there a more varied accumulation of the newer rocks than in the English plain. Between London and Chester a traveller would cross in regular succession deposits of all ages, from the early Tertiary down to the beginning of the New Red. The centre of the plain, round Birmingham, consists of New Red Sandstones and Clays, and these deposits spread from this point in three directions: along the lower Severn towards Bristol; through the Cheshire Gap to Liverpool; and along the lower Trent and Yorkshire Ouse to the mouth of the Tees. Westward and northward the New Red formation laps round the Cambrian and Pennine uplands, where their rocks sink into the ancient floor underlying the clays and sands of the plain; but eastward and south-eastward it is overlaid by an edge or escarpment of Jurassic limestone, and borings have proved that it extends for some distance in these directions under the covering of later deposits (Fig. 47). The Jurassic escarpment curves across England from Cleveland in the north to the Cotswolds in the south-west, and the limestone beds, which are cut short along its front, dip gently eastward and south-eastward, to disappear finally under a belt of clays, with interbedded sands. These clays and sands, of upper Jurassic age, form the ground under Oxford and Bedford, and in their turn dip under a Cretaceous escarpment, which runs from Flamborough Head through the Chilterns to West Dorset, curving sympathetically with the Jurassic escarpment to north-westward of it. The beds of the soft limestone known as chalk, whose edges are exposed on the face of the Cretaceous scarp, slope eastward and south-eastward, in accordance with the regional tilt, and pass under the thick clays of early Tertiary date, of and upon which London has been built. At several points deep borings for water have pierced the London clay to the underlying chalk. The eastern halves of Norfolk and Suffolk are characterised by a late Tertiary formation, called the Crag, which rests directly upon the chalk, the London

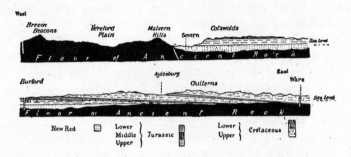

FIG. 47.—West and East Section through the English Plain.

clay having apparently been removed from this district before the Crag was deposited.

As a consequence of this structure the English plain has a grained surface, like that of sawn timber, and consists of alternating belts which have very various powers of resisting denudation (Fig. 48). Owing to the fact that water cannot pass through beds of clay, the rainfall is discharged from clay districts mainly by surface drainage, and the fine substance of the clay is steadily removed by turbid brooks. Sandstones and the softer limestones, on the other hand, allow much of the rainwater to percolate downward, and so greatly reduce the erosive power of the streams. Thus the more porous rocks, by yielding a ready passage to the moisture, preserve a comparatively high resistance to denudation, whereas the impervious clays are rapidly degraded. By these processes, the English plain, formed of more and less resistant belts, has been scoured, like grained wood

worn with age, to a ribbed surface of alternating upper
and lower strips. Two broad belts of upper ground,
formed of Cretaceous and Jurassic limestones, each
limited westward and north-westward by a considerable
escarpment, sever three lower belts, consisting chiefly

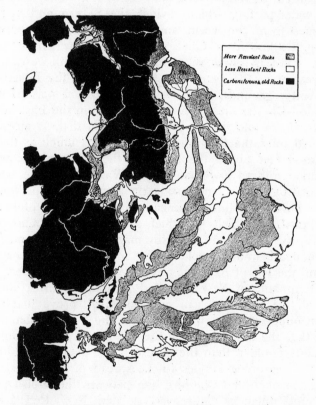

FIG. 48.—The more and the less resistant belts of the English Plain.

of clay-bottomed vales, broken here and there by sandy
and even limestone rises. Such rises are Hampstead and
Bagshot Heaths amid the London clay, Woburn Heath
and Shotover Hill amid the Oxford and Aylesbury clays,
and Cannock Chase and Delamere Forest in the wider
district of the New Red clay. Owing to the tilt of the

beds, the top of the chalk does not stand higher than the Jurassic escarpment, although it is composed of deposits which rest upon the Jurassic rocks.

The belts of lower clay ground, having been denuded chiefly by running water, remain a little higher near the sources of the streams than elsewhere. Therefore on the water-parting which divides the Severn and upper Thames from the Trent and Wash rivers, or, roughly, along the line from London to Chester, the ribs of the plain stand in lower relief than further south-westward, by reason of the generally higher level of the intervening softer grounds. To the north-east, however, of the London-Chester line, in East Anglia and in the East Midlands, the whole surface is depressed, so that, as already pointed out,[1] the hills nowhere rise to as much as three hundred feet above the sea, and the intervening lower grounds sink so low that, in the Wash, they have been invaded by the sea, and, over large areas, their constituent clays have been buried beneath marshy flats of alluvium and peat, of which the chief are the Fens round the Wash, the Louth and Grimsby marsh along the Lincolnshire coast, and Hatfield Chase and the ring of marsh round the Isle of Axholme at the head of the Humber.

Remnants of New Red and Jurassic deposits, along the shores of Glamorgan and Somerset, prove that the plain once extended where is now the Bristol Channel, and that the break between the Welsh and the Devonian uplands is older than the oldest of the plain formations. Similar reasoning applies to the spread of the New Red strata through the Cheshire gap between the Welsh and Pennine uplands. Moreover, isolated New Red areas exist in the Cumbrian Vale of Eden, in the 'North Welsh Clwyd Valley, and in the Irish County Antrim, and Jurassic remains have been preserved under the basalts of Mull and Skye.[2] These facts suggest a former continuity of the newer rocks, from Cheshire, through the Irish Sea and the North Channel, into the Hebridean seas, and they reveal the probable antiquity of the break between

[1] See p. 61.　　　　　　[2] See p. 75.

the Scottish and the Irish uplands. Salt is a characteristic mineral of the New Red deposits, and the distribution of the British salt mines—in Cleveland, Worcestershire,
Cheshire, and Antrim—is thus dependent on some very
ancient events in the history of British geography.

It must not be supposed, however, that the conditions
of the plain-area have been wholly restful since New Red
days. An important fault, striking north and south along
the eastern foot of the Malvern and Abberley Hills, has
let down the New Red rocks, underlying the Severn
Valley at Worcester, so that they end with a broken edge
against the Archæan, Cambrian, and Ordovician masses
which constitute the little mountain ridge of Malvern.
West of the Malverns, as far as the Welsh border, is a
district, unique in England, in which the older rocks have
presented little resistance to denudation, and have been
worn to a lowland. To find equivalents to the Old Red
plain of Herefordshire we must go to the Scottish lowlands of similar date in Strathmore, Moray, Caithness, and
Orkney.

Long after the fracture which produced the Malvern
boundary fault, the whole of that portion of the plain
which runs eastward from the Devonian uplands to the
Weald of Kent was subjected to considerable disturbance,
apparently due to pressure from the south. To understand the effect of the rock-movements which took place,
it must be remembered that the chalk of Southern England was laid down in continuity with that of Northern
France ; indeed, the lower chalk must still extend without
break beneath the shallow Strait of Dover, a fact which
it has been proposed to utilise for the piercing of a
Channel Tunnel. Prior to the epoch of disturbance, a
thick sheet of chalk, more or less buried under subsequent
clays and sands, spread from France, across the site of
the English Channel, and over much, if not all, of the
English plain. To-day, on the French coast—north and
south of Boulogne—and right across Southern England,
from Dover Cliff and Beachy Head almost to the

Mendips, are the denuded remains (Fig. 49) of a much flattened upfold of these chalk strata, edged by two lines of usually sharp down-flexure. The broad top of the uplifted beds seems to have been slightly creased by minor folds (Fig. 51) parallel to the main axis of up-heaval, and was very gently domed, so as to culminate in the neighbourhood of Tunbridge Wells, where some 3000 feet of rock appear to have been denuded from the summit of Crowborough Beacon, a hill which still rises 800 feet above the sea. Along the northern line of bordering flexure, marked by the chalk range of Surrey

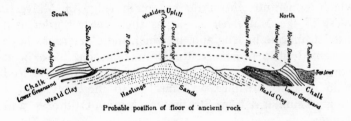

FIG. 49.—Section through the Wealden Uplift in Kent and Sussex.

and Kent, the strata bend suddenly downward and then spread into the nearly horizontal floor of the London basin, from under whose clays and sands the chalk emerges again in a long upward tilt, to end in the great Chiltern escarpment already described (Fig. 50). Owing to the south-westerly curve of the Chilterns as contrasted with the straighter westerly trend of the North Downs, the London basin narrows westward, and its pointed end is occupied only by the valley of the Kennet. The East Anglian and Kentish shores, following the general lie of the hills, impart a similar form to the Thames estuary.

The line of flexure which determines the southern edge of the Wealden uplift carries the chalk down beneath the clays and sands of the Hampshire basin, along whose axis lie Spithead, the Solent, and the Frome valley of Dorset (Fig. 50). Beyond the almost level floor of this downfold, the chalk strata rise once more in a line of

very sharp flexure, running west and east through South
Dorset into the Isle of Purbeck, and through the Isle of
Wight. The grandly upcurving beds, marked by lines of
flints, are conspicuous in the white cliffs of Swanage, the
Needles, and Culver Point, but the sea has now removed
the southward extension of the raised strata, except in
the salient angle of the Isle of Wight, where the chalk top
of St. Catherine's Down remains to indicate the flattened
character of the original uplift. It is convenient to speak
of the more southern of the two belts of chalk upheaval
as the Vectian uplift, from the ancient name of the Isle of

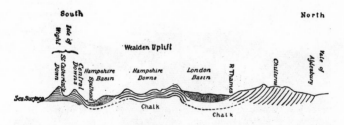

FIG. 50.—Section through the Wealden and Vectian Uplifts in Berkshire
and Hampshire.

Wight, while the more northern has been referred to as
the Wealden uplift.

Both the superficial and the coastal features of the
area south of the Kennet-Thames and east of Devon and
Somerset, with the single exception of Dungeness, have
been carved by denudation from the great sheet of deposits,
which has thus been embossed with two shallow basins expanding eastward and two belts of flattened uplift. While
the lower, western end of the Wealden uplift still retains—
in Salisbury Plain and North Hampshire—a complete
roofing of chalk, the higher portion of the dome, in
Surrey, Sussex, and Kent, has suffered greater degradation.
Either by the action of weather, or perhaps by marine
erosion during a period of partial submergence, the dome
was planed down, so that the strata lying beneath the
chalk were exposed (Fig. 51). These underlying beds

having been affected by the same rock movements as the chalk, the plane of denudation intersected several concentric domes of alternating clays and sandstones, whose cut edges produced a graining of the denuded surface, arranged in oval—eastward and westward—concentric rings. The subsequent more rapid destruction of the less resistant rocks has of course left the harder edges salient in relief. In the centre, from Hastings to Horsham, is a hilly nucleus, chiefly of sandstone, known as the Forest Range, which rises to 800 feet. Round this, upon the

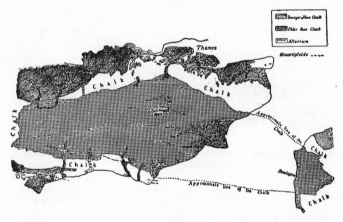

FIG. 51.—Sketch of the structure of the Weald and the Bas Boulonnais.— *After* TOPLEY.

Weald clay,[1] is a ring of lower ground (Fig. 48), incomplete towards the east, because the land has there been breached by the Channel. This is in turn enclosed by a ring, similarly incomplete, of greensand, which is especially prominent to the north and west, where Leith Hill and Hind Head nearly reach 1000 and 900 feet respec-

---

[1] The chief divisions of the Wealden and Cretaceous Series are—

The Chalk and Upper Greensand.
The Gault Clay.
The (Lower) Greensand.
The Weald Clay.
The Forest (or Hastings) Sands.

tively. The thin layer of gault clay produces only a narrow—as it were incised—ring of valley, separating the greensand hills from the chalk downs, but it spreads exceptionally into a little plain near Farnham in the north-west. Finally, a chalk escarpment, whose cut face looks inward, frames in the whole district, except to the south-east, along the coast between Beachy Head and the South Foreland. On the French shore opposite—grasping the little coastal district of exposed sub-Cretaceous rocks, which is known as the Bas Boulonnais—is a significant remnant of the section that is missing of the ring of chalk escarpment.

The details of the topography of Southern England depend very largely on the varying steepness of the dip of the strata along the lines of flexure. In the North Downs, for instance, between Farnham and Guildford, where the dip is very steep, the ridge, known as the Hog's Back, is narrow and comparatively low; but beyond Guildford, where the northward dip begins to take a rather lower angle, the Downs gradually broaden into a belt of upper ground, seven or eight miles wide, with a southward escarpment, from 600 to 800 feet high. Beyond Chatham and Maidstone, the direction of the range changes abruptly from ENE. to SE., and here the chalk surface is again narrow, but it rapidly widens into a terminal cliff-ended plateau, occupying the triangle between Canterbury, Deal, and Folkestone. Thanet is a fragment of chalk upfold, cut short by the waves along the Margate and Ramsgate cliffs, and divided from the main range by a clay-filled downfold, through which ran the former sea-strait of Wantsum, now silted up. The line of flexure, which has produced the North Downs, is continued westward along the northern edge of the plateau of Hampshire, where the chalk roof of the Wealden uplift, still complete between Winchester and Basingstoke, dips down beneath the Tertiary sands and clays of the Kennet Valley of South Berks. As it enters Wiltshire, the flexure begins to take the character of a complete upfold, so that near the point where the three counties of Berks, Hants, and Wilts adjoin, denudation has left a height of nearly 1000 feet at Inkpen Beacon, the highest summit of the chalk. A little further westward the chalk has been worn through along the axis of this upfold, and the underlying rocks have been exposed in a little "weald," known as the Vale of Pewsey. Devizes is here built in a greensand valley, defined on either hand by chalk escarpments. In the Isle of Wight the surface of the Vectian uplift has suffered similar denudation, and the underlying deposits have been exposed between the line of chalk flexure, which crosses the island, and the chalk table on St. Catherine's Down.

Thus the English plain consists of two structural systems. (1) Within the Midland quadrilateral, defined by the estuaries of the Mersey, Severn, Thames, and Trent, the topography has been shaped by denudation acting upon rocks grained in curves from north to south-west. East Anglia and Eastern Yorkshire partake of the Midland type of structure. (2) South of the Kennet-Thames, on the other hand, denudation has worked upon material whose graining was determined by the Wealden and Vectian uplifts, striking eastward and westward. The form of the London basin and the outline of the Thames estuary are due to the juxtaposition of these two systems. In the north of Wilts, where the chalk ranges of the two areas converge to form the Marlborough Downs, the strata rise from the narrow downfold under the upper Kennet Valley, on the one hand, northward into the escarpment which overlooks the Vale of the White Horse, a feature of the Midland system, and on the other hand, southward into the escarpment which commands the Vale of Pewsey, a member of the southern system.

The floor of ancient rock which underlies the deposits of the plain has been reached by not a few borings for water and coal. The rocks struck are in some cases Carboniferous and in others Old Red or Silurian. It would appear, therefore, that prior to the deposit of the

newer rocks, the older formations were not merely folded
and faulted, but also planed down by denudation, with
the result that along the axes of upfold the deeper strata
were exposed, and in the troughs of downfold rocks of
somewhat later date were preserved. In other words, the
ancient surface, upon which the newer deposits rest, is
itself grained like the plain above. The precise pattern
of the graining is a matter of deep interest, for it is possible that coal seams may be treasured in some of the
downfolds.

There are two opportunities of inferring the nature of
the underlying rocks in addition to that of actual boring.
On the one hand, the structure of the uplands is not likely
to change abruptly where it sinks below the sheath of newer
deposits ; on the other hand, the New Red part of the
plain-formations, being relatively thin, is pierced by occasional upthrows of the older rocks. Along a broad belt
extending from the Tees to the Mendips, it is therefore
possible to describe in general terms the topography of
the buried floor.

In the coalfields of Durham and the West Riding, the
New Red strata rest on the upturned edges of the Coal
Measures, but between Leeds and the Tees is an interval
in which coal is absent, and the New Red rests directly
on the Millstone Grit (Fig. 52). It is clear, therefore, that
the coal had already been removed from this intervening
district when the New Red clays were deposited. The
alternative hypothesis that no coal was there formed may
be dismissed, on account of the general correspondence
of the coal-bearing strata of Durham and of the West
Riding, and the detailed evidence that they were once
continuous. We must believe, consequently, that with
the upheaval of the Pennine fold, forces acting from
the north and south threw up a fold at right angles
to it, striking east and west, through what is now the
North Riding of Yorkshire, and that the Coal Measures
were worn off the crest of this fold precisely as they were
removed from the Pennine crest. When the New Red
rocks were subsequently deposited they rested impartially

upon the upturned edges of the Coal Measures along the
Pennine flanks, and upon the Millstone Grit forming the
denuded axis of this buried ridge. As a consequence,
the coal of Durham dips eastward from the Pennine axis
and *northward* from the buried axis, while that of the West

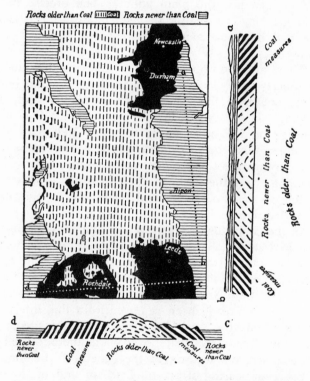

FIG. 52.—The Intersecting Upfolds of North Western Yorkshire.

Riding dips eastward from the Pennine but *southward*
from the buried axis. On the assumption that in other
directions the coal-beds rise against other buried ridges
—perhaps far to the eastward under the North Sea—we
speak of the coal-*basins* of Northumberland and Durham,
and of the West Riding.

In the Midland district, west of the Jurassic escarp-

ment, a series of upfolds of the Carboniferous and older
rocks radiate from the broad end of the Pennine Range,
like the fingers of an outspread hand (Figs. 48, 53). In the
intervals are shallow basins of New Red clay and sandstone, beneath which recent investigation has revealed
considerable areas of hidden coal. The first of the
radiating upfolds bears the granitic mass of Charnwood
Forest and the Leicestershire coalfield ; the second up-
bends the coal of the Tamworth and Nuneaton field ;
between these is a New Red basin occupied by the plain
of Leicester. The third lifts to the surface the South
Staffordshire coalfield and produces the Clent and Lickey
ridges ; between this and the second is the New Red

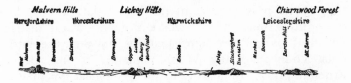

FIG. 53.—West and East Section through the Midlands.—*After* LAPWORTH.

basin of Warwickshire, whose clays were once covered
with Shakespeare's Forest of Arden. The fourth is productive of the Wrekin and the Shropshire coalfield ; while
the fifth is the axis of the North Staffordshire coalfield.
A fertile basin of New Red deposits fills most of Worcestershire between the Abberley-Malvern and the Clent-Lickey
axes. It is noteworthy that the three counties of Leicester,
Warwick, and Worcester, each in turn overlooked by the
Jurassic escarpment, should each coincide with a geological
basin.

The Bristol coalfield resembles on a smaller scale the
Durham and West Riding fields, in that it is a rock-basin
in the ancient floor, partly buried beneath the newer
deposits. The ridge of Carboniferous Limestone through
which the Clifton gorge is cut constitutes its western rim,
and the Mendip upfold runs to south of it, but the
eastern rim is hidden beneath the Cotswolds.

As long ago as 1858 Godwin Austin threw out the

brilliant suggestion that there might be coal under Southern England, along the line between Bristol and the coalfields of Belgium and Northern France. A recent boring at Dover has proved the correctness of his surmise. Coal has been struck at a depth of about 1100 feet, and a second boring nine miles to northward, on the road to Canterbury, has also reached the Coal Measures. They appear to dip gently from a buried upfold underlying the North Downs, doubtless belonging to the same system as the Mendip upfold further west. It seems, therefore, likely that a belt of several basins, some it may be containing coal, occupies the surface of the buried floor under London, Berkshire, and North Wilts. Should the seams prove to be of adequate importance, it is possible that at no distant date a busy field of industry may extend where now are rural districts unsullied by collieries, and that the unity of the buried floor connecting the Welsh Upland to the Belgian Ardennes, now visible only to the geological imagination, may become patent in the facts of economic geography.

Note on authorities.—In addition to the works mentioned in the note appended to Chapter VI., the following may be named as pertinent to the subjects discussed in the foregoing chapter :—"The Coal-fields of Great Britain," by Professor Hull ; "The Geology of the Weald," by the late Mr. William Topley ; and "A Sketch of the Geology of the Birmingham District" (printed for the Geologists' Association), by Professor Lapworth. Information with regard to the Dover Coalfield may be found in a paper by Professor Boyd Dawkins, printed in the Handbook to Dover of the British Association, 1899.

CHAPTER VIII

THE PHYSICAL HISTORY OF BRITAIN

THE British polity is made of institutions dating from all centuries in the last thousand or more years. In like manner, natural features of widely different geological age co-exist on the present surface of Britain. But as the derivation of the race and blood and the political organisation of a people present two more or less separate objects of historical inquiry, so there are two distinct questions of date concerning the deposits of which a land is built. The epoch of the original formation of a rock-bed may be vast ages earlier than that of its subsequent folding and faulting, and rocks of several different materials and epochs may be involved in the same upheaval. In British geological history there have been at least five unrestful periods productive of geographical revolution, and each of them has left monuments of the changes effected, whose seared and broken remains have become the chief features of the existing surface.

Throughout Scotland, in North and Mid Wales, and in all the Irish uplands but those of the south, the prevalent grain of the rocks is from north-east to south-west. In these districts, as already pointed out, the effect of denudation, acting upon strips of unequally resistant material, has been to impart a south-westerly trend to many of the details and to some of the larger elements of the land-relief and coastal outline. The most ancient of these features, and indeed the most ancient of all Britain, appear to be the half-submerged gneissic ridge of the Outer Hebrides and the worn sill along the west coast of the northern Highlands. Masses of pre-Cambrian sandstone have filled certain hollows in the ancient

7   97

surfaces, and imply by their position that the Archæan rocks had been previously ridged into a mountain system —the "Huronian" range of Bertrand (Fig. 54).   In Carnarvonshire Cambrian deposits, composed of Archæan fragments, have been heaped against buried Archæan slopes, in such manner as to suggest that the denudation of a north-western land was in progress during the Cambrian epoch. Rocks of Archæan age in Norway and Canada have a similar constitution and relations, the Lofoten Islands especially presenting a close analogy, both of lie and build, to the Long Island of the Hebrides. It may therefore be that after the first period of great movements of which any record remains to us, the Huronian mountains extended north-eastward across the site of the Atlantic ocean, skirting the southern edge of a continental "Atlantis," of which Greenland and the Scoto-Icelandic rise may be remnants.

FIG. 54.—The main axes of rock-folding in the structure of Britain.

In the period which ensued continued depression, accompanied by the deposition of thick sediments off the old shore, characterised much of the British area: this process was, however, interrupted by numerous upheavals, the most important of which appear to have taken place at the close of the Ordovician epoch. There is conclusive evidence in the deposits of Southern Scotland that the bulk of the land lay to the north-west, where pressure from the south-east had crumpled the Cambrian deposits against the edge of the northern continent, and raised the "Caledonian" system of mountains, more or less parallel to the already denuded Huronian ridges. The Scottish Highlands and the mountains of North-western Ireland, together with the Scandinavian Uplands round the Sogne Fiord, are the basal wrecks of these Caledonian Alps. So powerful was the pressure that the strata were not merely folded and over-folded, but in places were fractured, and the broken edges were thrust north-westward for several miles over the adjoining beds. The very substance of the rocks was re-arranged and indurated by stress and possibly by partial fusion, so that the resistant gneisses and schists were formed, which to-day constitute the Scottish Highlands. That the great longitudinal faults of Glenmore and the Scottish Rift belong in the main to this or an immediately succeeding age is made probable by the fact that the valleys produced by the down-thrust of the faulted strata were filled, in the Old Red epoch, by unconformable sandstones.

The Southern Uplands of Scotland appear to have been raised chiefly towards the close of the Silurian epoch, but in Wales, except along parts of the border towards England, the Cambrian, Ordovician, Silurian, and lower Old Red strata seem to have been deposited without any very marked interruption, for they overlie one another with tolerable regularity from Plynlimmon to the Herefordshire plain. In North Wales, however, the upper beds of the Old Red group rest upon the worn edges of older strata, and the same is true of the upper Old Red rocks of many parts of the British Isles. It would appear, therefore, that after the deposit of the Silurian rocks, and again after that of the lower Old Red sandstones, there occurred third and fourth periods of rock-movement, and that mountains were then thrown up parallel to the pre-existing Caledonian and Huronian ranges. The Southern Scottish Uplands, the mountains of the counties Down and Armagh, the Lake Mountains, most of the Welsh Upland and the mountains of the Wicklow group are the remaining fragments of these systems.

Thus in four several epochs the rocks of North-western Europe were folded and faulted along lines extending from north-east to south-west, and in each the border of Atlantis must have advanced a stage over the area now occupied by Britain, although it is possible that even in Archæan times there were islands in the sea off the continental coast-line.

With the end of the Old Red period a new phase of rock deposition set in. The complete absence of Carboniferous deposits in Greenland and in the Scandinavian peninsula, except in its southernmost promontory, suggests that the northern continent was still unsubmerged. Southward, however, a regional depression extended from Ireland to Russia, and in the sea which occupied this were formed vast sheets of Carboniferous limestone. The Caledonian range may still have presented a generally unbroken edge, but the more southern ridges, folded in the Silurian and Old Red periods, had already been broken into detached blocks, which stood above the rising waters as an island or group of islands, occupying more or less of the space still set with the Welsh, Wicklow, Cumbrian, and neighbouring hills. The preservation of these insular masses in advance of the Caledonian shore has involved so many consequences that " Proto-Britain " may perhaps be a justifiable name for them (Fig. 55). In the end they must have been almost wholly buried amid the sediments of the Carboniferous sea, and under the Coal Measures formed in the vast swamps which subsequently took the place of that sea. But the induration of their crushed rocks imparted to them such solidity that, even when buried, they appear to have resisted the subsequent movements in the crust around.

Towards and at the close of the Carboniferous epoch took place a fifth period of great movement, known to the continental geologists as "Hercynian." Simultaneous pressure from the east and from the south upfolded the Carboniferous and lower strata along two series of axes at right angles to one another. The Pennine range and the Malvern-Abberley ridge were due to forces acting from the east, and in consequence strike from north to south. The corrugation of Munster, on the other hand, along eastward and westward lines, was due to forces from the south, and was part of a movement which raised the "Armorican" range of Suess, extending eastward under South Britain and Northern France into Belgium. On the partly buried floor of the English plain, from South Wales to

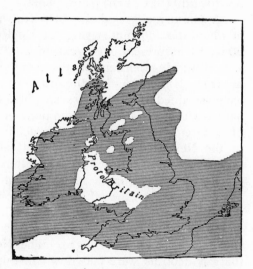

FIG. 55.—The British region during the Carboniferous epoch. The approximate area of the sea is indicated by the hatched surface.

Northumberland, upfolds of the two series intersected one another and produced the basin-structure characteristic of that area. The floor of the rift valley of Scotland was also crumpled, and the effects on the existing contours have been the more marked, because, interbedded with the ordinary deposits of Old Red and Carboniferous date, were here thick layers of hard volcanic material, which have shared in the folding and have resisted denudation. But the Carboniferous rocks of Central Ireland, under the lee of the Wicklow-Welsh (proto-British) masses were undisturbed, and their subsequent even denudation has produced the Irish plain. Moreover, it would almost appear as though the Hercynian pressures had come, like those of earlier date, from the south-east, and that it was the resistance of proto-Britain which resolved them into forces from the east and from the south, and thus first imparted to the area that triangular arrangement of south-westward (Huronian and Caledonian) and eastward and northward (Hercynian) feature-lines.

A continental period of quiescence was now interposed, in which the floor underlying the English plain was worn down to its present level, except in East Anglia, where a northward extension of the Ardennes was still prominent. High ground of the Armorican system must also have remained in the south-west. The climate appears to have been dry, so that the conditions prevalent were those of a desert. At this time were accumulated the sands of the New Red series, and a salt lake seems to have branched from the sites of Worcester and Birmingham eastward of the Pennine range through Yorkshire on the one hand, and, on the other hand, westward of that range through the Cheshire gap and the Irish Sea to Edendale and County Antrim, while a third branch extended through the Bristol Channel (Fig. 56). The New Red clays and the salt deposits were laid down in this lake. It is thus clear that the gaps now occupied by the estuary of the Severn, by the Cheshire plain, and by the North Channel was already open, and it is not uninteresting to note that Nithsdale, which crosses the Southern Uplands in a depression parallel to the North Channel, contains the little coalfield of Sanquhar, and had therefore been formed before the close of the Carboniferous epoch.

As time progressed the sea gained an entry to the salt lake, and a subsidence of the district set in, so that the Jurassic deposits were thrown down in a wide gulf which penetrated through the North Channel to the sites of Skye and Mull. Thus the existing Minch, North Channel, and Cheshire gap are a connected chain of features dating in essence from the New Red and Jurassic epochs. There is no evidence to show whether the gap now occupied by the St. George's Channel as yet existed.

The occurrence of the upper, but not the lower, Jurassic strata in the deep borings of the eastern counties and the metropolitan area, indicates that in the Jurassic age the East Anglian Upland was gradually removed and the gulf of the southern sea still further widened. After an emergence, marked by the deposit, in fresh water, of the local sands and clays which now form the surface of the Weald, there occurred the second great "regional" depression, which in some respects

FIG. 56.—The British region during the Jurassic epoch. The approximate area of the sea is indicated by the hatched surface.

repeated the conditions under which the Carboniferous limestone was laid down. The chalk must have slowly accumulated on the bed of a relatively deep sea, extending from the Crimea over the English plain and through the Cheshire gap. Only the upper chalk, however, was deposited in Antrim, so that the Cretaceous sea probably occupied the Hebridean gulf only during the maximum submergence towards the close of the epoch. In the opinion of so cautious a geologist as Prestwich, Atlantis still spread from Greenland to Norway, and the Highlands were probably a part of it.

The surface which emerged from the Cretaceous sea

was that from which the existing features of Britain have
been carved. The London clay, deposited upon the chalk
in a local sea, contains no pebbles derived from Jurassic
rocks, and from this and other data it is inferred that
a mantle of chalk often more than 1000 feet thick
enveloped the English plain, and wrapping round the
ancient shoulders of the Welsh and Pennine masses
extended through the Cheshire gap into considerable
recesses beyond. The Hebridean volcanoes soon rose
to heights of perhaps 10,000 feet above the surface
of the Tertiary continent, and preserved beneath their
lavas certain thin beds, containing the remains of plants,
similar to those of the same age found in Greenland.
Traces of a river course of this time have been left in
the island of Eigg, the flow of which seems to have come
from the west or north-west. These and other indications make it probable that land spread at this time from
Brittany to Greenland and Scandinavia, and that the two
great basins of the Arctic and Atlantic areas were still
severed by a wide tract (Figs. 18, 57). A relatively weak,
"posthumous" renewal of the pressures which at the
close of the Carboniferous epoch had raised the Armorican
range, bent the chalk strata of the south into the shallow
basins of London, Hampshire, and Paris, and slightly
lifted the intervening Wealden and Vectian districts.

The denudation which has formed the present surface
of Britain has been in progress in Scotland and Ireland
ever since the close of the Carboniferous epoch, except
for a partial interruption during the Cretaceous depression.
The Coal Measures have been almost wholly stripped
from the Irish plain and from great areas in Scotland
and the north of England. Rocks to the depth of at
least 2000 feet have been removed from Kinder Scout,
the tabular summit of the Peak of Derbyshire. But it
was not until Tertiary times that the features of the
English plain began to take outline. The relatively thin
strata of the chalk along the Pennine and Cambrian slopes
were then worn through, and the underlying Jurassic
strata exposed. These in turn have been cut back from

over the New Red deposits of the West Midlands, and thus the recession of the two great midland escarpments, the Chilterns and the Cotswolds, was inaugurated. The incipient denudation of the Wealden dome must have been contemporary.

The crags of Norfolk and Suffolk were formed, late in the Tertiary epoch, in the North Sea, a marine area of whose origin no record is known. Deposits contemporary with the crags have been pierced by a deep boring at Utrecht to a depth of several hundred feet. At first the eastern waters seem to have had no communication with the northern and western seas, but in the upper crag occur fossils of American and Atlantic molluscs

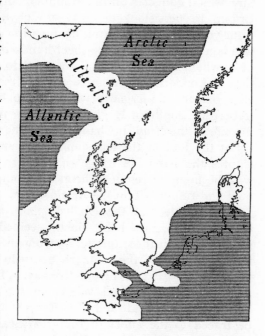

FIG. 57.—The British region in the middle of the Tertiary epoch. The approximate area of the seas is indicated by the hatched surfaces.

previously absent from this region. It is therefore probable that very late in the later Tertiary epoch the connection between Scotland and Norway collapsed, and that the Arctic and Atlantic basins invaded the land, the division between them subsiding into the submarine Scoto-Icelandic ridge. No mere inspection of the chart could have suggested the recent origin of the vast slope by which the ocean bed dips down from the British plateau to the abyss.

In the penultimate stage of the evolution of Britain a remarkable event intervened, which drew a curtain between all the great past and the present. For reasons still disputed, Britain temporarily underwent a climate similar to that of Greenland in the present day. The south-west winds brought up from the ocean vast supplies of moisture, which collected on the mountains of Scandinavia and Britain in persistent deposits of snow. Accumulating from year to year, and from century to century, this snow was compressed into an ice-sheet hundreds of feet in thickness, which overwhelmed all the land to the north of the sites of London and Berlin, and doubtless extended to the edge of the submerged platform, there breaking away in icebergs. Southern England, from Cornwall to Kent, and the site of the English Channel, were then a moss-covered sill at the foot of the ice, similar to that which now constitutes the habitable fringe of Western Greenland; this was the home of reindeer, bears, and other animals which now find refuge within the Arctic circle.

The glaciers of the English plain, as traced by the boulders transported by them, seemed to have been nourished from three quarters—from the Welsh Uplands; from a section of the southern Scottish Uplands through the Cheshire gap; and from Norway. The generally low level of both hills and valleys in the district between Flamborough Head and the Essex flats may perhaps be traced to the effect of the great Scandinavian glacier which here intruded upon Britain.

When the climate grew milder, and the ice retreated to the uplands, Britain emerged in broad connection with Europe, and the animals and plants of the mainland advanced freely northward. Even the floor of the North Sea appears to have been land, for the bones of the mammoth, the reindeer, the elk, the bear, and many other animals, have been dredged from the surface of the Dogger Bank. Ireland, separated from Great Britain by a relatively deep channel, seems to have been early detached. Comparatively few living beings had time to reach it, for alike as regards mammals, birds, reptiles, and flowering plants, Ireland is poor in species when compared with Great Britain. Then at last, after the renewed submergence of the North Sea area and the inthrust of the Channels, the Strait of Dover was cut by the waves through the Wealden axis, probably where the Downs had been breached by river-gaps similar to those of Guildford and Freshwater Gate in the Isle of Wight. Britain carried adrift with it a fauna and flora consisting of rather fewer species than those of the opposite Continent, but in other respects almost identical. Of mammals, birds, and reptiles there is only one conspicuous example, which is British and elsewhere unknown. The red grouse of Scotland, Ireland, Wales, and the North of England, is specifically different from the allied species even of Scandinavia. Conclusive evidence of the recent origin of the Narrow Seas is to be found in the fact, that in the western mouth of the English Channel there are deposits of land shells belonging to species which still live in the neighbouring lands. On the mountains of Scotland are Arctic plants and the Blue Hare, isolated remnants of the glacial flora and fauna. In Ireland and Cornwall occur plants of Lusitanian species, but they are all minute-seeded, and may well have been transported across the Bay of Biscay on the feet of migrating birds.

The physical history of Britain, as embodied in its present geographical relations, is defined by geographers in the statement that the British Isles are a "recent continental" island group. They are, in other words, a fragment of the neighbouring Continent, and have been divided from it only in a recent epoch. Their structure can be understood only if regarded as continuous with that of the Continent: they have the same fauna and flora, and the seas which separate them from the Continent are shallow.

Ultimately, however, Britain was based, not on the existing continent to south and east of it, but on a vanished northern land, and the crucial events in its history have been the folding of the Huronian and Caledonian mountains on the southern border of that land; the folding and subsequent definition of Wales and the other uplands of Mid-Britain ; the Hercynian folding from the east and from the south against the resistant blocks of Wales and its smaller neighbours ; the collapse of the Scoto-Norwegian and Scoto-Icelandic bars of land ; the posthumous Hercynian uplift of the Weald ; and the erosion of Dover Strait. The triangular outline of Britain is thus the embodiment of her history, and the oldest feature of her storied surface, the Long Island of the Hebrides, stands significantly on the far oceanic border, while Dover Cliff, the newest, is at the continental angle where the Narrow Seas meet.

Note on authorities.—In addition to the books named in the notes at the end of Chapters VI. and VII., the following works bear on the discussion in the foregoing chapter :—" Das Antlitz der Erde,' by Professor Suess ; " The Building of the British Isles," by A. J. Jukes Browne ; "Island Life" (Chapter XVI.), by A. R. Wallace ; and "The Origin of the British Flora," by Clement Reid. The third volume of Suess's great work has yet to be published, but a French translation of the first two volumes, by De Margerie and Bertrand, has already appeared under the title of "La Face de la Terre." In a paper on "The Geological Structure of the Malvern and Abberley Hills," published in the *Quarterly Journal of the Geological Society*, vol. lvi., some valuable remarks have been made by Dr. T. T. Groom on the dates of the Hercynian movements and kindred subjects.

CHAPTER IX

THE RIVERS OF BRITAIN

DENUDATION acting upon grained and unequally resistant rocks has shaped the present surface of Britain,
and the history of the exposure of this surface is obviously
additional to that of the original deposition or of the
subsequent graining of the constituent rocks. From the
very nature of the process, the record of its vicissitudes
has in the main been obliterated, but significant clues are
to be found in the lie of the river-courses and in the
relative altitudes of the summits. Since the products of
denudation are carried away by the streams, it is clear
that the river courses must, at each stage, have been
intimately adjusted to the form of the developing surface,
and that the summits cannot surpass the height of the
original surface upon which the denudation began, unless
as a result of subsequent crust-movements or of volcanic
action. The evidence to be considered does not consist
of isolated facts ; for the rivers of a land usually form, in
varying degrees of symmetry, a system, or systems, with
a majority of courses tending to certain dominant directions ; and in Britain, at any rate, as already pointed out,[1]
the higher summits of each district usually touch or
approach the level of an imaginary plane, which is
exceeded by none of them. Upon these bases a theory
may be built, which explains so much with such con-
sistency, that it can hardly be false as a whole, although
it lacks conclusive proof and, as regards details, even
suggests certain difficulties. The English plain, owing
to its wider expanse and to the relative simplicity of

---

[1] See Chapter V.

its structure, presents in this connection a less complicated problem than do the ancient land-fragments along the oceanic border.

As might be inferred from the position of the uplands, the rivers of Great Britain are longer on the eastern than on the western slope. An apparent exception is to be found in the Severn, but the head-waters even of this river—the Vyrnwy, the upper Severn itself, the Teme, the Wye, the Usk, and the Taff—come down from the Welsh uplands *eastward* in the direction of the Thames, and it is only in the English plain that their flow is intercepted by a cross channel—the Warwick Avon and lower Severn—which escapes westward through the gap between the Welsh and Devonian uplands (Fig. 58).

The great divide of the English drainage must be considered, therefore, to run, not from north to south through the midst of the land, but from the Cheviot Hills, along the Pennine range—nearer to its western than to its eastern edge—and, curving round the southern boundary of Cheshire, into the Welsh mountains, between the basins of the Dee and the upper Severn.[1] It does not coincide everywhere with the line of greatest height. The divergence is especially notable where a rise in the ground connecting the Peak with Wales lies to the south of it, and is, in consequence, cut through by a gorge at the foot of the Wrekin, by which the upper Severn escapes south-eastward. But the upper Severn, flowing parallel to the divide, has an exceptional character, and the general arrangement of the rivers is, for some purposes, better indicated by carrying the dividing line across the Severn basin, past the sources of the Teme and Wye (Fig. 58).

A long series of streams descend, eastward and south-eastward, from the Pennine-Cambrian divide—the Tyne, the Wear, the Tees, the Swale, the Ure, the Nidd, the Wharfe, the Aire, the Calder, the Don, the Derwent, the Dove, the Trent, the Tern, the Vyrnwy, and the Severn. Of these the first three flow independently into the North

[1] See note on watersheds at p. 143.

Sea ; the next seven are intercepted by the Yorkshire
Ouse, and carried southward in a channel parallel to the
Jurassic and Cretaceous escarpments of Yorkshire ; the
Trent collects three more, and follows the western foot
of the Jurassic escarpment of Lincolnshire northward to
its confluence with the Ouse. Together, the Trent and

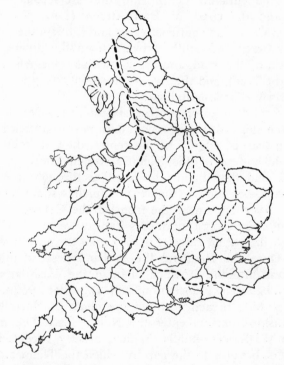

Fig. 58.—The river-systems of England. — — — — major divides.
— — — — — minor divides.

the Ouse form the Humber, which resumes the eastward
flow of the source-streams, making a breach through both
Jurassic and Cretaceous escarpments. The upper Severn
and the Vyrnwy, as already said, are intercepted by the
Warwick Avon and lower Severn, which flow, like the
Trent and the Yorkshire Ouse, along the foot of the
Jurassic escarpment, here raised high into the Cotswold

Hills. Thus there are three considerable rivers, the
Yorkshire Ouse, the Trent, and the Avon-Severn, whose
combined courses form a curve, extending across England
from north to south-west in a direction roughly parallel to
a series of apparently correlated feature-lines—the south-
eastern shore of the Irish Sea, the Pennine-Cambrian
divide, the Jurassic escarpment, the Cretaceous escarpment, and the coast of East Anglia (Fig. 58). The
Pennine-Cambrian source-streams and the Humber, which
flow eastward and south-eastward from the divide, cross
the grain of the land, and are known as transverse. The
Ouse, the Trent, and the Avon-Severn, following the grain,
are described as longitudinal.[1]

A second series of south-eastward head-streams flows
down the slope of the Jurassic limestones from their north-
western scarped edge. In the centre, the Cotswolds bear
the head-waters of the Thames, which converge upon
Oxford, and flow thence to Reading through a gap in
the chalk escarpment (Fig. 59). Further southward the
Bristol Avon rises near the front of the Cotswolds, and,
bending completely round, cuts its way westward at Bath
through the parent ridge (Fig. 63). To the north-east, the
Great Ouse, the Nen, and the Welland descend into the
Fens and into the drowned plain of the Wash, at whose
mouth, between Hunstanton and Gibraltar Point, they
make a wide breach through the chalk of Norfolk and
Lincolnshire, and so enter the North Sea. The mouth
of the Wash corresponds, in fact, exactly, except in the
matter of breadth, to the gap by which the Thames passes
through the Chilterns between Oxford and Reading.
Although transverse near their sources on the Jurassic
limestone, and again where they pass through the chalk
at the mouth of the Wash, the rivers of the Fens exhibit
long reaches in which they run between the great escarpments and parallel to them.

Beyond the chalk escarpment is a third series of
transverse source-streams descending eastward and south-
eastward—the Yare, the Waveney, the Orwell, the Stour,

[1] See note on river-origins at p. 144.

the Blackwater, and the Chelmer. These East Anglian rivers enter the sea by separate mouths, and are, therefore, comparable to the Tyne, the Wear, and the Tees among the Pennine rivers.

Thus three successive orders of transverse streams flow across the English plain eastward and south-eastward, the first from the Pennine-Cambrian divide, the second from the summit of the Jurassic escarpment, the third from that of the Cretaceous escarpment (Fig. 58). The first series is collected by three longitudinal rivers, the Yorkshire Ouse, the Trent, and the Avon-Severn. The Ouse and the Trent ultimately escape transversely by the Humber, which crosses the line of both the great escarpments. The second series, with the exception of the Bath Avon, is gathered up by the Thames and the Wash, both of which traverse the chalk escarpment. The third series consists of streams which, having no scarp to encounter, flow independently to the sea.

The rivers of the South of England belong to a system distinct from that of the Midlands, for the second of the English divides strikes from Wilts to Kent along the line of the Wealden uplift, throwing the waters northward into the Thames and southward into the English Channel. The Wey, the Mole, the Darent, the Medway, and the Kentish Stour are the chief streams of the northern slope ; the Salisbury Avon, the Test, the Itchen, the Arun, and the Sussex Ouse are those of the southern slope. All the more eastern streams of this system, whether belonging to the northern or to the southern slope, rise in the centre of the Weald near the Sussex frontier, and cut gaps through the North or South Downs, near the towns of Guildford, Dorking, Sevenoaks, Maidstone, Ashford, Arundel, and Lewes. These gaps are identical in character with those made by the Thames and the Wash through the chalk escarpment of the Midlands.

The Kennet and the Thames below Reading occupy a unique position among the rivers of the English plain (Fig. 59). They flow eastward along the trough in which the south-eastward slope from the Pennine-Cambrian divide

8

meets the northward slope from the Wealden divide. The tributaries of the Kennet-Thames belong, therefore, both to the Midland and to the Wealden river systems. On the left bank are the upper Thames, the Colne, and the Lea descending from the Jurassic and Cretaceous escarpments; on the right bank are the Wey, the Mole, the Darent, and the Medway coming down from the midst of the Weald. A close connection is thus evident between the scheme of river-drainage and the events related in the last chapter by which the plain was grained according to distinct Midland and Southern patterns. It is possible that the Solent and Spithead mark the drowned valley of a river similar to the Kennet-Thames, whose sources were the Frome and the Dorset Stour.

The most striking phenomenon presented by these facts is the manner in which the transverse rivers cut, in so many instances, through the belts of higher ground. Between Oxford and Reading, or more accurately between Wallingford and Reading, the bed of the Thames has an elevation of little more than 100 feet above the sea, yet it makes a gap through a hill-range rising on either hand to heights of 700 and 800 feet (Fig. 59). The strata of chalk were deposited upon the sea-bed in continuous sheets, and it follows that they must once have been coherent across the gap to which the river valley is here narrowed. No fractures have been detected which are sufficient to account for the break in the hill-range, and the only adequate suggestion is that the river has itself worn the passage. The chalk once extended further to the north-west, in the direction of the Cambrian upland, a fact proved by the occurrence of detached, chalk-capped hills in front of the main escarpment, as at Sinodun near Wallingford. In Tertiary times the Thames must have flowed over a table-land raised high above the level of Oxford, and at least flush with the present summit of the Chilterns. Here, therefore, as often elsewhere, the river is older than the hills. The Chilterns were notched by the Thames, when their scarcely perceptible ridge lay far to westward of its present alignment, and the deepening gap has travelled eastward together with the receding and growing escarpment.

North-eastward of the Thames "water-gap" the Chiltern escarpment exhibits a series of remarkable notches, through which are carried, in a north-westerly direction, the railways, the roads, and the canal connecting London with the Midlands. No rivers pass through these "wind-gaps," but a short distance south-eastward of them rise streams which

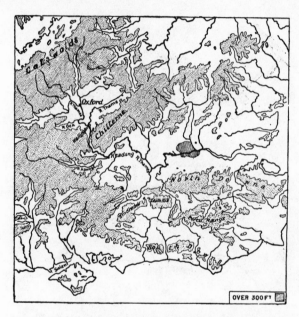

FIG. 59.—The Wealden drainage and the basins of the upper and lower Thames.

descend to the lower Thames. It is obvious that when the chalk spread further westward, a wide area over the site of the vale of Aylesbury must have been drained by these transverse channels, and the gaps in the existing ridge are doubtless sections of the decapitated valleys. Now, however, the longitudinal Thame has pushed its source back from the upper Thames along the unresistant clays which have been exposed by the recession of the chalk edge. The

Chiltern escarpment, in fact, and the Thame Valley are correlative features, both being incident to a comparatively advanced stage of denudation. The original drainage-system was independent of the graining of the rocks and "consequent" only on the smooth south-easterly tilt of the planed surface of the newly raised land. The Thame was of "subsequent" development, and its valley necessarily followed the graining of the rocks. When a consequent

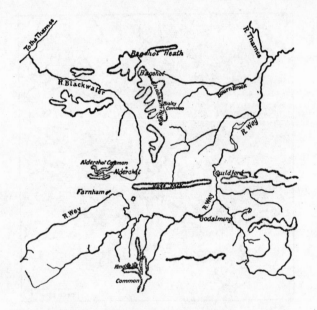

FIG. 60.—The River Wey of Surrey and its relation to the Blackwater tributary of the Berkshire Loddon.

river happens to cross the grain of the land, as does the Thames between Oxford and Reading, it is likely to incise its transverse valley at least as fast as the land is worn to a ribbed surface of longitudinal valleys and ridges. An arborescent system is thus developed, consisting of a consequent trunk-stream which breaches the ridges, and subsequent, lateral tributaries from the longitudinal valleys. The Thames between Oxford and Reading, and its right and left tributaries, the Ock and the Thame, are an example of this arrangement.

A similar explanation is to be given of the Wealden drainage. The rivers of Surrey, Kent, and Sussex once flowed from the axis of an uplift whose more resistant elements have become the North and South Downs, Leith Hill and Hind Head, and the Forest Hills about Tunbridge and Hastings. As the less resistant matter was removed and the general level of the river basins was lowered, water-gaps were formed through the upstanding ridges, and subsequent, lateral channels were thrown out from the original, consequent streams. Some of these subsequents have been more successful than others in capturing source - streams : a subsequent stretch, for instance, of the upper Wey, developed from Godalming to Farnham, has probably decapitated the Blackwater, which now rises just north of the chalk, near Aldershot (Fig. 60). North of Reigate and at Caterham are wind-gaps in the Downs, heads of valleys opening northward to Croydon, through which may once have flowed streams now transferred to the Mole.

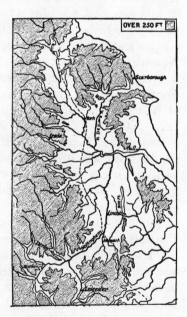

The Humber breaches both the Jurassic and Cretaceous escarpments, thereby indicating that a plateau, at least as high as the Wolds of Lincolnshire and Yorkshire, once extended westward, across what are

FIG. 61.—The basin of the Humber.
- - - - - The East Coast Railway from London to Edinburgh.

now the Vales of York and Nottingham, to the flank of the Pennine Range (Fig. 61). The Pennine rivers may then have reached the sea independently, by roughly parallel eastward channels, as the rivers of Northumberland and Durham yet continue to do. In the end, however, as the clays along the foot of the Jurassic escarpment were degraded, a single transverse estuary, the Humber, throwing out subsequent, lateral channels, the Ouse and the Trent, robbed in succession its transverse rivals, and united all the head-streams into one great Humber basin, which draws its sources from more than a hundred miles of the Pennine-Cambrian divide.

The Witham must have long persisted as a competitor of the Humber. Its diminished head-stream still traverses the Jurassic escarpment by the gap at Lincoln. From Burton to Newark the flow of the Trent is aimed precisely at this gap, and a well-marked belt of gravel, derived from the pebble beds of Cannock Chase and its neighbourhood, still indicates the course formerly held by the Trent between Newark and Lincoln. This course was abandoned when a subsequent channel, developed from the head of the Humber along a belt of yielding clays, tapped the river at Newark and offered a more deeply worn path to the sea. After unusual rainfall, when the flow of the waters is impeded, the Trent floods still spread from Newark towards the Witham, and it is recorded that in 1795 the lower parts of Lincoln city were inundated with Trent water. In the gravels of Norfolk are fragments of carboniferous fossils, which can only have been brought thither, by some such stream as the Trent-Witham, from the hills on the Pennine-Cambrian divide.

The rivers of the Fen country, the Nen, the Welland, and the Great Ouse, are in the main subsequent channels, developed from the former Trent-Witham. They have doubtless seized what were the sources of the East Anglian rivers, and diverted the drainage of the Jurassic belt from the estuaries of the Yare, Orwell, and Blackwater to the broad gap in the chalk occupied by the Wash entry.

Although no south-eastward river now crosses the Cotswolds, an inspection of the map leads inevitably to the suggestion that, in view of the whole character of

the Midland river system, the Severn above Tewkesbury
may have been the head-water of the Thames (Fig. 62).
The Warwick Avon and lower Severn have all the appear-

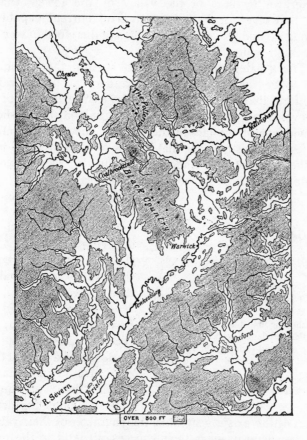

FIG. 62.—The basin of the Severn, showing the narrowing of its
transverse valley at Coalbrookdale, and the relation of the
longitudinal Warwick Avon to the transverse head-streams
of the Thames. The comparatively high level of the
Black Country and the Potteries is incidentally shown.

ance of a subsequent river, developed from the Bristol
Channel north-eastward along the foot of the Cotswolds,
and this may have cut the Thames short by the capture

of the upper Severn. That event, however, must have taken place before the Ice age, for glacial drift occurs in the valley at Tewkesbury. There is abundant evidence in the gravel terraces of the valley of the lower Thames that that river once had a powerful current capable of moving coarse gravel, and that it may therefore have come from high-lying sources.

The greater the volume of a stream, the wider will tend to be the curves of its meandering. It is evident, therefore, that if the streams on the eastward slope of the Cotswolds originated in the Welsh upland, there should be evidence of the fact in the form of the existing valleys. Professor Davis believes that he has obtained this evidence in the case of the Cherwell, Windrush, Evenlode, and Colne tributaries of the upper Thames (Fig. 63). The minute irregularities of these streams are in striking discordance with the swinging curvatures of their valleys. Moreover, these valleys contain abundant gravel deposits, derived from rocks in the basin of the Severn, and recent investigation has made it probable that these deposits are fluviatile, rather than marine or glacial. Thus the articulation of the existing streams, the character of their valleys, and the deposits near their sources, all tend to the hypothesis of an original consequent drainage from Wales to the Thames. But further criticism of the data in this crucial instance is still to be desired.

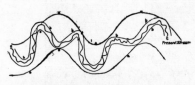

FIG. 63.—Diagram of a portion of the Colne Valley of Gloucestershire, showing the diminishing radius of the meander-curves corresponding to a supposed shrinkage in the volume of water.—*After* BUCKMAN.

a. Original high level valley; *b.* smaller valley at lower level; *c.* present stream.

Two rivers of the Midland system present an additional complexity: the Bristol Avon and the Yorkshire Derwent. Both of them break through the Jurassic escarpment in a direction apparently opposed to the original drainage slope. In process of the development of an escarpment, the drainage of the actual front of the scarp is thrown by torrents into the subsequent river at its foot, whereas the water from immediately beyond the summit is carried down the dip slope by shortened consequent streams. The scarp torrents are apt to eat into the range, forming coombes, often filled with dense wood, which are the most picturesque features both of the Cretaceous and the Jurassic hills. Occasionally they win a channel right through the belt of upper ground, and throw out lateral, subsequent tributaries along the clay belts which lie beyond; these tributaries in turn may capture the head-streams of the original consequent drainage of the dip-slope. The term "obsequent" has been invented, on the analogy of "consequent" and "subsequent," for the rivers which commenced as scarp torrents. The Bristol Avon appears to be obsequent at Bath, subsequent between Bradford and Chippenham, and consequent above Malmesbury, where it seems to have captured a source of the Thames (Fig. 64). The obsequent Derwent has seized upon the southward drainage of the North York Moors, and carried it westward through the Vale of Pickering into the Ouse, away from what appears to have been its former exit near Scarborough (Fig. 61). The Little Ouse of East Anglia is also an obsequent.[1]

Thus it may be said that, although definite proof of the precise courses followed in past times by the rivers of the English plain is rare, yet the apparent disorder of the existing channels admits of reduction on simple principles and of consistent explanation. The evolution of the present Midland system from a great series of roughly parallel rivers descending from the Pennine-Cambrian divide to the North Sea must have taken place between the emergence of the chalk plateau in early Tertiary times and the on-coming of the Ice age. It is just possible, however, that the diversion of the Trent from the Witham to the Humber may have been an event of even later date.

The river-systems of Northern and Western Britain are more difficult of analysis, on account both of the

[1] See note on the Bristol Avon at p. 145.

greater complexity of the rock structure and of the more ancient emergence of the land. Portions of the higher uplands may have remained unsubmerged by the Cretaceous sea, and the direction of some of the existing valleys may perhaps have been determined in pre-Cretaceous ages. But the high elevation of these districts has been the cause of a rapid incision of the drainage lines, and of many successive adjustments to the structure of the very different rocks

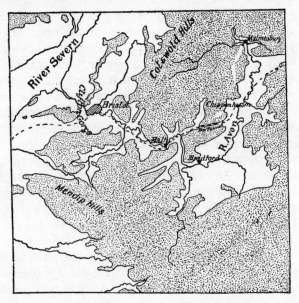

FIG. 64.—The Bristol Avon. – – – – – Great-Western Railway.
over 250 feet.

from time to time exposed. From evidence already referred to,[1] it appears, however, certain that the existing drainage did not commence upon the Huronian, Caledonian, and Welsh mountain-ranges, but upon the slightly undulating plains of grained rock to which denudation reduced these mountains. Re-emergence converted the plains into plateaux upon whose tilted surface the original drainage was consequent.

[1] See Chapter V.

The most markedly transverse river in Wales is the
Wye, whose general direction is south-eastward across
graining of Ordovician, Silurian, Old Red, and Carboniferous
rocks.   An isolated tableland, from 600 to 900 feet high,
known in part as the Forest of Dean, stands athwart the
lower valley, between Monmouth and Chepstow, and has
been trenched by the river, in limestone gorges, almost to
sea-level (Fig. 65).   Below Builth, in the upper valley, an
even deeper gap has been cut through a ridge of Silurian
and Old Red rocks.   It would appear, therefore, that with

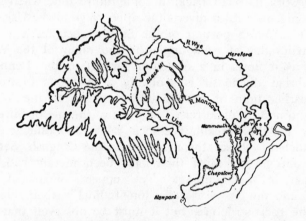

FIG. 65.—The Hereford Wye, showing the Gorge between
Monmouth and Chepstow.   – – – – – Possible future
diversion of the upper Wye into the Usk.

the exception of portions of the great loop through Herefordshire, the Wye is transverse from its source in Plynlimmon to its mouth at Chepstow, and that it must be
older than the low-lying Hereford plain, through which it
winds before entering the Monmouth gorges.   With the progress of denudation the carboniferous mass of the Forest
of Dean has been left outstanding, except where cut by
the river, while the general level of the country around
has been gradually lowered.   Thus the Wye is in all probability a consequent stream, whose earliest course was
over a grained plateau with a south-easterly tilt.   The

Monnow may perhaps represent a portion of the original direct channel, for the loop through Herefordshire has the aspect of a subsequent diversion.

The Usk has a shorter, but roughly parallel, course through a gap in the Old Red Sandstone escarpment of the Black Mountains. In Brecknockshire, above this gap, it is approached by the Wye, and a deep longitudinal depression connects the valleys. The Wye is here flowing at a higher level than the Usk, and in the ordinary process of development, a subsequent tributary of the latter may work its head back, in some future time when man is negligent, until it diverts the upper Wye to the Usk.

The Welsh portion of the Severn occupies a longitudinal valley at right angles to the valley of the Wye, and as it flows in a direction parallel to the Pennine-Cambrian divide, it is probably a subsequent stream. In earlier times it must have emerged from the Welsh upland upon a plain raised high above the site of Shrewsbury, for the Wrekin, Wenlock Edge, and other ridges parallel to these, through which the English Severn has cut gorges, must have been merely resistant streaks in the graining. The upper courses of the Teifi and the Towy are also longitudinal in their relation to the rock structure, but it must be observed that the plateau into which they have been worked, as reconstructed by Ramsay from the levels of the hill summits, had a north-westerly tilt. The Dee appears to be longitudinal in Merionethshire, but in Denbighshire it turns into the transverse Vale of Llangollen. A single transverse feature, however, in a river course. which is otherwise longitudinal, is as likely to have been obsequent in its origin as consequent, and, if the Vale of Llangollen were obsequent, the Merionethshire Dee may have had an exit through the Clwyd, for a wind-gap connects their valleys.[1] The Conway cuts through the lower northern end of the Snowdon axis, detaching the Great Orme's Head, but it may none the less be a subsequent river, for its course is along the line where the Ordovician rocks of Carnarvon-

[1] But see note on Bala Lake at p. 146.

shire emerge from under the Silurian rocks of Denbigh-shire, and the Silurian sheath may have formerly extended to the sea westward of the Head. The Clwyd also, of the Vale of St. Asaph, may be subsequent, for its valley has been re-excavated in a strip of relatively soft New Red rocks, which had been deposited in a pre-existing depression.

On the whole, then, the one long consequent valley of Wales appears to be that of the Wye, which rises near the western sea and flows south-eastward to its interception by the subsequent Avon-Severn. Most of the other rivers, except the Usk and the Taff, seem to have adopted subsequent channels. But the Conway and the Clwyd are anomalous in direction, even if subsequent.

New Red and Jurassic deposits along the shores of the Bristol Channel show that this entry is of ancient—perhaps Carboniferous—date, and that it has been re-excavated by denudation from a sheathing plain, comparable to that which still covers the floor of the Cheshire gap. Through this plain the subsequent Severn must have worked its way inland, transferring the Welsh drainage from the eastern to the western sea. As the Jurassic and New Red rocks were degraded, the Mendip ridge was laid bare, and a way was maintained through the resistant lime-stone by the development of a water-gap at the constriction of the channel marked by the Steep Holm, a detached Mendip fragment.

In the Devonian peninsula, the Exe and the Tamar, flowing southward to the English Channel from sources close to the Bristol Channel, appear to be consequent streams indicative of a general southward tilt of the earlier upland within which the resistant rocks of Exmoor and Dartmoor were buried. The Tone, on the other hand, and parts of the Tawe are parallel to the Lundy-Exmoor upfold, and the Torridge seems to have captured one of the southward-flowing source-streams of the Tamar. The Devonian peninsula is, however, the mere skeleton of a land, and the granitic masses of Dartmoor and Cornwall, exposed by denudation, have developed local drainage systems of little general significance.

As already pointed out, the water-shed follows the western edge and not the axis of the Pennine upland, and certain facts suggest the conclusion that it once held a still more westerly position.   In Derbyshire two more or less longitudinal streams, the Dove and the Derwent, have insinuated their valleys northward from the southern end of the range, but the Wye still flows eastward from Buxton completely across the limestone core.   Further north, the Aire appears to have been robbed of its head-stream by the obsequent Ribble, and the deep gap between Carlisle and Newcastle may once have been traversed by the Tyne.   This gap is ultimately due to a local downfold transverse to the range, and it is noteworthy that the northern shore of Solway Firth, from the mouth of the Nith eastward, follows precisely the same straight line as does the Tyne from the gap to Newcastle.   Perhaps the Nith and the Annan were the former head-streams of the Tyne.   In any case, the valley of the Eden appears to have a subsequent character : it has been re-excavated, along a line parallel to the divide, from a pre-existing depression filled with unresistant New Red deposits (Fig. 37). The Lune has in the main a longitudinal course, and the radiating streams of the Cumbrian dome have originated under purely local conditions.   There are no important consequent features in the Mersey, the Weaver, or the lower Dee.   Therefore it may be concluded, provisionally, at any rate, that the Pennine-Cambrian divide has gradually shifted its position, eastward and south-eastward, from near the coast of the Irish Sea.   It is still almost exactly concentric with the coastal curve.

In Scotland a clue to order is perhaps to be detected in the south-easterly courses of the Esk, Annan, Nith, and Dee, which descend from the Southern Uplands to Solway Firth and the Irish Sea.   The Nith has its source in the northern slope of the range, through which it cuts a transverse valley, followed by the Glasgow and South-Western Railway.   Several of the valleys of this region —markedly that of the Nith—are of ancient date and have been re-excavated from wedges of New Red and even Carboniferous rock preserved in faulted troughs. The Teviot, the Tweed below Kelso, the Ettrick, and the Yarrow flow in longitudinal valleys at right angles to the Nith, and Gala Water has the normal south-easterly direction of the transverse streams. But the upper Tweed, between Peebles and Kelso, is anomalous: it has an eastward flow, conforming to neither of the prevalent directions, but roughly parallel to the Don and the Dee of Aberdeenshire. Except where indented by the head of Clydesdale, the water-parting strikes from sea to sea along the northern brink of the upland belt. At one point, however, a loop extends to the summit of the Pentlands, to embrace the source of Lyne Water, a transverse head stream of the Tweed. The sum of all these facts is consistent with the idea that a mountain system with a south-westerly strike was here reduced to a grained level, which was subsequently uplifted with an initial tilt to south-eastward.

The valley-system of the Grampian Highlands presents essentially the same elements as does that of the Southern Uplands. The transverse rivers flow south-eastward across the grain of the land, while the longitudinal rivers follow the grain, either north-eastward or south-westward: the former must be the consequent and the latter the subsequent members of the system. But there are a few striking cases of due eastward or westward flow, comparable to that of the Tweed above Kelso. Of these the Dee and the Don have been cited, and to them may be added the Tummel and Glen Leven. Possibly these anomalous courses are due to the re-excavation of ancient, overlying channels, belonging to some earlier system, for Old Red deposits still occur at an elevation of 1400 feet in the valley of the Avon, an anomalous northward river which, if we may judge from the map, has apparently captured the head-stream of the Dee. It should be noted, however, that these eastward and westward valleys are parallel to the clean-cut shore-lines which extend eastward of Cape Wrath and of Inverness, and also to

the shore and river-line of Solway Firth and the Newcastle Tyne.

The Tay has a special interest on account of the rapid
alternation of transverse and longitudinal sections of its
course (Fig. 66). Rising in Ben Lui, in the extreme west
of Perthshire, it runs for a short distance north-eastward
to Tyndrum, then turns transversely to Crianlarich, where
it enters the long subsequent valley which is occupied, in
its middle third, by Loch Tay. At the confluence of the

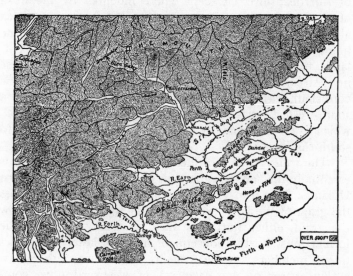

FIG. 66.—The basin of the Tay.

Tummel, below Pitlochry, the Tay turns south-eastward,
and emerges transversely from the Highlands, near
Dunkeld. It now bends south-westward, thus accepting
the longitudinal course of its tributary, the Isla, and flows
for a short distance through the lowland of Strathmore.
At Perth it once more becomes transverse, making a
breach through the Sidlaw range. Finally the Firth of
Tay extends past Dundee north-eastward, along the axis of
a denuded upfold and, therefore, longitudinally. The Tay
is clearly older than the great depression of Strathmore.

Before the denudation of the relatively unresisting Old Red Sandstones, the Sidlaw and Ochil ranges must have been buried in an upland, whose surface may have continued the south-easterly tilt of the Highland plateau. The course of the Tay was determined in that epoch, and the main consequent channel appears to have been that which descends from Athol, past Pitlochry, under the successive names of Garry, Tummel, and Tay. The pass, or gorge, of Killiecrankie is the narrow gap made by the transverse Garry at a point where it encounters a very resistant belt of rock. It is not improbable, as suggested by Sir Archibald Geikie, that the Earn, the Teith, and the Forth are the lower courses of streams whose transverse head-waters have become feeders of the subsequent Loch Tay. There are several suggestive wind-gaps in the ridges north of the shortened rivers, through one of which the Callander and Oban Railway passes, between Kinlochearn and the Tay Valley.

The Northern Highlands are drained chiefly eastward and south-eastward into Moray Firth and Glenmore. As the trend of the rock graining is here more nearly northerly than in the Grampian Highlands, the streams of this slope must be considered as transverse, while the sea-lochs of the west coast may represent obsequent valleys opening into the longitudinal Minch. The river Ness of Glenmore, and the Findhorn and Spey, are obviously subsequent channels, in part re-excavated from the Old Red Sandstones deposited along pre-Devonian valleys.

It is now generally agreed that both the Northern and the Grampian Highlands are the dissected remains of grained plateaux, of which the highest portions still rise to about 3500 and 4500 feet respectively. The Old Red Sandstones in Glenmore rest in nearly horizontal beds up to a height of 2300 feet, and it is therefore probable that at no very remote period in geological time, the longitudinal valley of Loch Ness may have been wholly filled with these deposits. The present superior elevation of the Grampian summits is due in the main to the resistant qualities of their granitic nuclei, and there

9

is no evidence to show that the plateau of slightly more
yielding strata in the Northern Highlands was not originally
of at least equal elevation. A gentle south-easterly tilt is indicated by the relative heights of the Grampian summits,[1]
and if this were formerly prolonged over the Northern
Highlands, streams which rose only a few miles from the
Minch may once have crossed in succession the northern
schists, the Red Sandstones filling Glenmore, the Grampian
schists and granites, the Red Sandstones filling Strathmore,
and a streak of volcanic rock marking the axis of the
buried Sidlaw-Ochils. With the denudation of Glenmore
and the development of the longitudinal rivers Ness and
Lochy, the transverse head-streams of the Grampian rivers
would be decapitated, and the drainage of the Northern
Highlands diverted to Moray Firth and Loch Linnhe.
Similarly, when a longitudinal tributary was insinuated
south-westward from the Garry-Tay, along a strip of unusually yielding schists, it must have seized what was left
of the consequent head-streams of the Earn, the Teith, and
the Forth, becoming at last a more voluminous water than
the consequent Garry, and therefore to be considered as
the master stream.

The Sidlaw Hills now rise to 1400 feet, in spite of the
fact that the axis of the upfold producing them has been
replaced by the Firth of Tay. The Ochils have a summit
of 2300 feet, and the Campsie Fells one of nearly 1900
feet. It is therefore very possible that the rivers which cut
the gaps at Perth and Stirling once continued their flow to
the Southern Uplands across thick carboniferous deposits,
now removed. Gala Water may perhaps represent one
of their lower courses. The chief apparent difficulty in
the way of such a reconstruction lies in the anomalous
course of the Clyde, which traverses the Ochil-Campsie
belt of hills, but in a direction opposed to that of the Tay
and Forth. In order to obtain a likely solution of the
problem as thus complicated, it is necessary to investigate
the lie of certain of the western sea-lochs.

The grain of the Grampian rocks tends to SSW. as

[1] See p. 50.

it approaches Ireland, and Loch Long is to be regarded
as a longitudinal glen invaded by the sea (Fig. 67).
About mid-way to its head, it is crossed by a more or
less transverse depression occupied by Loch Goil and
the Gare Loch, the former a branch of Loch Long, the
latter a curiously back-set gulf, rather than tributary, of
the Clyde, with a deeply cleft wind-gap at its head leading

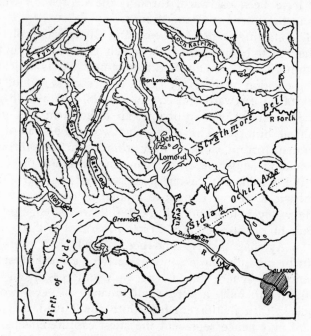

FIG. 67.—The Sea-lochs at the mouth of the Clyde.

over to Loch Long.   Such a combination of features can
only be explained on the assumption that a south-eastward,
consequent valley (the Goil-Gare) was intersected by the
subsequent Long Valley, and that the streams had made
some further progress with denudation before the district
underwent a depression and partial submergence.   The
incision of the wind-gap at the head of the Gare was arrested
when the Goil stream was diverted by the intrusion of

the Long Stream. Here, therefore, is distinct evidence of a consequent river flowing in the usual south-eastward direction. The river Leven, draining Loch Lomond, enters the Clyde at a similar angle to that of the Gare Loch, and both channels are aimed at the gap in the hills above Dumbarton, which is now traversed in a reverse direction by the Clyde. Beyond the hills the flow of the old river may have been eastward, through the depression which ends in the Forth at Grangemouth.

The starting-point of the existing Clyde was probably in the reach below Greenock, which is in line with the Strathmore belt of Old Red Sandstone. As is indicated by the position of the Holy Loch, this reach was once the valley of an eastward consequent stream, and a wind-gap below Greenock was probably an episode in the geographical history. The next stage would be that of an obsequent torrent, working back from Loch Long through the yielding sandstone, so diverting in succession the Gare and the Leven, and taking possession of the gap above Dumbarton. From Lanark to a point below Glasgow the Clyde valley is longitudinal, for it follows the edge of the Lanarkshire coal-basin in a direction parallel to the upfold on the Ayrshire border,[1] and here, therefore, a river-bed might be cut either in a south-easterly or a north-westerly direction. Where the Clyde now emerges from the Southern Uplands, a very small change of level would suffice to turn its torrent head into the Tweed, and this torrent may hence represent the latest capture effected by the usurping Clyde.

It is quite possible that the Tweed may be the lower course of a river which once had its sources in the Western Highlands. The Nith may have received other of the waters of Argyll, perhaps from the Crinan depression and the Sound of Bute, or it may be from the Sound of Mull and the Pass of Brander. If the Nith were continued into the Tyne,[2] the courses of the Nith-Tyne and the Goil-Gare-Tweed may have exhibited sympathetic eastward curves. The Teith-Forth and the Tay make

---

[1] See p. 70.   [2] See p. 126.

corresponding curves, and it may be suggested that the Don and the Dee of Aberdeenshire represent the lower, easterly components of rivers of the same series, whose upper, south-eastward courses have been obliterated by the subsequent Spey, Findhorn, and Ness.

Thus all the consequent drainage of Scotland seems to have originated on a single, wide-spreading plateau, grained from north-east to south-west, but it is impossible to speak with certainty of the geological date of this departure. There is, however, remarkable evidence of the rapidity of subsequent denudation. In the early Tertiary period great cracks radiated from the volcanic centres of the Hebrides, through the South-Western Highlands, the Midland Rift Valley, and the Southern Uplands. These cracks were injected with molten lava, which solidified into buried walls, known as dykes. The cut edge of one of these dykes can be traced from the western shore of Loch Lomond into the summit of Ben Lomond on the other side of the water, and, therefore, when the lava was still molten the walls of the crack must have been continuous from the bed of the loch to the summit of the mountain. Consequently, the Lomond Glen must have been excavated to a depth of at least 5000 feet since the early Tertiary epoch. In the same space of time the river-system of the English plain has undergone its entire development.

It is equally impossible to infer how far westward and northward the plateau may have spread into the area now occupied by the ocean. The horizontal basaltic beds are piled upon one another to a height of 3200 feet in Ben More of Mull; and the Minch may once have been flooded to its brim with solidified lava sheets, resembling those of the Snake Plains in North America, of the Western Deccan in India, and of Laikipia in East Africa. In view of the very recent submergence of the barrier between the Atlantic and Arctic abysses,[1] it appears likely that, north-westward, at any rate, even the hundred fathom line does not mark the limit of the vast tabular block from which Scotland was carved.

[1] See p. 105.

The most conspicuous element in the drainage-system of Ireland is the great river Shannon, the longest of all British rivers.   It rises within twenty miles of Donegal Bay, not far from the upland which may be regarded as an extension of the Grampian Highlands, and flows southward with a slow stream over the central plain, as far as Killaloe at the exit from Lough Derg (Fig. 68).   Here it

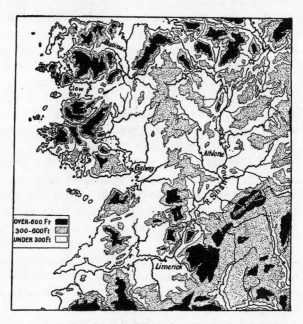

FIG. 68.—The basin of the Shannon, showing the Gorge at Killaloe, between Lough Derg and Limerick.

cuts a passage, marked by rapids, through a group of lofty hills, and finally turns westward from Limerick through a fiord-like estuary, sixty miles in length, to the Western Ocean.   Apart from geological history, it would be difficult to understand why the Shannon should not have crossed the unbroken plain from Lough Ree to Galway, or to Dublin, instead of cleaving the gorge of Killaloe through a group of isolated uplands 2000 feet in height. It must, however, be assumed that the Shannon already existed when the plain was still buried deep under deposits, wherein most of the present mountains lay hidden like the bones in the flesh.

The drainage of the greater part of Leinster and Munster constitutes an obvious and nearly regular system : the Avoca, the Slaney, the Barrow, the Nore, the Suir, the Blackwater, the Lee, and the Bandon all flow through southward transverse courses, but some of them, and notably the more western, also exhibit great lengths of longitudinal eastward channel, making sharp elbows with the southward reaches (Fig. 69). The build of Munster is relatively simple, and presents a perfect harmony between the rock-structure and the river system. The eastward channels follow the downfolds : the southward channels cross the upfolds in gorges. Wind-gaps occur in the ridges which separate the longitudinal valleys. The whole corrugated surface must, therefore, once have been buried in the substance of a plateau tilted gently southward. Parallel rivers flowed over this, heedless of the underlying complexities of rock. At a later time the surface became weathered and ribbed, and subsequent channels began to develop along the more yielding strips of limestone preserved in the downfolds of the Devonian strata. Thus the Suir may have captured the upper Blackwater ; the Blackwater, with its long subsequent valley, may have decapitated the Lee at Fermoy and the Bandon at Mallow ; while the Lee may have robbed yet another length of the Bandon. It is even conceivable that the Shannon may once have flowed through the deep gap south of Mallow, to Cork or Kinsale harbour ; for its present westward estuary has the appearance of a subsequent channel which has intercepted the upper river at Limerick.

The rest of the rivers of Ireland are of less general interest. Local systems of drainage necessarily arose, when the ring of coasts was complete, where denudation had exposed the mountain groups. The Boyne and

the Liffey flow through the central plain, the latter from
the mountains of Wicklow, the former from lower sources.
The Laggan, and the Blackwater tributary of Lough
Neagh, have a longitudinal position in the depression
which extends into the Rift Valley of Scotland.   The
lower Foyle is longitudinal with reference to the ridges
of Donegal.   The Bann, however, holds an exceptional
north-north-west course, parallel to the western border of
the lava plateau of Antrim, with reference to which it

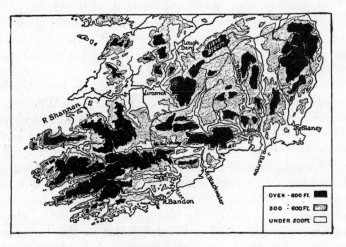

FIG. 69.—The rivers of Southern Ireland. .... The Great Southern
and Western Railway from Dublin to Cork.

may perhaps count as longitudinal.   The Erne at Enniskillen follows a line of fracture at the junction of the
Carboniferous limestone and the Old Red sandstone.
In all these courses there is no important obstacle pierced
by a stream in such manner as to indicate a consequent
origin.

A special characteristic of certain of the Irish rivers
is a tendency to expand into wide lakes of irregular
outline.   Nearly half of the course of the Shannon above

Killaloe is through the three Loughs Allen, Ree, and Derg. Lough Erne and upper Lough Erne constitute one half of the entire course of the Erne River. Along the foot of the mountain rim of Connaught are the Loughs Corrib, Mask, and Conn, occupying a position at the junction of geological formations which is comparable to that of the curve of great lakes in North America, or of the lake belt of north-western Russia. All these loughs and others smaller, in addition some that have been choked with bog-moss, have been formed in the plain by the solution of the Carboniferous limestone in the river waters. Lough Neagh, on the other hand, the largest of British lakes, is probably due to the obstruction of the off-flow by the lava-sheet of Antrim.

The lakes of Great Britain are smaller than those of Ireland. They are almost all of glacial origin. In the plains northward of the Thames, and especially in Cheshire and the Midland Valley of Scotland, were formerly numerous little waters ponded by moraine and drift material. Some of these have been blocked with peat and others have been emptied by man, so that few now remain, but among these is Loch Leven of Fife. The Archæan floor of gneiss, exposed along the western edge of Sutherland and Ross, and the Harris end of Long Island, are sown with almost countless rock tarns, and a few such tarns are scattered over the eastern Grampians, the Southern Uplands and the Welsh mountains. But the most interesting of the glacial lakes occur in the glens of the Highlands, west of the meridian of Killiecrankie, and in the dales of the Lake Mountains of Cumberland and Westmorland. They are usually long and deep, their beds sinking into one or more rock basins. At the upper end is a delta, gradually encroaching on the water, while a rock bar closes the lower end except for the notch by which the stream escapes. They occur both in longitudinal and transverse valleys. A vigorous controversy has long centred on the origin of these glen lochs, but, on the whole, Ramsay's view that they are ice-made is now gaining ground. Their distribution in Great Britain is, however, peculiar, and it is not easy to understand why they should be so rare in the eastern Grampians, the Southern Uplands and the Welsh mountains. Probably they were produced by the valley glaciers at the close of the ice-age rather than by the continuous ice-sheet. For climatic reasons, and because of the steeper descent of the valleys, such glaciers would, doubtless, have greater effect in the west. As might be expected, many submerged lake-basins are traceable in the beds of the sea lochs and kyles of the Hebrides.

Despite their importance in the landscape and upon the map the lakes of Britain are of adventitious origin, and have constituted no essential factor in the development of the drainage system. Of far greater significance, could their channels be traced with certainty, would be the rivers which formerly coursed over the plains, now sunk under the Narrow and Irish Seas. One of these must have been derived from the shallow sill between the Hebrides and Ireland, and must have passed southward through the North Channel, and by the line of deeps off the east coast of Ireland, to the continental edge westward of Cornwall.[1] No quite clear and continuous furrow can be detected on the bed of the St. George's Channel, but the slight transverse rise in that constriction may have caused a lake in the western Irish Sea. The course of the sunken river must have been symmetrical with that of the Shannon, and its estuarine reaches were doubtless longitudinal with reference to the rock graining produced by the Armorican corrugation. Tributaries may have been received from the Bristol Channel and from the western end of the English Channel ; or the three Channel streams may have formed a group of ria-inlets on a fringed coast, like that of south-west Munster. Having regard to the probability of a long persistent union of the lands now broken into Brittany, Cornwall, and Munster, it may well have been that, following the lie of the still earlier Hebridean gulf,[2] the North Channel river passed

[1] Compare p. 32.   [2] See p. 103.

in remote pre-glacial times through the Cheshire gap, rather than the St. George's Channel.

However speculative many of the points in this attempted reconstruction of the British consequent drainage, the cumulative effect of the evidence appears to be reasonably clear. The preceding analysis has shown that all the important consequent streams now remaining—in the Midland Plain of England, in the Devonian Peninsula, in Wales, in the Pennine Isthmus, in the Southern Uplands, in the Midland Valley of Scotland, in the Grampian Highlands, in the Northern Highlands, and in Ireland—have south-easterly courses, tending to easterly in the Pennine region and along the eastern margin of Scotland, and to southerly in Ireland. Only the streams of the Wealden uplift are exceptional. The subsequent valleys, unless where special and explicable local conditions have compelled an anomalous flow, have a generally north-eastward or south-westward direction, but round the Pennine upland they tend to become northerly and southerly, and in the south of Ireland easterly and westerly. The consequent and subsequent channels of the existing rivers are thus in detailed harmony with one another. Evidence of the process of development of the subsequent rivers has been exceptionally preserved in the cases of the Trent-Witham and the Clyde. There are clear indications that the mountainous districts of Wales, the Southern Uplands, the Grampian Highlands, and the Northern Highlands are dissected plateaux. The immensity of recent denudation along the oceanic border is testified by the gorges of the Wye and Shannon, and by the position of the Old Red Sandstones and the Tertiary Dykes of Scotland ; while the relatively undenuded condition of the English plain in Tertiary times is evidenced by the absence of Jurassic fragments in the London clay, and the presence of carboniferous fossils in the Norfolk crag. No consequent rivers enter the Irish Sea except from the north-west, while from the south-eastern shores of this sea appear to be receding in concentric curves the Pennine-Cambrian divide, and the

Jurassic and Cretaceous escarpments of the Midlands.
Even the vanished river of Eigg came from the west or
north-west, and the Scoto-Icelandic rise has only recently
been submerged. The conclusion seems inevitable that,
except in the south-eastern corner of England, the present
river system of Britain has been developed, from a series of
roughly parallel channels, on the grand terminal slope of
a continental Atlantis
spreading south-east-
ward from Greenland.
The Welsh river Wye
would, therefore, appear
to be an older geogra-
phical feature than the
mile-high continental
slope which now de-
scends, west of Scot-
land, into the Atlantic
abyss. The existing
Irish Sea and Cheshire
gap, the Midland Plains
of Scotland and Ireland,
and Glenmore and the
Minch must have been
re-exposed in the pro-
cess of recent denuda-
tion. In a more funda-
mental sense, therefore,

FIG. 70.—Probable flow of the rivers in the
period of extensive emergence, immediately after the Ice Age.

than that of mere remoteness, the oceanic border may
be regarded as at the back of the land, for the rock-
structure and the river-systems of all Britain, except the
Weald, have grown from north-western origins.

Two hydrographical features of the British area
remain for consideration, the course of the Rhine over the
bed of the North Sea, and the Wealden watershed, neither
of them being related to the main drainage-slope of

Britain.   The rivers of the Rhine system now spread their
deltaic "distributaries" over all Holland from Terschelling
in the north to Flushing in the west, but there is evidence
to show that in early historical times the main channel
continued the direction of the river above Wesel, instead
of bending as at present to the west.[1] The principal
mouth must have been midway along the south coast
of the North Sea, and it is difficult to decide whether the
further course would more probably trend to the east or

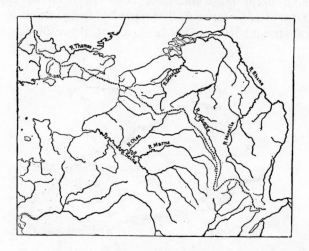

FIG. 71.—The Belgic and Wealden Divide, between the sources
of the Solent and Seine on the one hand, and those of the
Thames and Western Rhine tributaries on the other

to the west of the Dogger bank.   If the latter were the
case, the Rhine may possibly have traversed the Silver
Pits, having the Elbe as a tributary (Fig. 70).   But
whether the Rhine received the eastern rivers of Britain,
or the Thames was the head of an independent stream,
all the rivers of the North Sea plain must have had a
late origin, unless the break in the Scoto-Scandinavian
land was of earlier date than is generally supposed.

The Wealden watershed was determined in the middle

[1] See Reclus, *Geographie Universelle*, vol. iv. p. 219.

of the Tertiary epoch by the "posthumous" uplift of the chalk. It extends beyond the Strait of Dover far into the continent of Europe, separating the north-eastward rivers of the Rhine group from the rivers which flow south-westward into the Seine (Fig. 71), for the Medway and the Kentish Stour must be regarded as belonging to the same drainage-slope as the Lys, the Scheldt, and the Sambre. When the glacial epoch passed away, Britain remained for a time in connection with the mainland. The Wealden uplift must still have been unbroken by Dover Strait, for it is remarkable that none but insignificant longitudinal streams have as yet been thrust, from the Channel

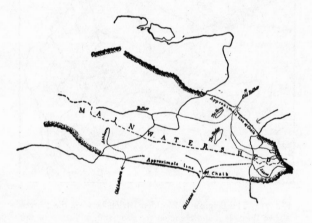

FIG. 72.—Diagram of the Eastern Weald and Bas Boulonnais, showing the probable lie of the features before the formation of the Strait of Dover.—*After* TOPLEY.

shore, along the clay belts which intervene between the chalk downs and the Forest range of Hastings. There were, doubtless, water-gaps in the chalk ridges which prolonged the North and South Downs into France, and it is possible that when a depression had admitted the Atlantic waters up the English Channel, the Strait was originated by the wash of the waves, which gradually widened the water-gaps, cutting them back into the cliffs of Beachy

Head and the South Foreland, of Cape Blanc Nez and the coast of Picardy (Fig. 72).

Thus the Kentish promontory—of such vital significance for the inhabitants of the islands—has a unique physical history, distinguishing it from the feature-system of all the remainder of Britain. Moreover, the continuation of its watershed into the continent is not unconnected with the boundary between the Romance and Teutonic peoples, which comes down to the coast opposite to Dover.[1] In the Middle Ages, when the Roman roads had fallen into decay, traffic was chiefly by boat on the streams, and the Teutons could maintain their position on the tributaries of the Rhine, lower Meuse, and Scheldt more easily than the French, who had to cross from the Seine.[2] There is an intimate causal relation, therefore, between the physical structure of the Wealden uplift and the pregnant historical facts (1) that the south-eastern corner of Britain approaches to within sight of the Continent, and (2) that the two great interacting races of European civilisation meet where the narrow seas are narrowest.

Note on Watersheds.—The word "watershed" denotes a line and not a slope : it is an adaptation, not a translation, of the German word "Wasserscheide." In almost any land two different systems of watershed may be drawn, the one parting the rivers according to their destinations, the other according to the grouping of their transverse headstreams. The latter is the more likely to suggest the character of the original drainage system, because subsequent channels may have diverted the lower rivers from their first destinations. In this book, watersheds of this type have been termed "divides," while the word "water-parting" has been reserved for watersheds drawn according to destination of drainage, which are the more important from the point of view of human movement and settlement. The Trent and the Severn flow through Staffordshire and Shropshire down the same drainage slope from the same Pennine-Cambrian divide, but their basins are separated by the great water-parting of England, for the one issues in the eastern and the other in the western sea. In other places, as for instance along the Pennine Range, watersheds drawn on the two plans may coincide.

FIG. 73.—Relation of a plain of denudation to contorted strata.

[1] See p. 10. [2] See note on the Linguistic Frontier at p. 146.

Note on River-origins.—It may be convenient to state in general terms the theory of river-origins, which is here applied to the explanation of the river systems of Britain. Denudation, whether marine or sub-aerial, marginal or superficial, is constantly tending to degrade every land, however mountainous, to a base-level. This level is usually grained, like sawn wood, because the plane of denudation intersects folds in the constituent rock-beds (Fig. 73). If land thus denuded be raised afresh by crust-movements, a series of streams is likely to be formed, which will flow over the plateau, following any initial tilt of the nearly flat surface, but unaffected by the perhaps complicated structure and varying quality of the rocks beneath. Such streams are described as *consequent* on the original tilt of the planed and raised surface. Denudation, commencing a fresh cycle of operation, soon furrows the plateau along the less resistant belts of the graining, leaving the more resistant as salient ridges (Fig. 74). The consequent rivers keep, however, to their first direction by maintaining notches in such of the developing ridges as are crossed by their paths, and these notches or *water-gaps* (*a.* Fig. 75) are incised

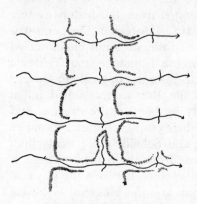

FIG. 74.—Incipient drainage system.

pari passu with the degradation of those of the valley reaches, which intersect the *longitudinal* furrows. Such rivers are said to be *transverse* to the grain of the land. They develop lateral tributaries to collect the drainage of the furrows, and these tributaries are described as *subsequent* to the consequent main stream. Should any consequent river, owing to physical peculiarities of flow or of under-lying rock, open a specially deep valley, its subsequent tributaries, having steeper channels, are likely to work their sources back through the furrows

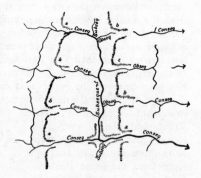

FIG. 75.—Mature drainage system.

of the graining, at the expense of the subsequents of the next system, and ultimately to tap and divert its main consequent stream (Fig. 75). Thus a single, more rapidly incised consequent may successively decapitate many of its neighbours, and form a great arborescent river-system. The abandoned notches in the ridges will cease to be incised, and will be left by the progress of denudation as high-level *wind-gaps* (*b*). Finally, since both sides of the longitudinal furrows must be drained into the subsequents, it follows that short streams are developed flowing in a direction opposite to that of the consequents, and Professor Davis has spoken of these streams as *obsequent*. The source of an obsequent stream may even work back through a ridge, most frequently at a wind-gap (*c*), and seize the subsequent drainage of the furrow beyond.

It is to be observed, therefore, that transverse streams may be either consequent or obsequent, and that longitudinal streams are most usually subsequent, but may be consequent. Conversely, subsequents must be longitudinal, and obsequents must be transverse, but consequents, which depend merely on the original tilt of the surface, may be either transverse, longitudinal, or oblique, *i.e.*, intermediate in direction between transverse and longitudinal.

Note on the Bristol Avon.—The explanation of the course of the Bristol Avon presents great difficulties. The account given in the foregoing chapter involves less improbability than does that of Ramsay, who postulated a temporary westward tilt of the whole region. But it is noteworthy that without any general change of direction the Avon traverses successively two gorges, at Bath and at Clifton, and in view of the rarity of important obsequent streams in the English plain, a straight river which is doubly obsequent would appear unlikely. Moreover, it cannot escape observation that from Bath to the sea the Avon flows in a direction parallel to the Mendip ridge. Perhaps it was formed as a subsequent river along the denuded axis of a slight upfold in the chalk, which may here have been relatively thin. The Vale of Pewsey is an existing valley of that character, and approximately on the same axis as the Avon Valley (allowance being made for a slight change of direction), but no subsequent river has as yet been developed in it. If the suggestion here made be the correct explanation, then both the Warwick and Bristol Avons are subsequent rivers developed from the Bristol Channel, the one along the Midland system of rock graining, the other along the Southern (Wealden) system.

Note on authorities.—A paper on "The River Valleys of the South of Ireland," by the late Professor Jukes printed in the *Quarterly Journal of the Geological Society*, vol. xviii. (1862), is classical, but was written when studies of this nature had made little progress. Many pertinent discussions by Ramsay, A. Geikie, Hull, and Topley are scattered through the works cited in the notes to Chapters VI. and VII. The important evidence of the diversion of the Trent from the Witham to the Humber is contained in a paper by Mr. Jukes-Brown in the *Quarterly Journal of the Geological Society*, vol. xxxix., and in a memoir of the Geological Survey, entitled "The Geology of the Country round Lincoln." We have to thank Professor W. M. Davis, of Harvard University, not only for systematising the terms and methods employed in these discussions, but for a valuable paper on "The Development of Certain English Rivers," published in the *Geographical Journal*, vol. v.

Papers bearing on the Severn-Thames problem are " The Drainage of Cuestas," by W. M. Davis in the *Proc. Geol. Assoc.*, vol. xvi. ; "The Genesis of the Severn," by S. S. Buckman in *Nat. Sci.*, April 1899 ; and "On the Origin of the High-Level Gravel with Triassic Débris adjoining the Valley of the Upper Thames," by Osborne White, in the *Proc. Geol. Assoc.*, vol. xv.

The Clyde problem was discussed by H. M. Cadell in a paper on "The Dumbartonshire Highlands," in the *Scot. Geog. Mag.*, vol. ii. For the Scottish Lochs, see Sir John Murray and F. P. Pullar, *Geog. Journ.*, vol. xv. For the Cumbrian Lakes, see H. R. Mill, *Geog. Journ.*, vol. vi.

Note on Bala Lake.—Since the account of the Dee given on p. 124 was printed, my attention has been called to a paper by Mr. Philip Lake in the *Geol. Mag.*, 1900, in which he shows that an alluvial plain exists at the present foot of the lake, and argues, from this and other circumstances, that the Merionethshire Dee formerly flowed S.W. into the Wnion, not N. into the Clwyd. But he indicates a former southward drainage system for the whole district, thus supporting the general theory developed in the foregoing chapter.

Note on the Linguistic Frontier.—The Walloon district of the Belgian Meuse is an exception which proves the rule (p. 143), for the passage across the watershed is nowhere easier than from the Oise to the Sambre.

CHAPTER X

BRITISH WEATHER

THE natural features of Britain have been determined by the interaction of two agencies, the one producing stresses in the earth's crust, and so raising, crumpling, and fracturing the rock beds, the other impelling the moist winds landward, and biting into the rock surface a configuration of coast lines and river basins. But just as the details of the drained surface are in the long run closely adapted to the underlying structure, so the winds and waves are guided by the surface features, and are conditioned by the very forms they are in process of shaping. Every hill has its influence upon the rains which are degrading its substance : every headland bends the currents which are reducing its salience. The solid features and the fluid circulations are, therefore, delicately adjusted to one another : a correlation which gives intricate unity to the varied theme of geography. Climate has closely co-operated with rock structure in determining the features of Britain, and these features are in turn among the chief causes producing variety of climate within the British area.

The average succession of weather in any region during the several seasons of the year is the climate of that region, and a study of the chief types of British weather is, therefore, essential to the understanding of the British climates. Changes of weather are in the main due to variations of atmospheric pressure.[1] When the air above a given spot is rarer than usual its pressure is reduced, and the weight of the column of air extending

---

[1] See note on the Physics of the Atmosphere at p. 162.

upward through the atmosphere is proportionately less. On the other hand, when the air is denser than usual the weight of the atmospheric column is greater. This varying weight is measured by means of the barometer, an automatic balance with a liquid counterpoise. If the atmospheric weight diminishes—if, that is to say, the air above becomes slightly rarer—the mercury in the barometric tube falls a little, but if the air becomes denser and its pressure greater, the mercury rises. Thus may the fluctuations in the air at a given spot be observed from hour to hour, and from day to day. If, however, observers at two different spots be equipped with barometers, it becomes possible to ascertain at an appointed moment the difference of atmospheric pressure in the interval between them. Scattered all over Britain are meteorological stations, at each of which the most essential instrument is the barometer, and every day at fixed hours telegraphic messages are sent from each of these stations to the Meteorological Office in London. The most important fact in each message is the barometric or atmospheric pressure, and this is entered upon a blank map of Britain. When the figures from all the stations have been received and entered, it is always found that, allowance having been made for variety of elevation and temperature, the pressure does not change from station to station without method. The differences are invariably related in so simple a manner, that it is possible to draw straight or simply curved lines, connecting all places with an equal pressure at the hour of observation. These lines, which are called isobars, or lines of equal pressure, can obviously never cross one another. A map thus marked is known as a synoptic weather chart.

A series of such synoptic charts are here shown in the form published daily in the *Times* newspaper. The first of them depicts the weather at 6 P.M. on the 1st of December 1898 (Fig. 76). The isobars are seen to run east and west in orderly succession. The southernmost crosses Devonshire and the Channel, and, as indicated by the number placed against it, connects all points whose atmospheric pressure was equal to a column of mercury thirty inches high. The northernmost crosses the Shetland Isles, and corresponds to a pressure of twenty-nine inches of mercury. The intervening isobars are placed at intervals marking a difference of pressure of two-tenths of an inch. Thus in the six hundred geographical miles which separate the latitude of Devonshire from that of the Shetlands, there was a steady diminution of pressure amounting in the aggregate to one inch. Meteorologists, borrowing a metaphor from road engineers, would describe

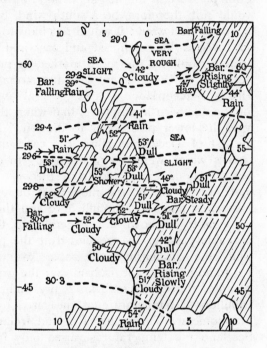

FIG. 76.—Synoptic Chart of the Weather at 6 P.M. on Dec. 1, 1898, showing a northward gradient.

Light wind, ⌐ Fresh or strong wind, → A gale, →→

this diminution by saying that there was a northward gradient of one-tenth of an inch in sixty miles.

Since no barrier divides the atmosphere into compartments, the fluid air is free to yield to the higher pressure in the south, and to flow northward towards the lower pressure. The northward movement of air, down the gradient from the Channel to the Shetland Isles, would constitute a south wind, strong if the gradient were steep and the isobars close together, light if the gradient were

easy and the isobars far apart. Owing, however, to the
rotation of the earth from west to east, all winds in the
northern hemisphere tend to swerve to the right hand. A
wind from the English Channel moving towards air of
lower pressure in the neighbourhood of the Shetland Isles
would not, therefore, be a south wind, but a south-west
or nearly west wind : it would not blow towards the north,
but towards the north-east and east, and the easterly de-
flection would be the more marked in proportion to the
steepness of the gradient and the strength of the wind.
This is in accordance with the general law of Buys Ballot
for the northern hemisphere, that when the back is to the
wind the lower pressure is to the left. In the chart for
the 1st of December 1898, the winds are indicated by
arrows which were drawn according to observation, and
not merely as calculated from theory. It will be seen
that, on the whole, the movement of air was from the
south-west and west, though here and there, from causes
too local to be shown in a general map, there were small,
probably passing, divergencies from the perfect regularity
which the parallelism of the isobars would demand.

In addition to the isobars and the wind arrows it will
be noted that the chart bears figures indicative of the distribution of temperature, as measured by the Fahrenheit
thermometer. Throughout England, Ireland, and Southern
Scotland the temperatures varied only from $51°$ to $53°$,
and even in the Shetland Isles nothing lower than $42°$
was recorded. For the time of year the weather was
warm, as might have been anticipated from the prevalence of south-westerly winds, which bring air from more
southerly latitudes and from the surface of the Atlantic
Ocean. In the autumn and winter the sea is always
warmer than the land, partly on account of its system of
currents, and partly because, owing to the high specific
heat of water, it retains more of summer warmth.

Lastly, in addition to the other information on the
chart, there are words showing that cloud and rain were
distributed over the whole of the British area. The wind
blowing from the warm south-west and coming from off

the ocean must have been nearly saturated with all the
moisture it could hold.   Passing north-eastward into
regions of less pressure it must needs expand a little, and
that expansion, by causing a slight lowering of temperature, would reduce the air's capacity for holding invisible
moisture. The
surplus mois-
ture, no longer
tenable by the
air, would be
thrown down as
cloud and rain.
    Thus at
6 P.M. on the
1st of Decem-
ber 1898, there
were light and
fresh south-
westerly winds
in Britain, while
the sky was
overcast, and in
places a warm
rain was falling.
On the 4th of
the same month
the distribu-
tion of pressure
had somewhat
changed, and

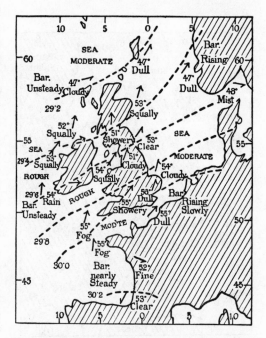

FIG. 77.—The Weather at 6 P.M. on December 4, 1898,
showing a north-westward gradient of pressure.

the isobars were, in consequence, drawn in a north-easterly
and south-westerly direction (Fig. 77).   The general aspect
of the chart for this day is one so often repeated that it may
be regarded as presenting the most frequent type of British
weather.   The high pressures had fallen a little eastward
in the continent of Europe, and the gradient was, therefore, in a north-north-westward direction from Kent
towards Iceland.   The wind, also, had veered a little,
and had become, on the average, south-south-west : the

weather was still dull, though, on the whole, finer than three days earlier.

A third condition of the air is represented in the chart for the 14th of January 1901 (Fig. 78). The gradient was here from east to west, the area of highest pressure being due east of Britain. The winds were southerly, and the weather was cool and clear, except along the oceanic border, where an unsteady barometer, accompanied by relative warmth, a dull sky, and a rough sea, indicated the passage of atmospheric disturbances over the neighbouring region of the ocean.

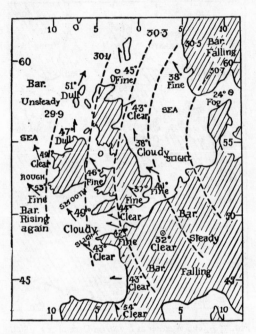

FIG. 78.—The Weather at 6 P.M. on January 14, 1901, showing a westward gradient of pressure.

Occasionally a patch of denser air extends and becomes detached from the area of high pressure on the continent. On the 25th of January 1899, such a centre of high pressure was established over the North Sea, and the isobars upon the chart for the day succeeded one another in concentric curves approximating to circles (Fig. 79). The isobar nearest to the centre indicated the very high pressure of 30.7 inches, and from this there was a gradual decrease to 30.3 in the Bay of Biscay. The air was, of course, streaming out in all directions from the region of

high pressure, and in obedience to the universal law
was everywhere crossing the isobars with a right-handed
swerve. A system of light winds thus blew spirally out
from the North Sea, and the direction of the spiral coincided with the movement of the hands of a watch. Such a
system of pres-
sure and winds
is known as
an anti-cyclone.
The air supply-
ing the wind
could obviously
come only from
the upper layers
of the atmos-
phere, and an
anti - cyclone
marks, there-
fore, a region of
falling air. The
upper portion
of the atmos-
phere, being
free from the
weight of the
underlying
layers, is both
rare and cold,
but as the air

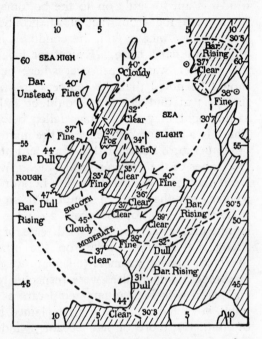

FIG. 79.—The Weather at 6 P.M. on January 25, 1899,
showing an anti-cyclone.

descends earthward it is compressed and accordingly
somewhat warmed. Even if saturated when above, the
moisture it contained would no longer suffice to saturate
it below, and therefore the air of an anti-cyclone,
though in contact with the sea, is relatively dry and void
of cloud. The peculiarities of anti-cyclonic weather
are due to this fact, for radiant heat traverses dry air
more easily than moist air. During the long days of
summer, therefore, the sun's rays are apt to generate
abnormal heat and drought in a period of anti-cyclone,

but a winter anti-cyclone is usually associated with bright cold days, and frosty, brilliantly starlit nights : it is the earth which then radiates heat into space during the long hours of darkness. In the valleys, however, the coldest, heaviest air, hardly stirred by the gentle anti-cyclonic winds, is apt to settle on to the bottoms, and to become laden with fog from the moist ground. This, as the chart shows, was, in fact, the condition in Britain on the 25th of January 1899. Except for local fogs and mists, the weather was almost everywhere cold and fine. It should be noted that the temperatures are set down for six P.M. : at mid-day they would be a little higher, and at midnight they would have fallen below freezing-point. There is a striking difference in the matter of distribution of temperature between this chart and that of the 4th of December of the previous year (Fig. 77). On the 4th of December the temperature in London measured 56°, whereas on the 25th of January it stood only at 36°, a difference of no less than 20°, due to the easterly continental winds on the south side of an anti-cyclone. Along the oceanic border, on the other hand, in the Shetlands and at Valencia (off south-western Ireland), the December temperatures were respectively 47° and 54°, as compared with the January temperatures of 40° and 47°, a fall, in each case, of only 7°, explained by the prevalence of southerly, more or less oceanic, winds on the western side of an anti-cyclone.

Far more frequent in the year history of British weather is a condition in every respect the opposite of anti-cyclonic. At 6 P.M. on the 27th of December 1900, for instance, there was relatively high pressure in Scandinavia, in Germany, and over the south of France, but the orderly succession of the isobars from the continent towards Iceland was broken by the invasion of a gulf of low pressure from the west, whose centre, as marked by the isobar indicating the very low pressure of 28.8 inches, lay just to the west of Ireland (Fig. 80). At 8 A.M. on the 28th it had reached the Isle of Man (Fig. 81), and at

6 P.M. on the same day had passed on to the North Sea.
During the whole of the twenty-four hours the winds were
swirling round the centre, accompanying it forward as the
tyre of a wheel goes forward with the axle.   The isobars
indicate a pressure rising in all directions from the centre,
and the air was, therefore, driven in towards the centre
by the marginal
high   pressure.
In obedience to
the general law,
however,   the
wind crossed the
isobars with a
right - handed
swerve, so that
the   rotatory
movement was,
in fact, an in-
ward swirl of
air turning in
the   direction
opposed to that
of the hands of
a watch.   In the
centre   the   air
must,   on   the
whole, have been
rising into the
upper atmos-
phere.   Such a

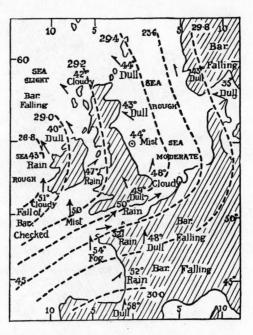

FIG. 80.—The Weather at 6 P.M. on December 27, 1900,
showing the approach of a cyclone from the west.

system of pressure and winds is spoken of as a cyclone,
or more simply as a barometric depression.   The word
"depression" is, of course, only metaphorical when
applied to the air, the fact being that the winds swirl into
a nucleus of rarer rising air.   But except in this respect,
an atmospheric cyclone is almost precisely similar to one
of the little dimple-centred eddies which may often be
seen floating down the surface of a turgid stream.

On examination of the charts for the 27th and 28th

of December 1900, it will be observed that the general character of the weather was overcast and rainy, except that on the 28th there are indications, in rear of—that is to say, to west of—the centre, that the weather had become showery and even fine over Ireland and Southern England. Throughout the area covered by a cyclone the circumstances are conducive to precipitation. The air moving in towards the central lower pressure, and there rising, is slightly expanded, and as a consequence chilled. If drawn from humid regions and generally saturated, it will precipitate cloud and rain on all sides of the depression, but it is in the eastern half, and especially in the south-eastern quadrant of a cyclone of the northern hemisphere, that the rainfall reaches its maximum, for the air is there drawn from south-west and west, from the warmer latitudes where the atmosphere normally holds a greater burden of invisible moisture. In the case of Britain, moreover, a vast ocean lies in the same directions.

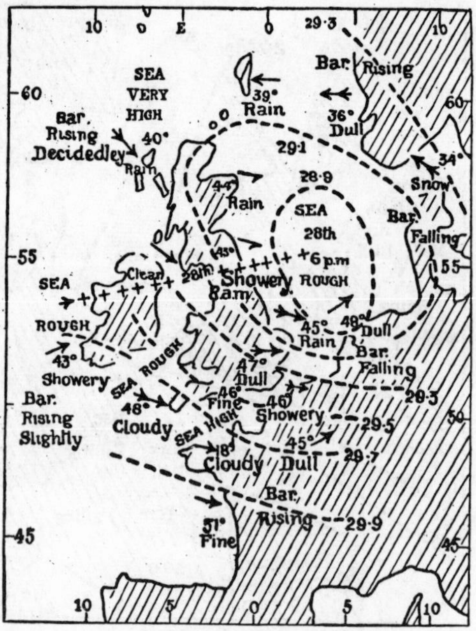

FIG. 81.—The Weather at 6 P.M. on December 28, 1900, showing a cyclone.

Track of the cyclonic centre, + + + + +

It will, of course, be obvious that, as the cyclonic centre journeys forward, the wind at any given point covered by the depression undergoes a change of direction. If the centre passes to the north of the point of observation the wind will veer from south-west to north-west, and the weather will clear somewhat and grow colder. A general change of this character may be observed in the south of Ireland and the south-west of England on comparing the chart for the 27th of December with that for the 28th. If, however, the centre passes to south of the point of observation, the wind will back from south-east, through east, to north-east, and finally to north-west, and, as in the other case, although less markedly, the sky will clear and the temperature fall. Such changes are visible in the north of Scotland on the same two charts. It will be noted further that on the 28th of December there was a marked contrast between the warm winds to the south of the centre, and the cold, easterly, continental breezes to the north of it.

The cyclone of the 28th of December was a well-developed storm: the gradients towards the centre were steep, especially on the southern side, and the winds were, therefore, strong, amounting in not a few places to a gale. Many depressions pass over the British area, some of which are known to come completely across the ocean from the coasts of America, but most of them are shallow, and produce merely a change of winds and weather. They need not cause storms in the usual sense of the word. Thirty or forty cyclones, ordinary and extraordinary, approach Britain from the west in the course of a year. The majority of them radiate from the oceanic area lying immediately south-westward of Ireland (Fig. 82). Of these, a few pass up the English Channel, a few cross England, and a few more strike diagonally through the Bay of Biscay and across Southern France to the Mediterranean, but the greater number move to the north-eastward along the oceanic borders of Britain and Scandinavia, following a very thoroughfare of storms. At certain seasons, in the autumn and winter, storm cyclones are apt to succeed one another in grand procession north-eastward along the last-named track, which may swing slowly on to and off the western shores of Britain.   A second, well-marked, path of cyclones enters the British Seas from a point to the south of Iceland and, passing by or through the north of Scotland, traverses the North Sea to Southern Norway or Denmark.   But the tracks thus indicated only express an observed tendency : it is impossible to foretell with certainty the course which will be taken by an arriving cyclone.

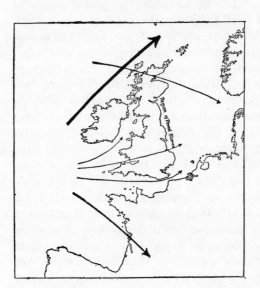

FIG. 82.—The more frequented Storm-tracks of the British Seas.

The thickness of the lines indicates the relative importance of the tracks.

Occasionally an atmospheric depression becomes lodged over Britain, embayed, as it were, in a back water, and there it lingers for a few hours, gradually dying away. With this fact may be correlated the circumstance that the storm-tracks about Britain are for the most part over the sea, for the winds are impeded by friction upon the land. Moreover, the energy of the cyclonic whirls appears to be due to latent heat derived from the moisture precipitated in the up-draft of air which has been drawn from the sea-surface.

An important contrast is to be observed in the general character of cyclones and anti-cyclones. Cyclones tend to advance with some rapidity and to follow one another in series, causing a spell of broken and rainy weather. Anti-cyclones, on the other hand, move slowly, and are apt to last long, while it is rare that the winds issuing from them have the strength of a gale. In order, however, to understand the manner in which these two systems of atmospheric phenomena co-operate to produce the changeable British weather, it is necessary to look far beyond the small area of Britain itself. In three directions, corresponding generally to the three sides of Britain, lie three permanent or alternating centres of atmospheric disturbance. Away to the north-west, beyond the oceanic border, is a nearly fixed centre of low pressure to the southward of Iceland. Eastward and south-eastward, beyond the narrow seas, is the monsoon area of Euro-Asia, a region of low pressure in the summer and autumn, and of abnormally high pressure in the cold winter and spring. South-westward, beyond the Channel entries, lies the Atlantic centre of permanently high pressure in the neighbourhood of the Azores. The Icelandic in-swirl and the Asiatic out-swirl are the dominant wind-systems during the cold season (Fig. 83). The atmosphere over Britain is then normally under the control of a north-westward gradient, and a great south-westerly current of air, moving in harmony with both swirls, brings moisture and relative warmth from the oceanic surface of lower latitudes. This current is troubled by many cyclonic eddies travelling for the most part north-eastward, which often carry their rainy south-eastern quadrants along the coasts of Ireland, Scotland, and Norway. The air ascending in each of the migrating cyclones must be assumed to flow eastward in the upper layers of the atmosphere, and to settle downward within the area covered by the continental anti-cyclone. In January and February the high pressures of Asia frequently extend westward through Germany into France, and a local anti-cyclone, or it may even be an extension of the great Euro-Asiatic system, may spread over the continental angle of Britain, producing calm, cold, and relatively dry weather. A fall of snow may mantle the ground, and a long frost may be inaugurated which yields only with difficulty to the impact of the cyclonic eddies from the west. At such times the heaths and downs of

Surrey are bathed in sunshine and crisp, clear air, while mists settle into the Thames Valley, making a silent and bitter gloom continuous through day and night. Among the Northern Hebrides, however, the sea may, at the same time. be lashed by cyclonic storm winds, and clouds may

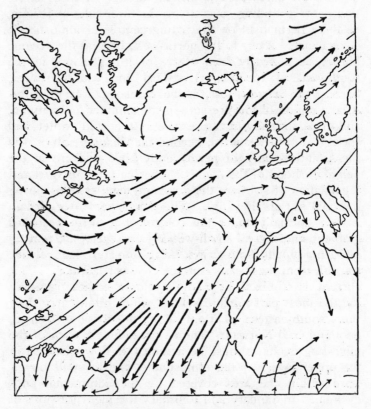

FIG. 83.—The prevalent Winds of Winter in the North Atlantic Area.
—*After the* DEUTSCHE SEEWARTE. (See note on p. 163.)

hang on all the slopes, while the verdure is maintained throughout the winter by persistent warm rains.

With the advance of spring the relative power of the three controlling centres—Icelandic, Asiatic, and Atlantic —is altered. The cyclones travel in a more easterly direction, often following the English Channel or crossing the Bay of Biscay, so that the east winds of their northern indrafts bring the dry biting air from the Russian plain which is characteristic of eastern, and especially of south-eastern Britain in the month of March.

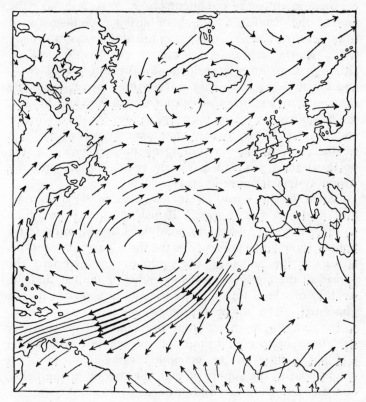

FIG. 84.—The prevalent Winds of Summer in the North Atlantic Area.
—*After the* DEUTSCHE SEEWARTE.

In the summer time the Icelandic depression and consequent wind-swirl are of minimum importance; while the North Atlantic system of high pressure obtains its most northward position and its completest development (Fig. 84). The prevalent winds of Britain become westerly

11

rather than south-westerly, being drawn eastward to the low pressures of Asia at the time when they are most vigorously expelled from the high pressures off the Azores. Moreover, the air spreading outward from the Azorean centre is less disturbed by travelling storms than is the winter air crowding into the Icelandic centre. Eddies continue to enter the continental area, often following the line of the English Channel, or striking south-eastward from near the Shetlands, but they are at this season usually feeble whirls, expressed in merely changeable weather, although sometimes intensified—locally and irregularly—and forming the secondary disturbances which bring the summer thunderstorms. Occasionally, in July and August, the Atlantic anti-cyclone may spread over Western Enrope and envelop South Britain, inducing a spell of brilliant weather. With the on-coming of autumn, however, the north-westerly gradient is slowly re-established, and the winter system resumes its sway.

Such is the *regime* of the weather in what may be described as the normal British year. From time to time, however, owing to conditions as yet imperfectly known, the relative influence of the three governing centres is varied, the paths of the cyclones are diverted, the spread of the anti-cyclones is extended or limited, and the weather of whole seasons may become in a certain degree abnormal. The power of forecasting exceptional seasons, to be obtained, perhaps, from the simultaneous study of the atmospheric equilibrium for the whole world, would add not a little to the economic value of Britain. It would control the supply of fuel, the sowing of the fields, and the stations of the fishing fleets.

Note on the Physics of the Atmosphere.—All the changes of weather and varieties of climate may be explained by the application of a few fundamental physical laws. These will be found carefully stated in such a handbook as Dickson's " Meteorology" (Methuen, 1893). For the convenience of students it may be well to give the following page-references to that book :—On atmospheric pressure generally, p. 23 ; on the reduction of temperature owing to the expansion of air, p. 25 ;

on saturation of air, p. 27 ; on the latent heat set free by rain, p. 28 ;
on the absorption of radiant heat in the atmosphere, p. 30 ; on the
effect of the earth's rotation on air-movements, p. 42.

Note on Figs. 83, 84.—The thickness of the arrows indicates the
average strength of the winds ; their length is proportional to the con-
stancy of the winds.

Note on Authorities.—The weather of Britain may be followed in
the Daily Weather Reports and the Monthly Pilot Charts issued by the
Meteorological Office. The chief types of weather will be found deline-
ated in the great Atlas of Meteorology by Bartholomew, Herbertson, and
Buchan (Edin. 1899).

CHAPTER XI

THE CLIMATES OF BRITAIN

CLIMATE is average weather, and although the weather of Britain is everywhere changeable, yet the average result of the changes is not the same for all parts. The south-east is as markedly contrasted with the north-west in the matter of climate, as in position, outline, relief, and structure. In their passage off Ireland and Scotland the storms frequently carry their rainy south-eastern quadrants over the land, and the oceanic border is, in consequence, the most rainy portion of Britain (Fig. 85). Anti-cyclones, on the other hand, which tend to produce drought, are rare along the shores of the ocean, although not infrequent, either in summer or winter, over the portion of Britain which lies opposite to the continent. But there is a second reason why the north and west should be rainy: they are the districts which contain the British uplands. When wind, sweeping over the plain of the sea, strikes a mountain slope, it must diverge from its former path either round the flanks or over the summit of the mountain. In so far as it is forced upward, the air, being relieved of pressure, expands a little and is chilled, and since it is saturated with oceanic moisture, it drenches the slope opposed to it with torrents of rain. Thus western Scotland and Ireland are moist, both because they are frequently traversed by the most rainy quadrants of cyclones, and because they are mountainous. For a similar double reason the English plain is relatively dry: it is a lowland district, and it lies beyond the most usual path of the cyclones.

The leeward side of mountains is drier than the

windward side, for the air which has passed over a ridge, having shed much moisture on the upward slope, is compressed and slightly warmed on the downward slope.[1]   This dryness to leeward of the heights has been termed their rain-shadow.   In Britain, where so much of the rainfall is due to cyclonic influences, even the leeward slopes receive abundant moisture ; yet the rain-shadows to east-

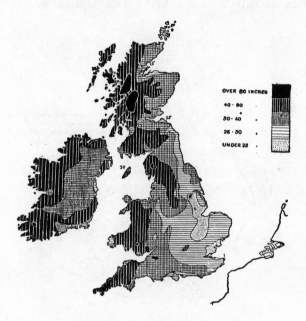

FIG. 85.—The Average Annual Rainfall of Britain.

ward and north-eastward of the hills are distinctly indicated upon the map.   They are evident in the form of areas of smaller precipitation to the east of Dartmoor and of Wales, and in the neighbourhood of Dublin ; but the most conspicuous is on the east coast of Scotland, and especially in Buchan and in the Straths of Dee, Don, and Spey, which lie under the lee of the Grampians,

[1] Compare the Foehn wind in the Alps.

the highest and most massively continuous of the British uplands. To the west of the Grampian summits the rainfall is probably the heaviest in Britain, and it is here, in consequence, that denudation has trenched the deepest and most numerous glens.[1]

Temperature is distributed over Britain, through the seasons, according to a somewhat different law.   In July

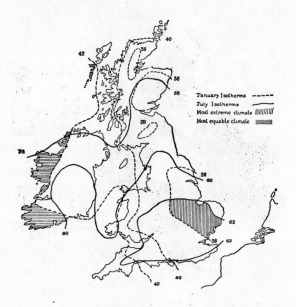

FIG. 86.—The Average Temperatures of the Air in Britain.

the isotherm, or line of equal temperatures, indicating an average of 60° Fahrenheit for the month, follows a sinuous course from west to east, through Ireland, Wales, and the North of England (Fig 86).   At this season of the year, direct sunshine counts as an important determinant of air-temperature even in Britain, and as

---

[1] Average annual rainfall at Ben Nevis Observatory, 151 inches; at Glencroe, Argyleshire (W. coast), 128 inches; at Nairn (E. coast), 24 inches.

a consequence, heat diminishes in the normal poleward direction.   In January, however, the isotherm of 40° Fahrenheit for the month strikes almost due southward along the west of Scotland and the east of Wales ; all points to the east of it have an average January temperature of less than 40°, while Cornwall, Wales, Ireland, and the Western Isles of Scotland have a temperature of more than 40°.   The winds from a relatively warm ocean,[1] and the latent heat set free by the frequent rains are the causes of the mildness of the western winter.

Britain may be divided into four climatic provinces, or quadrants, by means of the July isotherm of 60° and the January isotherm of 40°.   In the south-eastern quadrant, round London, the summers are warm and the winters cold, the average temperatures of January and July differing more than 20°, and the climate being, therefore, relatively extreme[2] and continental in type. In the north-west, on the oceanic border, the winters are mild and the summers cool : they differ in average temperature less than 20°, the climate being equable and oceanic in type.   The north-eastern and south-western quadrants have intermediate characteristics.   At Aberdeen, in the north-east, the winter is cold and the summer relatively cool, the average temperature for the whole year being comparatively low.   At Waterford and Plymouth, in the south-west, the summer is warm and the winter mild, the average temperature for the whole year being relatively high.   If a statement of the rainfalls be

[1] This warmth is not due to the Gulf Stream, as is commonly stated.   That very definite current ceases to be distinguishable a little to the east of the Newfoundland Bank, fully 1500 miles from the nearest shore of Britain.   The warm water west of Britain is due merely to the general north-eastward drift of the ocean surface, propelled by the winds from latitudes in which the sunshine is powerful.

[2] The climate even of South-eastern Britain is only *relatively* extreme, as is shown by the following statement : Moscow—January average temperature, 13° ; July average temperature, 67°.   London—January average temperature, 39° ; July average temperature, 63° Fahrenheit.

added to the variation of temperature, the four provinces may be thus defined :—

The south-east, containing London, Norwich, and Lincoln, is relatively extreme and dry. The north-east, containing Aberdeen, Edinburgh, and Newcastle, is dry, but somewhat cooler and less extreme than the south-east. The north-west, containing Stornoway, Londonderry, and Galway, is very equable and moist. The south-west, containing Waterford and Plymouth, is equable and moist, but, on the whole, warmer than the north-west.

The isotherms drawn across Britain exhibit characteristic curves in correlation with important physical features. The July isotherm of 60° bends northward over Ireland and England, and southward over the Irish Sea, for in

Fig. 87.—The Average Maximum Temperatures of July days.—*After* Gaster and Scott.

summer the land is warmer than the sea.   The January isotherm of 40°, on the other hand, exhibits an eastward bend over the English Channel, for at this time the sea is warmer than the land.   These lines, however, which indicate the average temperatures throughout the twenty-four hours, give smaller indication alike of the contrast between south-east and north-west, and of the influence of the channels and the uplands, than do other

lines drawn according to the mean minimum temperature
of the January nights and the mean maximum of the July
days (Figs. 87, 88). On an average January night the
Land's End is ten degrees warmer than is the region of
the East Midlands in the neighbourhood of the Fens,
whereas the highest temperature of an average July day
in this midland district is ten degrees warmer than on the
coasts of nor-
thern Scotland at
the same season.
Moreover, the
charts which bear
these lines of
mean *minima* and
maxima make ap-
parent, with
almost diagram-
matic clearness,
the influence not
merely of the
Irish Sea and
the English Chan-
nel, but of the
constrictions of
Great Britain at
Glenmore, the
Midland Valley
of Scotland, and
Solway Firth, and
they also show
the influence of

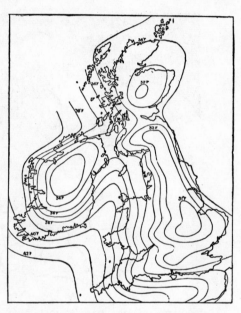

Fɪɢ. 88.—The Average Minimum Temperatures
of January nights.—*After* GASTER and
SCOTT.

the Cheshire Gap and the estuaries of the Severn and
Thames.

The diminution of winter temperature in Britain, from
west to east rather than from south to north, is a part
of one of the most striking climatic phenomena on the
globe. In the month of January a great northward
spread of oceanic warmth covers all the eastern half of

the entry to the Arctic Basin (Fig. 89). It is due to a
wind-driven set of the oceanic surface in a poleward
direction, moving on the average perhaps four and a half
knots a day. The limit of the consequent warmth in
the atmosphere may be assumed conveniently at the
January isotherm of 32° Fahrenheit. This line leaves
the North American coast south of the latitude of New-

FIG. 89.—The Winter Gulf of warmth over Britain.

The shaded area has an average January temperature below
freezing-point (32° Fahr.).

foundland, and, running just east of Iceland, attains to
its northernmost point in the neighbourhood of the North
Cape of Scandinavia. Thence it turns sharply southward
and follows the Norwegian coast, cutting through the marginal fringe of islands and peninsulas, and, continuing still
southward through Denmark, and across Europe almost to
the head of the Adriatic, turns finally south-eastward and
eastward along the Balkans. As seen from another planet

in an average January, the earth north of the fortieth parallel of north latitude—north, that is to say, of New York, the Pyrenees, and the Balkans—would present a generally shining surface, indicative of snow and ice, and into this would be thrust north-eastward to the seventieth parallel a dark pointed gulf, wherein the waters would be free of ice and the lands of snow ; but the northern extreme of this gulf would be hidden in the midwinter night.   Britain is placed not far ,from the centre of the area of abnormal warmth of winter, and the British winters are, in consequence, milder than those of any other region under the same northern latitudes.

Other minor, but not unimportant, determinants of climate exist, and of these the influence of elevation is the most significant.   Alike in summer and in winter temperature tends to decrease upward.   The winds also, being less impeded by friction, are on the whole stronger on the peaks than on the plains, and bright sunshine— more effective for the growth of plants than the diffused light from a grey sky—is rarer on the clouded uplands. In all these respects of relative temperature, wind, and sunshine, the oceanic border would be less favoured, by virtue of its mere position, than the continental angle of Britain, but the contrast is accentuated by the uplands of the north and west, and the plain of the south-east (Fig. 90).   On the eastern or corn-growing side of the country the greater length of the summer day in the north is not without appreciable agricultural value.

Local causes of still more restricted operation are aspect, the character of the soil, and the nature of the vegetation.   In a latitude so northerly as that of Britain a hill-slope facing southward receives the sun's rays more directly than does a flat surface or a slope tilted north- ward.   As a consequence, the southern faces of hills are more sunny — in the winter time more genial, in the summer time more burnt ; and this influence of aspect is the more important in proportion to the amount of sunshine—more effective, therefore, in the English plain than among the uplands of the oceanic border. Moreover, a slope, of whatever aspect, is exposed to less rigour in a frosty night, because the heavy cold air glides away from it into the valley bottoms. A sandy surface is the cause of greater extremes of temperature than is a heavy clay soil, for the air in the interstices of the sand is a bad conductor of heat, and temperatures, either high or low, are accumulated in the surface layer, whereas the water in clay, having a high specific heat, prevents a rapid rise of temperature, and checks a fall. Vegetation tends to equability, because of the stratum of air which is detained by the foliage, and by reason, also, of the evaporation of moisture from the vast surface of the total leafage.

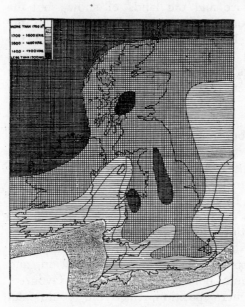

Fig. 90.—Sunshine in Britain. The gradation of tints from white to black indicates a diminution of average sunshine per annum from over 1700 hours in the S.E. to less than 1200 hours in the N.W.—*After* Dickson.

Instrumental observations permit of the tabulation of the different factors which go to form climate, but the general character of the vegetation is the clearest and most subtle index of their combined effect.   Only five per cent. of the total weight of the wheat crop is said to be derived from the soil, the remainder wholly from the atmosphere.   The approximate conditions of active vegetable growth in British latitudes appear to be a temperature of not less than 42° Fahrenheit, and a rainfall of at least eighteen inches. If the number of degrees be set down by which, on the average of the twenty-four hours, the temperature of any day exceeds the minimum of 42°, and the total of such numbers for all the days in the year be added together, a sum of "day degrees" is obtained which expresses roughly the vegetative potentiality of the climate. At Rothamstead, near St. Albans, a record has been kept since 1878 of the number of day degrees accumulated in each year between the 1st of January and the date of the wheat harvest. In eighteen years (1878–1895) the mean number obtained was 1900. When we bear in mind how late in the warm season British wheat is harvested, it will be seen that there is no large margin of climatic power available. Maize will nowhere

FIG. 91.—The months of maximum Rainfall in different parts of Britain.—*After* BUCHAN.

ripen in Britain, but it can be grown as a fodder crop. On the other hand, owing to the longer summer days and to the late season of the maximum rainfall, the conditions suffice for the maturing of both wheat and barley even in parts of Scotland (Fig. 91).

The excess of moisture along the oceanic border causes oats to be generally substituted for wheat and barley in all but the eastern counties of England and Scotland. Wheat, being deeply rooted, can withstand both the frosts and the droughts of the English plain, but it has there always been

considered a precarious crop, owing to the occasional defect
of adequate summer heat and to the frequency of thunderstorms. In those portions of Scotland and the north of
England in which wheat can be grown at all, it is perhaps
more secure on the average of years than in the south,
both on account of the comparative rarity of thunderstorms and of the more marked equability of the seasons.
Barley may be raised under rather less favourable conditions of temperature than wheat, and will endure a
greater amount of moisture, but it matures best in the
wheat districts of the east of England, although in dry
season it suffers more from drought, being less deeply
rooted than wheat.

Pasture grass is, however, by far the most characteristic
crop of Britain, and the best suited to its climate. The
humidity of the air maintains its verdure : the frequent
rains supply its growth. Neither the frosts nor the droughts
of the English plain permanently injure it, although they
may check its productivity, but it grows with greatest
luxuriance in the lowland portions of the west and north,
where frosts and droughts are rare and short. It is probably less dependent than the cereals upon direct sunshine, and thus flourishes along the oceanic border, where
the annual total of day degrees of temperature is high,
but the heat is largely dark heat, brought by the winds
from the sunshine of more southern latitudes. On the
uplands even grass is displaced by bogs of peat moss,
and moors of heather, gorse, and bracken.

According to the actual vegetation of to-day Britain
belongs to three zones of climate (Plate II.). The lowlands of the east and south-east are largely agricultural
and devoted to cereals. The lowlands of the west and
north are pastoral, or given to the cultivation of
oats ; while the uplands, especially in the north and
west, are clothed with bog and moor. Like the continental areas immediately to east and south of it, Britain
seems to have been densely forest-clad in pre-historic
times, and tree trunks are frequent in the peat bogs
of Scotland and Ireland. All the world over, however,

forest has been found to thrive under conditions which do not permit of an easy restoration of tree growth should it once be removed. Trees afford shelter to one another and to the undergrowth, but on naked, wind-swept uplands the saplings are bent, the soil is washed away by torrential rain, and the young shoots are eaten by cattle and sheep. In the populous lowlands of Britain few relics remain of the primeval forest, but there are many small woodlands of recent plantation.

In a highly civilised land, with artificial and luxurious modes of life, climate acquires an added geographical significance by determining the position of the health resorts. In the region of the Channel-entries a place of southern exposure, in the neighbourhood of Torquay or Penzance, has an exceedingly mild but moist winter. Further to eastward such places as Brighton and Folkestone have winters a little colder, marked, however, by more sunshine, and by a less humid air, for the temperature of the Channel surface is maintained, not by a wind-driven set, as is the case further to westward, but by the periodic intermingling of oceanic water, due to tides sweeping in upon the submerged platform. In the north-east of Scotland are conditions of a very different nature. Owing to the high barrier of the Central Grampians about Cairn Gorm, Ben Macdhui, and Lochnagar the rain-shadow is very pronounced, and it is possible to obtain summer coolness at high levels without the excessive rainfalls which characterise the heights almost everywhere else in Britain : hence the popularity of Braemar and other resorts in the glens of the Dee, the Don, the Avon, and the Spey.

Thus it is true in utmost detail, as in the large, that the climates of Britain are related to the features of its configuration. The connection may be traced with equal facility in the maps illustrative of the distribution of pressure, of temperature, of storm tracks, of rainfall, and of sunshine. From end to end the land is divided—by the belt of greater uplands, extending northward and southward from Sutherland to Devonshire—into western windward, and eastern leeward sides, but each transverse gap in the high ground admits the western influences through to the east. The broadest generalisation, however, is that, based on the frequency of cyclones in the north-west and of anti-cyclones in the south-east, which accumulates yet another contrast between the continental angle and the oceanic border.

Note on Authorities.—Bartholemew's Meteorological Atlas contains in convenient form most of the data needed for the understanding of the British climates. On the agricultural results of climate a paper by Mawley may be cited, on " Weather Influences on Farm and Garden Crops" (*Journ. Roy. Agric. Soc.*, vol. x.).

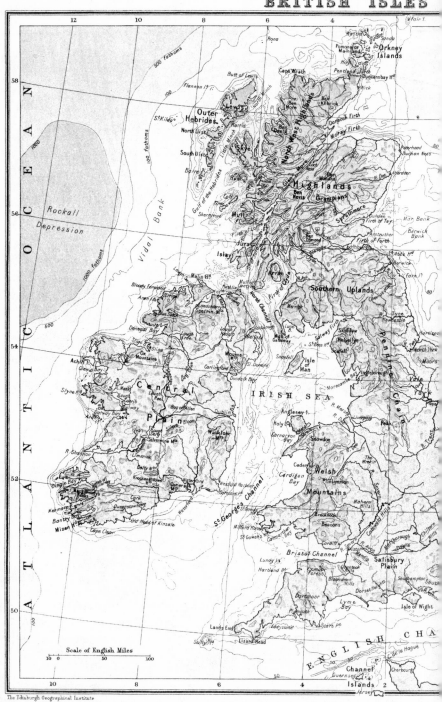

Scale of English Miles

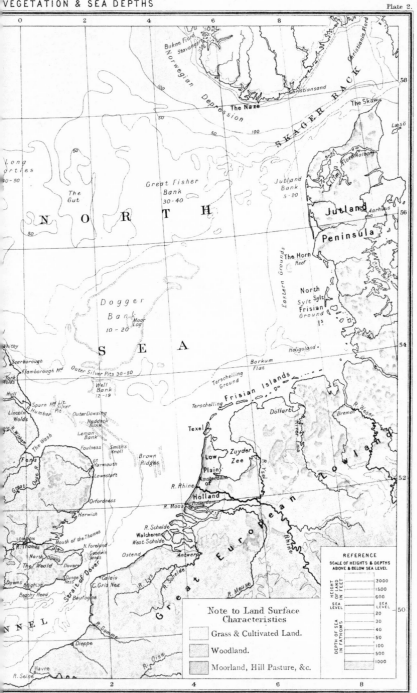

Bukne Fiord
Stavanger
Norwegian Depression
100
Christiania Fiord
Christiansand
58
The Naze
SKAGER RACK
The Skaw
50
50
100
Læsö

Long
orthes
30-50

The
Gut
50
Great Fisher
Bank
30-40
Jutland
Bank
5-20
Liim Fiord
Aalborg
Jutland
Aarhus
56

N   O   R   T   H
Peninsula

50
The Horn
Reef

Eastern Grounds
North
Syle
Sylt
Dogger
Bank
10-20
Moor
Log
Frisian
Ground
Is
R. Eider
54

S   E   A
Heligoland

Whitby
Scarborough
Flamborough Hd
York
Wolds
Borkum
Flat
Terschelling
Ground
go
Hull
Outer Silver Pits 30-50
Well
Bank
12-19
Silver
Pit
Terschelling
Frisian Islands
R. Weser
Bremen
Spurn Hd
Humber
Lincoln
Wolds
Outer Dowsing
Haddock
Bank
Texel
Dollart
R. Ems
R. Jade
R. Weser
The Wash
Leman
Bank
Foulness
Smiths
Knoll
Brown
Ridges
Low
Plain
Zuyder
Zee
R. Yssel
52
Fens
Great Ouse R.
Gt
Yarmouth
Lowestoft
Amsterdam
or
R. Rhine
R. Maas
Rotterdam
Holland
Orfordness
Great European Lowlands

LONDON
R. Thames
Mouth of the Thames
Harwich
R. Schelde
Walcheren
West Schelde
Ostend
Antwerp
R. Rhine
North
Downs
The Weald
N. Foreland
Goodwin
Sands
Dover
R. Lys
R. Schelde
R. Meuse
Downs
Brighton
Beachy Head
Dungeness
C. Gris Nez
Calais
Boulogne
Strait of Dover
50

NNEL
R. Somme
R. Oise
Dieppe
R. Seine
Havre

Note to Land Surface
Characteristics
Grass & Cultivated Land.
Woodland.
Moorland, Hill Pasture, &c.

J.G. Bartholomew

CHAPTER XII

RACIAL GEOGRAPHY

THE lie of the rock features of Britain and the interacting currents of the surrounding sea and air constitute the physical environment of one of the great nations of Europe. Regarded from this point of view, Britain has the appearance of being little more than a severed, marginal fragment of the vast continent known as the Old World. But the history of their development, based on the lost Atlantis of the north, has endowed the British Isles with more significant characteristics than those of a mere segment of the existing continental slope. The uplands of their oceanic border are to be thought of rather as the clipped edge of a vanished northern plateau than as the true margin of Euro-Asia, and the lowland of England was deposited as a coastal plain at the foot of the Welsh and Caledonian ranges, precisely as the coastal plain of the Atlantic States of America was formed in front of the Alleghanies. It has thus happened that the more accessible and habitable side of Britain is turned inward to Europe, not outward to the ocean, and that the flow of the consequent drainage, breaching the hill ridges, is in the same southward and landward direction. A provincial grouping of outline and relief has been settled in the process of rock-folding and denudation. The oceanic shore has been cleft by the North Channel into Scottish and Irish sections, and on either hand, secluded among the faulted uplands, are two detached plains, Scottish and Irish, to which access from within is afforded by the Vale of York and the geologically ancient gaps at Chester and Bristol. Ireland has been further separated by the St. George's Channel, while certain of the consequent rivers, such as the Severn and the Shannon, have been diverted westward into subsequent estuaries, thereby increasing the aloofness of the oceanic borderland.   On the other hand, the head-streams of the Ouse, the Trent, and the Thames have been collected eastward to the Narrow Seas, a change to which the uplift of the Weald along the south coast has contributed. Moreover, the submarine plateau, by magnifying the tides, has facilitated communication between England and the Continent, while the median uplands have presented a partial barrier to internal movement.   In many respects, therefore, the east and the west of Britain have stood further apart from one another in bygone history than has the metropolitan angle of England from Flanders and the Netherlands.

The climatic conditions of Britain, regarded as the environment of a human society, are no less exceptional than the features of the outline and relief.   As already indicated, the position is near the centre of a northward gulf of winter warmth, and to windward of the broad entry to the Arctic Sea. The weather is, therefore, open throughout the year, interludes of frost being comparatively rare, while the cyclones in their more frequented paths bring such moisture from the western ocean as suffices for the maintenance of a rich perennial vegetation.   Originally, the whole surface was covered with forest ; when this was removed, pasture became the natural crop, except where heather and peat-moss clothe the highlands and corn is cultivated in the plain of the continental angle. The soil of this plain is of unusual fertility, owing to the rapid succession of tilted, overlapping strata of limestone, sand, and clay, whose substance is easily mingled in due proportion for profitable tillage.   Beneath is the buried floor of ancient rock, cross-grained in the Hercynian epoch of disturbance, and hence preserving a wealth of coal between the intersecting upfolds of its structure.

Thus the essential qualities of the British environment are—

(1) Insularity, which has tended to preserve the continuity of social organisation ;

(2) Accessibility, which has admitted stimulus from without, and prevented stagnation ;

(3) Division into a more accessible east and a less accessible west, which has made for variety of initiative, and consequent interaction ;

(4) Productivity of soil and climate, the necessary basis of a virile native growth ;

(5) Possession of a vast potential energy stored in deposits of coal, the mainspring of modern industrial life ; and

(6) Interpenetration by arms of tidal sea, giving access to the universal ocean-road of modern commerce.

We have now to trace the connection of the British nation, in its successive phases and component elements, with the British physical environment as thus analysed.

In most regions of the world there are preliminary questions to be answered with reference to the fauna and flora, which present problems in many respects different, by reason of their greater antiquity, from those involved in the distribution of man and his works. In Britain, however, owing to the havoc wrought by the ice-mantle, no ancient forms of life have survived from Atlantis to be compared with the Marsupials of Australia or the Lemurs of Madagascar. The existing plants and animals advanced from the south contemporaneously with early man at a time when the island was still adherent to Europe. When Britain was subsequently insulated, two processes commenced which have continued to the present day. One after another, the species have been exterminated which constituted the rich European fauna of Britain, and, on the other hand, fresh human races, with their several breeds of domestic animals, have entered the island, usually from the south-east.

The evidence bearing on the establishment of successive races of men in Britain has to be drawn from five or six more or less independent fields of research, and there is still a conflict of opinion as to the co-ordination of the events thus severally recorded. At the present moment, however, the various inquiries appear to be on the point of converging, and, while it is yet desirable to state independently the evidence drawn from anatomy, language, archæology, history, and folk-lore, it may be permissible to attempt such a reconstruction of the history of the immigrations as shall interpret the existing facts of British racial geography.

The earliest tribes appear to have entered Britain overland. They came as hunters with the reindeer and the musk ox, which have now retreated with the ice into the polar north. To these animals succeeded the elephant, the mammoth, the rhinoceros, the hippopotamus, the lion, the bear, and great herds of migratory bison and horse. Little has been certainly learnt of the physical characteristics of the Palæolithic, or "ancient stone" peoples. We know them chiefly by their roughly chipped implements of flint, and by the sketches of animals, often of hunting scenes, which they have left upon their bone utensils. A blood relationship with the Eskimos of Greenland has been attributed to them, mainly on account of the similarity of their graphic arts.

Britain had already become insular before the immigration of the Neolithic race of men, whose weapons and implements were of finely-polished stone. With these were introduced the breeds of cattle prevalent in the islands until the time of the Teutons, for the Neolithic men were herdsmen, and not merely hunters. They seem to have brought with them, in addition to the ox, also the dog, the sheep, the goat, and the hog; and from these, by escape to the forests, have been derived the Chillingham ox, the St. Kilda sheep, the wild boar, and the wild goat. Many of the larger wild animals had by this time disappeared, yet the Irish elk was still extant, and also the reindeer, the bison, the brown bear, the wolf, the beaver, and the stag. The remains of Neolithic man are especially frequent in the submerged forests along the English shores, and in the carses or raised beaches of Scotland and northern Ireland, for there have been subsequent fluctuations in the level of the land, notably a slight elevation of Scotland and an equivalent depression of England. In the more open portions of the country, too, Neolithic man left many marks of his residence in the form of entrenchments, underground dwellings, and long, more or less egg-shaped burial barrows. Traces of his civilisation have been discovered in almost all parts of Europe, and there can be little question that the men of the new stone age came to Britain from the south and south-east.

What, however, imparts to Neolithic man one of the chief points of his interest is the preservation of his skeleton, and, therefore, of a knowledge of some, at least, of his physical characteristics. The structural feature which is transmitted by man with the most unerring heredity, supplying the surest clue to the source of his blood, is, undoubtedly, the shape of his head. There are two well-contrasted types of human skull, the one relatively long and narrow, the other short and broad. They may be distinguished as the long skull and the round skull. In Europe, the long skull is prevalent both in the north and in the south ; in Scandinavia, northern Germany, and Britain, no less than in Spain, Barbary, Corsica, Sardinia, Sicily, and southern Italy ; but there is an intervening " Alpine " belt of round-skulled population, extending from Asia through the centre of the continent into France, which is usually ascribed to an intrusive race. One of the most surprising facts in connection with modern Britain is the uniformity with which, in all parts of the country, the long-skulled type predominates. No distinction whatever can be drawn in this respect between the most thoroughly Teutonic .and the most completely Celticised districts. The Neolithic peoples of ancient Britain were of the long-skulled group.

A second feature, almost as constant as the shape of the skull, is the pigmentation of the hair and eyes. Men of the European races may be classified either as light or dark, blonde or brunette, and from recent investigations it would appear that a cross between the two races tends to redness. A map of Europe showing the relative frequency of the light and dark types, presents a very different aspect from one giving the distribution of skull forms. On the whole, the percentage of the darker type increases steadily from Scandinavia southward and south-westward. Among the long-skulled peoples of Spain, Barbary, and southern Italy, dark colouring becomes almost universal, whereas the lighter type forms nearly

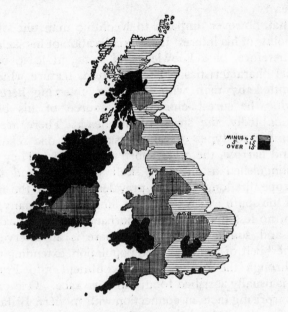

FIG. 92.—The Relative Nigrescence of the British Population.
(For explanation of index, see note 1, p. 193.)

the whole of the equally long-skulled population of Scandinavia. It would appear, therefore, that by a combination of the two criteria, skull form and colouring, the races of Europe may be analysed into three strains, a Mediterranean strain, long-skulled and dark, a Scandinavian or Teutonic strain, long-skulled and blonde, and an Alpine strain, round-skulled and of intermediate colouring.

The facts as regards Britain are very striking. A large majority of the population is here everywhere long-skulled, but in Ireland and the neighbouring portions of Scotland, in Wales, in Cornwall, and generally in the south-west of England, dark colouring is prevalent, whereas in the north and east of Scotland and in the east of England the blonde type is more conspicuous (Fig. 92). The natural inference is that the aboriginal population of Britain was of Mediterranean origin, and that the only blend which has seriously modified the race was due to the immigration of the Teutons within historic times.

In the plain of England and in southern Scotland, are found the remains of a third race—obviously later than the Neolithic—whose implements were of bronze, who buried their dead in round, not long, barrows, and whose civilisation was clearly on a higher plane than that which had preceded. The skulls of these " bronze " men were almost uniformly of the round order, and they represent the only considerable immigration of round-headed men which is known to have occurred in Britain, either in historic or pre-historic times. The most probable source of the intrusion lies in the Netherlands, where the round-skulled population of central Europe reaches its most northerly extension.

If we now turn to the evidence of language, we shall find that whereas the Teutonic dialects of Britain have everywhere coalesced into some form of English, the Celtic tongues of the west present a fission, which is of more than dialectical value. The Erse of Ireland, the Manx of Man, and the Gaelic of the Scottish Highlands, forming the Goidelic group, differ far otherwise from the Cymric of Wales, the Breton of Brittany, and the old Cornish tongue—which together constitute the Brythonic group—than does the talk of a Dorset Saxon from that of a Yorkshire Anglo-Dane. The area occupied by the Celtic languages has long been diminishing (Fig. 93). The names of rivers and of most other physical features are Celtic throughout Britain ; the village names are Celtic all over Ireland, in Wales, in a strip of England which adjoins Wales, in the Scottish Highlands, and throughout the Buchan promontory (Fig. 94). On the other hand, it is a remarkable fact, according to Rhys and Morris Jones, that there are many non-Aryan peculiarities of syntax in all the Celtic languages of Britain, an indication which may be correlated with the very significant contrast of physical structure presented by the broad-skulled Celts of

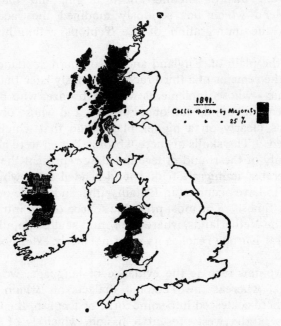

1891.
Celtic spoken by Majority
● ● ● 25 %

FIG. 93.—The Celtic-speaking Districts of Modern Britain.

Gaul and the long-skulled Goidels and Brythons of Britain. It would appear, therefore, that, while Britain has been subjected to overpowering Celtic influence, the amount of Celtic blood is probably not very great. In the main, the races of Britain are either Teutonic or aboriginal and pre-Celtic.

Three additional considerations, to be obtained from history and folk-lore, must be taken into account before an attempt can be made to piece together the evidence derived, on the one hand, from physical characteristics and arts of life, and, on the other hand, from language. (1) When Cæsar invaded Britain he found men of Belgian race established in the south-eastern angle of the country. These may well have been the broad-skulled " bronze " men of the round barrows, but if we are to judge from the comparative rarity of round skulls in the modern population, the Belgians, if such they were, can never have been more than a ruling caste. In any case, being inhabitants only of South Britain, they must have been more or less completely submerged during the Roman occupation.[1] (2) In the eighth century Bede speaks of two Celtic races, the Scots of Ireland and the Britons or Cymry of Cornwall, Wales, Cumberland, and Strathclyde. But in his time there lived in the Highlands of Scotland an enigmatical people,

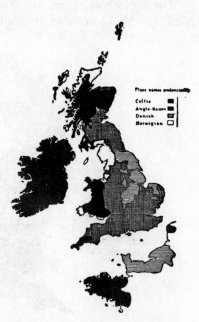

FIG. 94.—The Distribution of Village and Town-names in Britain.—*After* TAYLOR (but generalised).

described as Picts, or Pechts, who do not appear to have been Celts at all. They are known to have dwelt also in Ulster, and were probably speakers of a pre-Celtic, non-Aryan language, which may have had Mediterranean, possibly Berber affinities. (3) It is believed by several of the authorities that memories of a pre-Pictish race linger in the dwarfs and fairies of the Celtic legends. Traces of such a race are probably to be detected in the prevalence

[1] See note on the Belgians at p. 193.

of short stature especially in South Wales and the neighbouring districts of England (Fig. 95). It is likely, in fact,
that several successive waves of immigrants are massed
under the term Neolithic, for it is hardly probable that
these dwarfs were Palæolithics.

On the whole, then, it would appear that when the
Neolithic Mediterranean tribes had ejected the preceding

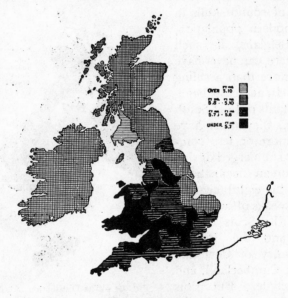

FIG. 95.—The Average Stature of the British Population according
to Counties.—*After* RIPLEY.

Palæolithic hunters, driving them to the hills and the
caves, and Britain had been occupied for the first time
by a race of herdsmen, successive hordes of warriors
swept into the islands from the south-east, assuming rule
and even imposing new tongues, but not displacing the
bulk of the aboriginal population. Of these conquering
races the first of which we have definite indication were
the Goidels, who penetrated to the Atlantic shores both
of Ireland and Scotland, absorbing the Pictish peoples,

still separable in the time of Bede. The second were
the Brythons who, in mass at any rate, won their way
no further than into Cornwall, Wales, and the south of
Scotland. The third may have been the Belgians. The
fourth were the Romans, whose dominion stopped short
at the edge of the Highlands (Fig. 98). In subsequent
centuries, when the English plain was possessed by the
Teutons considerable migrations appear to have taken

FIG. 96.—The Relative Position of the Races in Britain in the
First Century, A.D.—*After* RHYS.

place in the historic obscurity of the Celtic uplands
beyond. According to tradition, the Goidels or Scots
entered Ireland through the Dublin coastal gap, and
first settled in the middle land of the plain, known later as
Meath (Figs. 96, 109). Thence they extended into Ulster,
a branch of them occupying the little territory of Dalriad
in the north of county Antrim. It was the Dalriad
Scots who crossed to Argyll, and passing thence, by

Glenmore and over Drumalban, gradually conquered and Celticised the Picts of the eastern Highlands. For a time, at least, a Brythonic speech may have been spoken in Leinster, but the extremest historic position held by the second of the Celtic races was at Alcluyd, or Dumbarton, the crag fortress which served as outpost to the Britons of Strathclyde. In the ninth century the population of North Britain might have been described

FIG. 97.—The Relative Position of the Invaders of Britain.

as containing still unmingled samples of all the successive British races (Fig. 106). The Brythons were tenants of Strathclyde, having driven a wedge between the Picts of the north-east and the tribes of Galloway, in all probability also Pictish. The Gaelic Scot had seized upon Argyll, and the Angle had displaced the Brython from Lothian, while the Norseman of Scandinavia may have already appeared in Caithness and the Western Isles.

A curious question relates to the distinction which has been established between the Picts of Buchan and of Galloway. The former, according to recent research, still show a frequent tendency to red hair, and they were described by Tacitus as red-haired giants. It was suggested thirty years ago by Pearson that there may here have been a pre-historic infusion of Teutonic blood, an anticipation of the subsequent Norse and Angle invasions, and it would seem that modern ethnological inquiry bears out his theory. In Galloway, on the other hand, there is a tall population, the tallest, it is said, on the average, of all Europe, but the dark colouring betokens the Irish and Gaelic influence which is denoted by the name of the district.

There remains to be traced the effect of the Teutonic invasions. They were derived from two sources, from the fiords of the Norwegian plateau, and from the shores of the plain on either side of the estuary of the river Elbe. In Britain the invaders of the different tribes appear to have retained the same position relatively to one another that they had held on the continent (Fig. 97). The Saxons, chiefly from the left bank of the Elbe, occupied southern England ; the Angles, from the right bank, took the British shore from East Anglia to Lothian. At a later time the Danes, from south of the Skager Rak, occupied the Danelaw, between the Thames and the Tees, whereas the Norsemen, from north of the Skager Rak, seized the Orkneys, the Shetlands, Caithness, the Western Isles, and the Isle of Man. A few Norse communities were planted on either side of the seas separating Ireland from Great Britain, notably at Dublin, Wexford, Waterford, and Milford ; and there was a large Norse colony on the shores of Solway Firth and Morecambe Bay, whence a wedge of Scandinavian population, if we may judge from the place-names (Fig. 94) and the prevalence of blonde types in the existing population (Fig. 92), was pushed through the Aire gap to the frontier of Danish Yorkshire. This fact, no doubt, explains the spread of Domesday Yorkshire, and of the great pre-

Reformation diocese of York, from the Humber north-westward to St. Bees Head (Figs. 102, 104). How complete must have been the Norse occupation of certain districts is indicated by the circumstance that alone in all Britain the river-names of Caithness, Sutherland, and Dumfriesshire are Teutonic, and not Celtic.

The blondè appearance and considerable stature of the population of the so-called Danelaw, extending from Essex to Durham, is a consequence of the double Teutonic conquest, first by the Angle, and then by the Dane. On the other hand, the general frequency of nigrescence in the west of England—in Wiltshire, Gloucestershire, Somerset, and Devon—may be attributed to the more humane character of the subjugation of the west, in the comparatively late period after the preaching of Christianity. There are, however, two exceptional phenomena in the maps indicative of the prevalent colouring and stature of the population (Figs. 92, 95). The one is the predominance of short, dark types in the West Riding of Yorkshire, probably due to the preservation in the Forest of Elmet of a percentage of the aboriginal population. The other is the existence of an island of similar short and dark peasantry, segregated to the north-west of London about Hertford and in the Cotswolds. With the latter may be correlated the circumstance that the boundary between the Saxon and Anglian dialects of English is to be found in the neighbourhood of Bedford and Huntingdon. The likely explanation is that during the earlier Teutonic raids the Thames road was closed by the Roman walls of London, and the invaders had to make their way to the interior by circuitous routes.[1] For whereas the peoples of Kent, Essex, and East Anglia remained relatively small —being pent in by the great forest of the Weald, by the fortress of London, by the forests about Waltham, and by the wide marsh of the Fens—the West Saxons, entering by Southampton Water, spread over the chalk of Hants and Wilts to the upper Thames, and effected settlements as far inland as Oxford, Buckingham, and Bedford,

[1] See Chapter XIII.

while the Mercian Angles, advancing from Humber and Wash, attained to the sources of the Trent and Great Ouse. The impetus of either invasion would naturally be weakest where it approached the other to the north-west of London, and there, protected in the great forests, a remnant of the earlier population no doubt lingered, until such time as the more drastic and murderous stage of the conquest had been exhausted.

Until recent times most men lived their lives in the neighbourhood of their birthplace, and except in a few centres of trade frequented by foreigners the population of each district was recruited in the main from an ancestry locally restricted. Fresh strains of blood were occasionally introduced by an invasion, as of the Normans, or by some great pacific immigration and settlement, as of the Jews, the Flemings, or the Huguenots, but the influence even of these was confined to certain spots. Only the Anglo-Danish invasions appear to have fundamentally changed the blood of whole regions, despite the many alterations of language and custom imposed at other times by conquering aristocracies. Except, therefore, in the case of London, and to a lesser degree of other seaports, each person alive a hundred years ago was descended, although along very many different lines, from a few hundred ancestors living in his own neighbourhood in the time of the Norman Conquest, and from a few thousand more scattered in groups over Britain and western Europe—each group being ancestral to some stranger who came to the neighbourhood and left offspring. Since the beginning of the present century pedigrees have become more complicated, owing to the frequent shifting of population in the process of economic readjustment. A national solidarity of blood is being gradually substituted for provincial solidarities, but there are still strongly marked local characteristics in the great majority of the humbler population, although the upper classes, at least of England, have already blended more or less perfectly into a common type. A hundred years ago the squires and the professional classes were still markedly provincial.

Since the eleventh century no permanent hostile settlement has been effected in Britain, but, on the whole, there has been a frequent inflow of foreigners both from the Teutonic and the Romance coasts across the Narrow Seas. Flemings were brought by the Anglo-Norman kings to the neighbourhood of Norwich and to the "Little England beyond Wales" in Pembrokeshire, while Germans from the Hanseatic cities became numerous in London. Within the last three centuries the Protestant Huguenots, driven from France, and the Jews have made notable and valuable additions to the population. To-day there is a steady immigration of Germans and Eastern Europeans, who fuse with the natives around in the second or third generation, preserving only foreign names.

But by far the most significant fact of the present, is the blending of the northern and western people, of Aboriginal, Celticised, and Norse blood, with the south-eastern population of an Anglo-Saxon and cosmopolitan origin. The Irishman, the Welshman, and the Scotchman are present everywhere, adding to the rich variety of temperament and genius, and a process of averaging is in rapid progress, induced by the mechanical discoveries of the nineteenth century. There may still, however, be distinguished some nine several provincialisms in the British population. There is (1) the Catholic Irishman, essentially a pre-Celt, even when he does Celtic Erse into English ; (2) the Ulsterman, not quite Teutonic, however Protestant ; (3) the Scotchman of the far north, almost a Scandinavian ; (4) the Highlander, pre-Celtic and mercurial, yet with elements in his character very different from Irish ; (5) the Lowlander, Teutonic in the main, but descendant neither of Norman nor Dane ; (6) the Welshman, with a strong pre-Celtic infusion, dark, and of emotional temperament ; (7) the Englishman of the north and east, an Anglo-Dane ; (8) the Englishman of the south and west, a Saxon verging, especially towards Corn-

wall, on Celtic and pre-Celtic ; finally, there is (9) the Londoner, the Cockney, originally East Saxon or Kentish, but now a cosmopolitan ; for London alone of British towns has been a city of " world " importance and connections through ten centuries, and the Londoner of to-day is either a recent immigrant from the country or from abroad, retaining his provincial or foreign characteristics, or else he is a hybrid of the most intricate ancestry.

Note on Index to Fig. 92.—This map is constructed, after Ripley, on a method devised by Beddoe. Each head of dark hair is counted once, each head of black hair twice, and each head of light hair negatively once.

Note on the Belgians.—Rhys does not appear to distinguish between the Brythons and the Belgians, and he may, of course, be right, for this is undoubtedly one of the points on which the correlation of the evidence drawn from different sources becomes very difficult. On the historical evidence concerning the Belgians in Britain, see Bullock Hall's edition of *Cæsar.*

Note on Authorities.—On the subjects dealt with in this chapter reference may be made to Boyd Dawkins, *Early Man in Britain;* Beddoe, *The Races of Britain;* Ripley, *The Races of Europe* (with an exhaustive bibliography) ; Isaac Taylor, *Words and Places;* and Rhys and Brynmor-Jones, *The Welsh People.* Much pertinent matter is also to be found in the Brit. Assoc. Reports (1893-97) on the *Ethnographical Survey of the United Kingdom.*

CHAPTER XIII

HISTORICAL GEOGRAPHY

THE organisation of a people only becomes accurate and permanent when founded on a territorial basis. The Saxons brought with them across the Narrow Seas an organisation according to families, hundreds, and tribes, dependent, that is to say, on blood relationship. But the settlement of these units in the conquered land gave rise to our later parishes, hundreds, and counties. Gradually the idea of domicile replaced that of clan as the principle of social order, and whereas the family, or the hundred of families were formerly responsible for the malefactor, the modern police have power of arrest within clearly defined county or municipal areas. Thus, while in later history the physical features of the country are in some ways less coercive, administrative divisions have grown more precise, and have become more constant elements in the machinery of government.

The modern divisions of south-eastern England are traceable as far back as the Belgian invasion, for it is a noteworthy fact that the districts occupied by the pre-Roman tribes appear to have roughly coincided with those settled some five hundred years later by the Angles and Saxons. The Iceni held what became East Anglia. The allied Trinobantes and Catuvelauni controlled the region which belonged afterwards to the East and Middle Saxons. The Cantii preceded the Jutes in Kent, and the Regni the South Saxons in Sussex, while the Belgæ were established in what are now the counties of Hants and Wilts, the centre and stock of the kingdom of the West Saxons. Berkshire[1] appears to have taken its name

---

[1] The pre-Norman form of this word is Bearrucscir, the Domesday form is Berrochescire. See *Oxf. Hist. Atlas.*

from the Bibroci, probably a clan of the Atrebates of Silchester, and Dorset was named from the Durotriges. It may have been that the same entries from the sea, and the same internal passages and barriers guided the two successive swarms of invaders from nearly the same continental sources, along identical roads, to identical areas of settlement. It may, however, have been that the connection of the earlier and later divisions was even closer, that the Romans, as in Gaul, to some extent adopted the Belgic territorial limits, and that the Teutons, overthrowing one after another of the Romano-Celtic units of administration, succeeded naturally to the abandoned districts.

Although London itself does not appear to have been a focus of organisation before the coming of the Romans,[1] yet the district in which it stands, the territory occupied by the Trinobantes and Catuvelauni, was evidently the nucleus of a small empire. Three physical features, radiating from this neighbourhood, gave to it the strategical advantage of the central position, and at the same time isolated the surrounding countries of the Iceni, the Cantii, and the Belgæ. Northward were the Fen marshes, eastward the great estuary of the Thames—marsh-bordered up to the site of London, and south-eastward the almost impenetrable forest of the Weald.[2] The Catuvelauni and the Trinobantes stood, therefore, between the divided Iceni, Cantii, and Belgæ, in a position equivalent, on a small scale, to that of the German Empire of to-day in the midst of the nations of Europe. It was thus by no mere accident that Cymbeline, commemorated by Shakespeare, ruled at St. Albans and Colchester. The overthrow of his dynasty marked the definite establishment of Rome in Britain, and as the modern English have adopted Buluwayo and Kumassi, seats of barbaric chiefs, to be capitals of their conquered dependencies, so the Romans replaced

---

[1] It has been sugggested that the name London is identical with Londinières in the French department of Seine Inférieure, and in view of the frequent duplication of Belgic place-names on either side of the Narrow Seas, the similarity may not be wholly fortuitous. See *Geog. Jour.*, vol. xiii. p. 299.

[2] See note at p. 230.

the Celtic stockades near Colchester and St. Albans by
the cities of Camulodunum and Verulamium.

Roman power extended through Britain to Wales
and the south of Scotland, but was not fully effective
except in the plains. In Wales, the Peak, the Pennine
Moors, the Cumbrian Hills, and the Southern Uplands of
Scotland, the contour-line of 500 feet, or somewhat higher,
may perhaps be regarded as roughly delimiting the area of
Roman civilisa-
tion. The legions
were posted in
the north and the
west ; hence the
Roman system of
roads and cities
was based on two
great strategical
needs. Lateral
communication
between the
legionary canton-
ments of York,
Chester, and
Caerleon was
essential for pur-
poses of mutual
support, and on
the other hand a
system of radia-
ting roads was
necessary from

FIG. 98.—Roman Britain.

the continent and Kent to the marginal outposts (Fig. 98).
Near Sandwich, Dover, and Hythe were the Roman land-
ing-places. At Canterbury, Rochester, and London were
river crossings. From London three trunk-ways diverged.
The first ran to Colchester, and thence round the western
border of the Fens to Lincoln, from which city, skirting
the edge of the marshes of the Isle of Axholme and Hatfield
Chase, it led to York. The second, known afterwards

as Watling Street, lay north-westward through St. Albans to Venonæ, now High Cross, in the centre of the land, whence it bifurcated north-eastward through Leicester to Lincoln, and westward to the Severn at Wroxeter, beside the Wrekin and Wenlock Edge. The third crossed the great gravel flat of west Middlesex to Staines, or "the Stones," and struck onward over Bagshot Heath to Silchester, the Swindon of the Roman road system, from which neighbourhood ways branched to Bath, to Cirencester and Gloucester, to Salisbury and Exeter, and to Winchester, Porchester, and Chichester. Lateral roads connected York with Chester, Wroxeter, and Caerleon, while Caerleon communicated with Bath across the estuary of the Severn at the point known as Old Passage. The Wall of Hadrian, from Wallsend to Solway Firth, was so placed as to protect eastward and westward communication through the Tyne gap of the Pennine range.

In such a system London rose inevitably to greatness. Bath may have been the Simla of the Romans, where the imperial race sought the consolation of hot baths in the winter, and York their Rawal Pindi in the threatened borderland ; but London became both the Calcutta and Bombay of the British province. In the latter part of the Roman epoch a Duke of the Britons governed the north and the west from the three legionary centres, while a Count of Britain held civil sway from London. Thus did the pregnant contrast between south-east and north-west find early expression in the arrangement of government and defence.

When the legions were withdrawn the command of the sea passed to tribes of the low German stock, Jutes, Saxons, and Angles, ancestors of the later Hansards and Easterlings. On the other hand, the great commercial city of London encompassed itself with walls, behind which the Roman provincials could set at defiance every likely enemy except starvation. In the first instance, the pirates seized upon Thanet and Wight, and the whole Teutonic history of England may be regarded as based upon these

islets ; just as Arab tyranny in central Africa has rested
upon the island of Zanzibar, European dominion in
India upon the island of Bombay, Dutch control of what
is now the State of New York upon the island of Manhattan,
and the French settlements in Canada upon the island of
Montreal.

In rear of Thanet, separating it from the mainland,
there flowed in early times a channel of the sea, known
to our forefathers as Wantsum, and the Stour river entered
this by an estuary navigable to Canterbury.   Roman shipping, bound to London from the great Gallic port of
Boulogne, avoided the North Foreland of Thanet by
traversing Wantsum, as in the Middle Ages men crossed
from Hamburg to Lübeck, rather than double the Skaw
of Jutland.   The heavy traffic for London proceeded up
the Thames, but Richborough, near Sandwich, whose
ruins still look across the green meadows replacing the
strait, was a port of call whence passengers and mails
travelled by the overland route through Canterbury and
Rochester.   When the Jutes crossed from Thanet, and
seized the Kentish road at the passages of the Stour and
Medway, they broke the communication between London
and the Continent.   The Roman settlement of Durovernum
on the Stour became Cant-wara-byryg, the borough, that is
to say, of the " men of Kent," a term still applied to those
inhabitants of the county who live east of the Medway.
The Wealden Forest and Romney Marsh were barriers in
the way of southward advance ; while the inhabitants of
London, from their fortified base, checked the march westward.   So was established and defined the first of the
English kingdoms in Britain.

Northward of the Thames the Saxons, finding the
main channel blocked by London, entered the estuaries of
the Colne and the Chelmer, founding at Colchester and
Maldon the kingdom of the East Saxons, or Essex.   Advancing through the forests, probably by a Roman way
from Colchester to St. Albans, they struck the great north-
westward road of Watling Street, and severed London
from the north.   There is no record of the ultimate fall

of London, but the name Surrey, the "southern realm," or "southern people," seems to indicate that the East Saxons crossed the Thames, placing themselves between Kent and Wessex. In A.D. 597, Rome sent missionaries to the heathen conquerors of Britain, who landed on the shores of Wantsum, and founded their first bishoprics at Canterbury, Rochester, and London. Canterbury, which has ever since remained the see of the Primate of all England, lay even nearer to the south-eastern corner of the land, and to the continental base of civilisation, than did London, which became the chief place in the East Saxon colony. Prior to recent changes, the diocese of London approximately coincided with the counties of Essex, Middlesex, and Hertford, denoting by its limits the kingdom of the East Saxons, from whom the Middle Saxons can have been but partially severed. It is, however, noteworthy that of all the northern tributaries of the Thames, only the Lea and the Colne flow for twenty miles southward through broad strips of marsh, and that these two rivers mark the eastern and western boundaries of Middlesex.

East Anglia was taken by two tribes or folks of the Angles, who seized the mouths of the Orwell and the Yare, and occupied districts which have become Norfolk and Suffolk. On the other hand, a tribe of Saxons entered the tidal channels, then more intricate and spacious than now, in the neighbourhood of Selsey, and pushing up thence past Chichester to the South Downs, established the kingdom of the South Saxons, or Sussex. The tribes of Kent, Surrey, and Sussex, spreading slowly through the Wealden Forest, met at last in its centre, and here, therefore, is drawn the line separating Kent and Surrey in the north from Sussex in the south.

The seven territories of Norfolk, Suffolk, Essex, Middlesex, Surrey, Kent, and Sussex, correspond in some degree, notwithstanding the difference of scale, to the thirteen original colonies which formed the United States. In each case small and rival settlements were founded along a coast-line, whence advance into the interior was checked by a belt of physical barriers. What the ridges and the forests of the Alleghanies were to the English of the Atlantic colonies, that the Wash, the Fens, the Epping and Chiltern Woods, the Roman Walls of London, and the Wealden Forest were to the ancestors of these English when newly come from the plains of Northern Europe. The destiny of Britain passed definitively to the Teutonic race only

FIG. 99.—The Teutonic Kingdoms of South Britain and the Older Divisions of Celtic Wales.

when the Saxons struck into the interior from Southampton Water, and the Angles from the Humber. Pursuing the comparison with North America, these two entries may be likened to the Mississippi and the St. Lawrence. It was only when the French settlements in the basins of these inner rivers had been crushed in war, that the English colonists of the Atlantic coast succeeded to the dominion of North America.

The county system of England appears to have arisen in Wessex by a process of swarming from the first settlement of the West Saxons at Southampton and Winchester. Hants was the original Wessex, the Jutish territory of Wight being absorbed into it. It was not, however, for a generation after the first landing that the Saxons advanced from the Itchen and the Test to the capture of the hill fortress of Old Sarum, near the point where the rivers of Wilts converge to form the Avon. The conquerors were, no doubt, the young warriors who had grown to manhood in the new country. They placed their " tun," or stockade, on the banks of the Wily at the spot since known as Wilton. Ten miles of barren chalk upland separated them from the nearest of the older hamlets, but though possessed of a certain degree of autonomy, they still owed allegiance to the mother settlement. Hence arose a dual organisation, and the necessity for some name to distinguish the older from the newer " shire " or share of Wessex.

Once commenced, the foundation of colonies was easily continued. From the central upland of Hants and Wilts the invaders crossed the belts of morass and forest in the Frome and Kennet valleys, to displace the Durotriges from the open downs of Dorset and the Bibroci from the downs of Berkshire (Fig. 100). Somerset, on the far side of the great forest of Selwood, was occupied later, but the west end of Somerset is already beyond the limits of the plain, and as the Teutons forced their way into the Devonian peninsula, their race became diluted with the Celtic blood of the uplands. The name Devon is that of a Celtic tribe, the Damnonii ; and Exeter, on a bluff looking westward across the Exe, must have marked for long the limits of the West Saxon kingdom. Cornwall has remained Celtic in spirit until modern times, and the Cornish tongue, kin to the dialects spoken in Wales and Brittany, died only two centuries ago. The people of the

east end of Cornwall are still said to talk of going to
England when they cross the Tamar.   Thus the kingdom
of Wessex included six settlements, and beyond them was
Cornwall.   These became the seven south-western counties,
balancing the seven of the south-east, but whereas the
south-eastern counties were originally organised as separate
kingdoms, and were only subsequently reduced by conquest
to the status of counties, the western group, with the

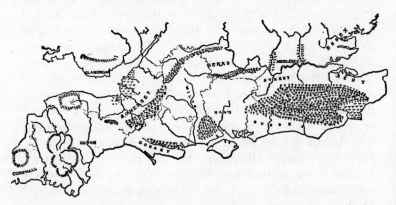

FIG. 100.—The Southern Counties of England as originated on the open
high grounds emergent from the forested lowlands.

exception of Cornwall, arose as a federal kingdom with
Winchester for its capital.

The Thames is unique among the greater English
rivers in being a boundary between counties almost from
its source to its mouth, whereas the Yorkshire Ouse, the
Trent, the Great Ouse, and the Severn intersect the counties
of their basins.   This exceptional frontier is a monument
of the time when a fortified London denied the Thames road
to the Anglo-Saxons, who elsewhere advanced up the streams
and up their tributaries, placing their boundaries rather on
the water-partings than along the water-ways.   London
compelled the West Saxons to march overland from the
south, and so led them to treat the river as a bulwark, which
they crossed only for a definite step of fresh colonisation
in what are now the shires of Oxford and Buckingham.

They traversed the open country in yet two other directions, eastward to Surrey, and north-westward across the Cotswolds to the valley of the Severn, where a sub-tribe, the Hwiccas, founded the three settlements of Gloucester, Worcester, and Hereford. But the northern and north-western territories of Wessex were subsequently lost to the Mercians, and the Thames became the permanent boundary (Fig. 99.)

The Anglian settlements north of the Tees were founded on a remote shore, but the great body of the Angle warriors pushed up the Humber, and up the rivers of the Wash system, to become neighbours of the Saxon, and to be involved in the history of the English plain. From the Trent and from the Witham they occupied Lindsey, or the Isle of Lindum, adopting for a centre the site of the Roman " Lindum Colonia." At Nottingham, higher up the Trent, they seized upon new ground, but at Leicester, where the Roman Fosse-way crossed the Soar, they took advantage of yet another Roman clearance. Near the sources of the Trent, at Lichfield and Stafford, they established their markland, or in the Latin of Bede, their Mercia, towards the Celtic border. From Stafford and Leicester they seem presently to have crossed the water-partings and to have placed themselves at Shrewsbury in a defensible loop of the Severn, within a short distance of the Welsh uplands, and at Warwick on the Avon. Kindred tribes working inland from the Wash and from the channels of the Trent basin settled in the valleys of the Welland at Stamford, of the Nen at Northampton, and of the Ouse at Cambridge, Huntingdon, Bedford, and Buckingham. Finally they appear to have incorporated the Hwicca settlements at Hereford, Worcester, and Gloucester, and also the West Saxon conquests about Oxford and Buckingham. Divided in the first instance into many rival peoples, the Mercians of Lichfield were able gradually to establish a supremacy among them, and to weld the whole of the Midlands, from Lincoln to Gloucester and from Bedford to Shrewsbury, into a single kingdom of Mercia.

From the Humber to the Forth lay a second Anglian realm, known from its position as Northumbria (Fig. 99). Alike physically and historically, this had a twin character and origin. The great basin of the Ouse, centred in the Roman city of Eboracum, became the kingdom, after- wards the sub-kingdom, of Deira. Further to the north, where the Tees, the Wear, the Tyne of Newcastle, the Tweed, the Tyne of Haddington, and the Esk of Mid- lothian flow eastward in separate channels to the sea, a series of coastal settlements coalesced to form the kingdom of Bernicia. But Bernicia included three more or less separate physical areas—(1) the low coastland of Northumberland and Durham, (2) the broad valley of the Tweed, opening seaward at Berwick between the Cheviot and the Lammermoor Hills, and (3) the coastal plain of Lothian, along the southern shore of the Firth of Forth. The Lammermoors come steeply down to the sea at St. Abb's Head, impeding communication from the south into Lothian ; but Tweeddale and the coastland of Newcastle are connected by an undulating sill, some ten miles wide, at the eastern foot of the Cheviots. Here, in the gateway to the subsequent kingdom of Scotland, was built the ancient capital of Bernicia, the castle of Bamborough, from whose ramparts the Holy and Ferne Islands are visible seaward. These islands may have been for the Bernician Angles what Thanet and Wight were at an earlier time for the Jutes.

The plain of Cheshire was conquered from the Britons by the Angles of Northumbria, striking through the Aire gap, and not by the Mercians. The effect was to divide the Britons of Wales from those of Cumberland. But Cheshire subsequently passed into its more natural con- nection with Mercia, and was included in the great Mercian diocese of Lichfield.

For a time the Northumbrians, the Mercians, and the West Saxons contested for supremacy over the English plain, but before any of them had won last- ing control a fresh race of more northern origin had obtained the mastery of the sea, and the power of harrying all the British coastlands. The first Danish settlement seems to have been in Thanet, which offered, as in earlier times, both insular security and rich booty from the Wantsum trade ; but the walls of half-vacant London no longer opposed an insurmountable difficulty, and the Danish raiders penetrated westward up the Thames and across the water-parting to meet the Danish fleets in the Severn Sea. Wessex, under great chieftains, struggled successfully against conquest, but from the Thames to the Tees the Angle dominions of Mercia and southern Northumbria passed so completely under Danish influence that for long afterwards the district was known as the Danelaw.

The Danish dominion gradually crystallised into three organisations : the kingdom of Guthrum in the south, from the Wash and the Fens to London ; in the centre a federation of five boroughs, Lincoln, Nottingham, Derby, Leicester, and Stamford ; in the north a kingdom of York, replacing Deira. Throughout the whole district, but especially in its more northern parts, the Danes have put their seal upon the map in the shape of place-names ending in "by," such as Derby, Whitby, Selby, Grimsby, and Spilsby.

The re-conquest of Mercia from the Danes was undertaken by Alfred of Wessex, and his son and daughter, and in recovering the Midlands they made England, at the same time bequeathing to us in almost final shape our county divisions. The war was carried in the first instance northward along the Severn, through the region of the Hwiccas, originally Saxon and not Angle, and so to Chester and the Ribble, thus dividing the Danes from Celtic allies in Wales. From this belt of Saxon Mercia, and from Wessex south of the Thames, the armies of Alfred's son and daughter, Edward and Ethelflaed, advanced eastward to the sea and northward to the Humber. Two treaties at an interval of eight years mark the gradual defeat of Guthrum. Of the first we know little, but it is supposed to have given Oxfordshire and possibly Bucking-

hamshire to Wessex. By the second, however, London
was acquired, and a boundary was drawn up the Lea to
its source, thence to Bedford, and up the Ouse to Watling
Street. From this point Alfred's territory marched with
that of the Five Boroughs, not of Guthrum ; and Watling
Street, whose pavement preserved a straight way through
the Midland forests, which still forms for thirty miles the
boundary between Warwickshire and Leicestershire, was

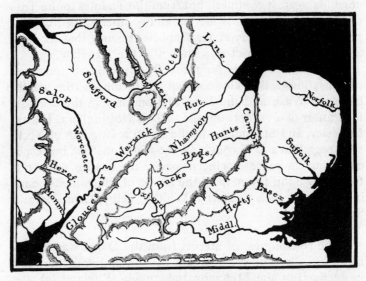

FIG. 101.—The Midland Counties of England as originated
round castles on the water-ways.

probably accepted as a frontier by some unrecorded treaty.
Year by year as the conquest was pressed onward, as one
Danish centre after another passed into Saxon possession,
fortresses were built and the country around was cut or
" shorn " into parts or shires to be administered from the
fortified centres. And so it came about that all through
the Midlands counties of roughly equal size are named
from their chief towns, Gloucester, Hereford, Worcester,
Oxford, Buckingham, Hertford, Bedford, Cambridge, Hunt-

ingdon, Northampton, Leicester, Nottingham, Derby, and Stafford. In the north-east and north-west the districts round Lincoln and Chester had always remained somewhat apart from Mercia, not infrequently appertaining to Northumbria rather than to the Midland kingdom. The large county of Lincolnshire and the old Cheshire, which included Flint and Lancashire to the Ribble, mark the end of the process by which Mercia was divided into artificial units, much as France was carved into departments in the revolutionary reconstruction. The process of county formation, begun unconsciously during the colonisation of Wessex, was continued by the reduction to the rank of sub-divisions of the once independent kingdoms of East Anglia, Essex, Kent, and Sussex. It became a conscious process of legislation when Mercia was shared among the forts of its Saxon re-conquerors.

The great size of the county of York is an indication of the late and incomplete subjugation of Northumbria by the West Saxon kings. In a region so remote from the base of operations the systematic, almost mechanical reorganisation of the Mercian plain could not be attempted. Yorkshire is the Danish kingdom of York which succeeded to the Angle kingdom of Deira. By the annexation of the Norse settlements between the Ribble and St. Bees Head, the Danes, acting through the Aire gap, extended Yorkshire across the island to the Irish Sea (Figs. 94, 102). An incipient but abortive division of the York kingdom into counties is probably recorded in the use of such local names as Cleveland, Holderness, Hallamshire, Craven, and Richmondshire.

Beyond the Tees what remained of Angle Northumberland was parted into at least three divisions. In the south, on the Wear, the great bishopric of Durham attained to a temporal jurisdiction which is the only equivalent in Britain of the ecclesiastical states, so frequent in Germany and Italy. In the north, Lothian and the Merse of Berwick gradually became independent, and together with most of the Celtic kingdom of Strathclyde, were ultimately annexed to Scotland. Between Durham and Berwick lay the earldom of Northumberland, the last remnant of a

dominion which had originally spread from the Humber
to the Forth (Fig. 102).

Such was the England which after 1066 fell to the
sway of William the Norman.   Towards the close of
his reign, when the conquest was at last complete, civil
reforms were undertaken which were the foundation of
the subsequent
unity and power
of the kingdom.
Domesday Book
was the result of
an inquiry with
a view to a more
r e g u l a r a n d
scientific admin-
istration, and in
Domesday we
find the present
county system of
England settled,
except that the
Ribble still shared
Lancashire be-
tween York and
Chester, that Rut-
land was still
divided between
Notts and North-
ants, and that
most of Cumber-

FIG. 102.—The Counties of the North of England
in the time of Domesday.

land and Westmorland belonged to Scotland.   The last-
named territories were ceded to William the Second,
and the modern Rutland, Lancashire, Westmorland, and
Cumberland cannot date from a later time than Henry
the First.   (For Durham, see p. 211.)

The ecclesiastical division of England, as it stood
before the rearrangement consequent on the Reformation, supplies an interesting commentary on the

history of the counties, for the diocesan boundaries are
in many instances older than those of the counties, and
originated in the kingdoms of the Heptarchy (Figs. 99, 104).
The dioceses of Canterbury and Rochester corresponded
to the old kingdom of Kent.   The bishopric of London

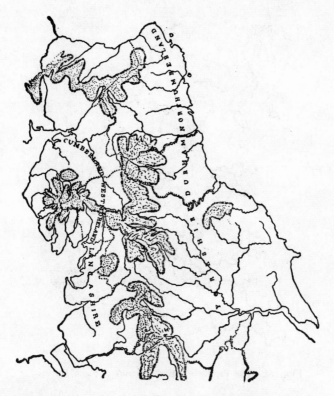

FIG. 103.—The Modern Counties of the North of England, ranged
along the East and the West Coast Roads.

was established beside the East Saxon kingship, and the un-
divided diocese of London nearly coincided, therefore, with
the counties of Essex, Middlesex, and Hertford.   Norwich
was the diocese of the East Angles, and included the
counties of Norfolk and Suffolk.   Chichester was almost

14

identical with Sussex, the kingdom of the South Saxons. But Wessex was divided into the two dioceses of Winchester and Salisbury. Of these Winchester comprised Hampshire and Surrey, thus indicating the early transfer of the last-named county from the East to the West Saxons, while Salisbury was equivalent to the three West Saxon

FIG. 104.—The Pre-Reformation Dioceses of South Britain.

colonies of Berkshire, Wiltshire, and Dorset. The relative isolation of Somerset was expressed by its coincidence with the diocese of Bath and Wells, and the peninsula of Devon and Cornwall was allotted to Exeter. The old Hwicca territory, of West Saxon origin although a Mercian conquest (Fig. 99), was divided between the dioceses of Hereford and Worcester, corresponding to the counties of Hereford, Worcester, Gloucester and south Shropshire.

But if we omit the small diocese of Ely, severed from Lincoln by the Conqueror, all the remainder of Mercia was ruled by two bishops ; for the diocese of Lichfield included Derbyshire, Staffordshire, north Shropshire, Cheshire, and south Lancashire, while the great diocese of Lincoln spread through all the east midlands from the Humber to the Thames at Oxford. The divisions thus far named constituted the archiepiscopal province of Canterbury ; but the relative independence of Northumbria was shown by a separate archbishopric of York. The inequality of area assigned to the two metropolitan sees would have been less conspicuous had not Northumbria been shared between the English and Scottish kings, and had not the territories of Lothian and Strathclyde been surrendered, as a consequence, to the ecclesiastical organisation of the northern kingdom. The immediate diocese of York corresponded to the shire in its Domesday extension, but included, in addition, the county of Nottingham.[1] Finally, the outline of the diocese of Carlisle denoted the southern limits of the kingdom of Strathclyde, won by William Rufus ; while the diocese of Durham was equivalent to the old earldom of Northumberland, from which the special franchise of St. Cuthbert, the later County Palatine of Durham, was already incipiently distinct in the time of Domesday (Fig. 102).

West of the Teutonic settlements of the English plain lies the peninsular upland of Wales. The word occurs also in Corn*wall*, in the *Valais* of Switzerland, and in *Wälsch* (non-German) Tyrol, and signified in the Angle tongue merely the foreign land. Wales falls naturally into three parts, and this triple division has constantly re-asserted itself in the history of the country. In the north-west, on either side of the Menai Strait, is the least accessible district, now consisting of the counties of Anglesea, Carnarvon, and Merioneth, but known before the Edwardian conquest as the Principality of Gwyneth

[1] For the relation of the dioceses of York and Lincoln to the water-ways, see pp. 242 and 278.

(Fig. 99). In the centre, lying open to the English plain, is the upper valley of the Severn, the land of Powys, within which was built, soon after the Conquest, the Norman castle of Montgomery. The remainder, constituting the southern half of the peninsula, was anciently known as Dinefawr, a region less secluded than Gwyneth, although less exposed to invasion than Powys. Apart from the Severn road through the heart of the country, ways led

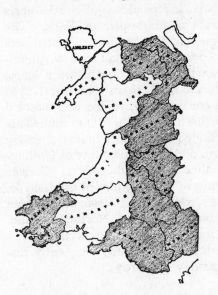

into Wales chiefly along the northern and southern shores, and accordingly we find the transition districts of Flint and Denbigh at the entry to Gwyneth, and of Gwent (subsequently the shire of Monmouth) at the entry to Dinefawr. A racial and linguistic distinction may once have differentiated the three divisions, for the Ordovicians of Powys appear to have had a Brythonic origin, whereas in the first century A.D., the inhabitants of Gwyneth and Dinefawr may still have

FIG. 105.—The Counties of Wales. The area of the former Marches of Wales is approximately indicated by shading, the Principality being unshaded.

spoken Goidelic dialects (Fig. 96). Of the ecclesiastical divisions, the diocese of Bangor corresponded very closely with the territory of Gwyneth, St. Asaph approximately with that of Powys, while the greater portion of Dinefawr was in the large diocese of St. David's, only the south-eastern district of Gwent and Morganwg constituting the diocese of Llandaff (Fig. 104). After the Norman Conquest of England great border earldoms were established in Cheshire,

Shropshire, and Herefordshire, a line of castles being built
at Chester, Shrewsbury, Ludlow, Hereford, Monmouth, and
Chepstow. From these bases Powys and Dinefawr were
gradually overspread by the Norman Lords Marcher, and
it was Gwyneth alone which retained its independence until
the reign of Edward I. This district, and the two detached
shires of Cardigan and Carmarthen, were then constituted
the Principality of Wales, and conferred upon the king's
son, and the Counties Palatine of Chester and Flint were
also assigned to the Prince. Thus the Marches of Wales
were divided into two unequal portions, the detached promontory of Pembroke being erected into a County Palatine
(Fig. 105). It was not until the reign of Henry VIII. that
the Welsh system of government was fully assimilated to
that of England. The separation of the land into thirteen
counties was then completed by the division of the greater
section of the Marches into five additional shires. Glamorgan was constituted from the old district of Morganwg
with the addition of the peninsula of Gower, Monmouthshire from the old district of Gwent, and Brecknockshire, Radnorshire, and Montgomeryshire respectively
from the Welsh portions of the valleys of the Usk, the
Wye, and the Severn. By the same Act of Parliament
which effected the change, Monmouthshire was for certain
purposes annexed to England.

The divisions of Scotland, owing in part to the greater
number of the immigrant races, and in part to the more
pronounced features of the land relief, are in some respects simpler than those of the southern kingdom. At
the beginning of history, North Britain was inhabited by
a pre-Celtic race of Picts or Caledonians, save in the
south-east, where the Britons had already occupied the
region which lies south of the Firth of Forth and eastward
of the Clyde. It was to this British district, of roughly
quadrangular form, that the Roman marchland in advance
of the wall of Hadrian appears to have been confined.
After the withdrawal of the legions, the east coast from
the mouth of the Tees to the head of the Firth of Forth,

together with the lower valley of the Tweed, was seized by Anglian sea rovers, and the breadth of the island in this region was thus divided between three several nationalities (Fig. 106). Along the eastern shore, to north and south of the royal seat at Bamborough, was (1) the English kingdom of Bernicia ; from the head of Edendale to the

FIG. 106.—The Divisions of North Britain prior to the Kingdom of Scotland.

mouth of the Clyde, was (2) the British kingdom of Cumberland, ruled from Dumbarton, or Alcluyd, and to some extent, no doubt, from Carlisle ; while the western promontory, now divided into the counties of Kirkcudbright and Wigtown, constituted (3) the isolated Pictish territory of Galloway. The Picts are known to have long maintained their separate identity in the neighbouring

corner of Ireland, in County Down, and according to
Rhys, Galloway was probably overrun by Celts of the
Goidelic strain, when as yet the whole of Ulster remained
Pictish (Fig. 96). Perhaps we are justified in imagining
a pre-historic episode of conquest round the Irish Sea,
when the Goidels, emerging by the gap of Chester from
the great plain of south-eastern Britain, occupied the
islands of Anglesey and Man, settled along the firths of
Galloway, and entered the Irish plain by the mouths of
the Liffey and Boyne. From Meath they would naturally
advance southward, in rear of the uplands of Leinster
into Munster, and northward, in rear of the Mourne
mountains into Ulster. Arrived again at the sea, near
the Giant's Causeway, they crossed within historic times,
under the name of Scots, to the isles beyond the North
Channel, and established the Gaelic realm of Argyll at the
expense of the northern Picts, whose remaining territory
became known as Alban or Albany. Thus it happened
that in the time of Bede, while Ireland was almost wholly
tenanted by Goidelicised Picts, Scotland had been shared
among no fewer than five peoples: the Angles of Bernicia,
the Britons of Cumberland, the Goidelicised Picts of
Galloway, the primitive Picts of Alban, and the Scots of
Argyll. Not long afterwards the complexity was still
further increased by the advent of the Scandinavian Vikings
from the Norwegian fiords, who conquered the Nordreys
(or Orkneys and Shetlands), the Sudreys (or Hebrides),
and the Isle of Man. For a time, they also overran all
Scotland north of Glenmore and west of Drumalban, but
their hold upon the mainland was of short duration, except
in the far north, where the Norse earldom of Orkney
long included the district of Caithness, then equivalent to
the two modern counties of Caithness and Sutherland. On
the water, however, they remained supreme until the thirteenth century, ruling the kingdom of the Isles, which
included the entire western archipelago, from the Lewis
in the north to Man in the south. The bishopric of Sodor
(Sudrey) and Man, and the revived bishopric of (Argyll
and) the Isles, together with the separate civil jurisdiction of

the Isle of Man, may be regarded as remnants of the Viking sovereignty which centred in the historic islet of Iona.

In North, as in South Britain, the effort for national unity appears to have been stimulated among the warring tribes by the influence of a religion common to all. Roman Britain was converted to Christianity some time before the departure of the legions, and, although the Romans never conquered Ireland, yet Christianity spread to the Scots of that island, and remained with them when the wedge of Anglo-Saxon pagandom had isolated their Church from the Christianity of the continent. During the generations of that strange detachment, Irish missionaries crossed to the northern Pict land and founded the mother church of North Britain in Iona, at the point where the sea-way from Ireland divides northward into the Minch and north-eastward into Glenmore. From Iona, whose sacred character may have dated from pre-Christian times, Christianity was preached to the Picts of Alban, to the Britons of Cumberland, and to the Angles of Bernicia, where a new Iona was founded on the Northumbrian islet of Lindisfarne. As has happened so frequently in subsequent history, the conqueror followed the missionary, and Iona became the basis of Gaelic Argyll, but in later days, under the stress of the Scandinavian raids, the alien Scots and the Picts, already united in a common faith, were able to blend Argyll and Alban into the kingdom of Scotland.

In the meantime, two changes of racial geography had been in progress in South Britain. The Angles and Saxons had driven their conquests across the island, and had reached the western seas at the mouths of the Severn and the Dee, thus isolating Celtic Cumberland from the Celts of Wales and Cornwall. On the other hand, the conquerors had themselves to submit to a Danish dominion, which did not, however, extend to Bernicia. Thus it came about that British Cumberland, unconquered by the Angle, and Angle Bernicia, unconquered by the Dane, were detached from the fate of the greater part of England. King Alfred and his descendants, basing their power on remote Wessex, welded all the Teutons of the south, Danes as well as Anglo-Saxons, into a common English realm, but when at last they approached the Tees and the Eden their resources began to fail. A series of obscure contests and negotiations, lasting to the time of William Rufus, resulted in a compromise by which the north of Bernicia, consisting of Lothian and the Merse, together with the north of Cumberland, consisting of Strathclyde and the dales of Annan and Nith, passed to Scotland, while the south of Bernicia, consisting of Northumberland and Durham, with the south of Cumberland, composed of those portions of the modern counties of Cumberland and Westmorland which are contained in Edendale, were permanently annexed to England. The border between the two countries remained without subsequent change, except that the town of Berwick, to north of the Tweed mouth, experienced vicissitudes of lordship, which finally resulted in its attachment to the English Crown, although technically not as a part of England. Long afterwards, in the reign of King James VI. and I., an abortive effort was made to express the union of Great Britain, by constituting a group of middle counties,[1] which would in a way have revived the old Bernician and Cumbrian "buffer-land" between the two kingdoms.

The Scottish kings, established in the Lothian fortress of Edinburgh, in rear of the threatened borderland, were soon assimilated to their Teutonic environment. Moreover, the English speech gradually spread westward into Strathclyde, and northward through Strathmore as far as Buchan and Moray, so that in time it occupied all the fertile lowlands, and confined the Gaelic to the highland glens. Thus Scotland became in large measure a second England beyond the Tweed, notwithstanding her Celtic name and origin. But the twin derivation of the Scottish blood, masked to some extent by the cross division of the English and Gaelic tongues, is still indicated by the frequency of the darker type of men in the south-west, especially in Argyll and Galloway, and of the lighter type in the Angle east and

---

[1] They were to have been Northumberland, Cumberland, Westmorland, Berwick, Roxburgh, Selkirk, Peebles, Dumfries, Kirkcudbright, and Wigtown.

Scandinavian north. It is remarkable that the blue eyes and fair hair of the Norseman are often to be seen among the more northern Gaels, and that in Sutherland even the river names are Norse, not Celtic. Perhaps the pre-Reformation division of Scotland into two archbishoprics, Glasgow and St. Andrews, the one spreading from the

FIG. 107.—The Mediæval Divisions of Scotland.

Lewis to Galloway, and the other from Cape Wrath to Berwick, may be accepted as embodying a racial distinction, no less than the obvious convenience of thoroughfare along the western and the eastern shores.

Ever since the fourteenth century Scotland has been sub-divided according to two competing systems, the one the basis of the king's administration and jurisdiction (Fig. 108), the other indicative of the ancient and long

preserved authority of the clan in the north and of the
noble family in the south (Fig. 107).   But when North
and South Britain were united by the accession of James
VI. to the throne of England, the sheriffdoms of the king
already coincided with the modern counties, save that
in the far north a single sheriff of Inverness controlled all

FIG. 108.—The Counties of Scotland.   The dotted areas indicate
Galloway, Lothian, and the old Sheriffdom of Inverness.

the land that is now sub-divided into the counties of Inverness, Ross, Sutherland, and Caithness.   With the exceptions of Fife, Argyll, Bute, Orkney, Ross, Sutherland,
and Caithness the Scottish counties are named after their
chief towns, and belong, therefore, to the category rather
of the Mercian counties than of the counties of Southern
England.

The counties of Scotland are ranged in two series along the eastern and the western sides of the country. On the eastern side, commencing from the English border, is (1) a group of four counties, of which Berwick is situated on the east coast road where it crosses the Tweed, and Roxburgh, Selkirk, and Peebles in succession up the basin of the Tweed. These counties correspond to the older districts of the Merse, Teviotdale, and Tweeddale, but Roxburgh includes, in addition, the little district of Liddesdale, on the Solway slope of the Cheviots. Next in order are (2) the three counties of Lothian, disposed along the southern shore of the Firth of Forth, their county towns, Haddington, Edinburgh, and Linlithgow, being set upon the east coast road to the north. Then follows (3) a belt of four counties, Stirling, Perth, Forfar, and Kincardine, with county towns upon the same eastern road to the north where it traverses Strathmore. The counties of this group extend up the Highland glens to the water-partings of the Mounth and Drumalban. Together they correspond to the districts of Menteith, Strathearn, Breadalbane, Atholl, Angus, and the Mearns. The county of Fife, clearly delimited by the coast line and the Ochil range, may be considered as supplementary to the third group, while the little adjoining sheriffdoms of Kinross and Clackmannan correspond to no natural units, and have their origin in purely historical circumstance. The counties (4) of Aberdeen and Banff represent the old divisions of Moray and Buchan, and the towns of Aberdeen and Banff stand at the points where the east coast road leaves the sea and approaches it again. Beyond these are (5) the counties of Elgin, Nairn, Inverness, Ross, and Sutherland, spreading over a great area, but with glens converging upon the lowland sill round Moray Firth, so that the county towns of Elgin, Nairn, Inverness, Dingwall, and Dornoch are placed within a very small compass along the east-coast road. Of the older divisions constituting this group, Moray and Badenoch are the most familiar ; together they form the counties of Elgin, Nairn, and most of Inverness. The county of Cromarty, now absorbed in Ross, consisted of a group of small liberties, and belonged historically to the same category as Kinross and Clackmannan. (6) Caithness and Orkney stand apart, approachable with difficulty, in the times before railways, except by sea.

On the western side of Scotland we have (1) a group of three counties, Dumfries, Kirkcudbright, and Wigtown, along the northern shore of Solway Firth. Of these, the two latter stand in the corner of the land, with their county towns on bays of the Firth, but Dumfries is traversed by the great west coast road through Nithsdale, and the town of Dumfries itself has a position corresponding generally to that of Berwick on the east coast, for it stands at the point where the way into Galloway branches from the main road to the north. (2) Ayrshire, consisting of Cunningham, Kyle, and Carrick, is drained into the Clyde Sea by short streams, which are crossed in succession by the west coast road. Next follows (3) the group of three counties belonging to the basin of the Clyde. Of these Lanarkshire occupies all the upper portion of the valley, and Dumbarton and Renfrew lie to right and to left of the estuary where it becomes too broad for convenient crossing. (4) Last are the counties of Argyll and Bute, consisting of a great series of Highland districts, mostly peninsular and insular, of which the most noted are Kintyre, Knapdale, Cowall, Argyll, Lorne, and Lochaber. Communication with these is of necessity almost wholly by water.

Ireland presents little of the complexity of Scotland. Except for the modern immigrations, it is inhabited from end to end by a single race of Goidelicised pre-Celts (*cf.* Figs. 92, 94, 95). The mountains are marginal, and there are, therefore, fewer internal barriers than in Scotland. The four provinces of Ulster, Connaught, Munster, and Leinster, corresponding to the tribal federations of the time of the Anglo-Norman conquest, were based upon the four corners of the island, each of which contains a nuclear group of hills, while a fifth district of Meath

lay wholly in the plain and spread from the lowland coast
of Dublin westward to the Shannon.   When the Anglo-
Normans landed in the island in the reign of Henry II.,
certain sub-divisions of these provinces had already become established, but, on the other hand, the limits of
the provinces themselves did not correspond exactly with

FIG. 109.—The Older Divisions of Ireland.   Limit of the Pale ⎼ ⎼ ⎼ ⎼

those shown upon the modern map.   Ulster excluded Cavan
and included Louth.   Its divisions were Tirconnel (the
present Donegal); Tirowen (the present Londonderry and
Tyrone) ; Ulster (in the narrow sense, equivalent to the
present Antrim and Down) ; and Uriel, which consisted
of the district now divided into the four counties, Louth,
Monaghan, Armagh, and Fermanagh (Figs. 109, 110).

Connaught, which included the county Cavan, had within it a district, about Connemara and Galway, known as Connaught in a special sense. Munster lay in three great divisions, corresponding to three systems of drainage. Thomond extended across the lower Shannon, and included the modern counties Clare and Limerick; Des-

FIG. 110.—The Counties of Ireland.

mond contained the southernmost basins of Ireland, now the counties Kerry, Cork, and Waterford; and Ormond was roughly equivalent to Tipperary, drained chiefly by the river Suir. Meath comprised, besides the modern counties Meath and Westmeath, also Longford and the northern portion of County Dublin, but the city of Dublin was included in Leinster. At the time of the landing of the

Normans, Dublin, Wexford, and Waterford, along the sea front of Leinster, were walled towns in the hands of the Norsemen. It is noteworthy that, whereas Meath has been annexed to the modern province of Leinster, and with it the county of Louth, originally a part of Ulster, yet the four archbishoprics of Armagh, Dublin, Cashel, and Tuam, otherwise corresponding to the four provinces, were so delimited that Meath was allotted to Armagh, and not to Dublin.

The Anglo-Norman dominion in Ireland attained to its maximum development early in the fourteenth century. The land had then been divided into a number of counties, corresponding to some extent, although not wholly, with the modern divisions. But the island almost recovered its independence during the Wars of the Roses, the English jurisdiction being confined to a small area round Dublin, known as the English Pale, including parts only of the counties Louth, Meath, Dublin, and Kildare. Beyond the Pale, Ireland was little cultivated, the wealth of the almost nomadic tribes consisting mainly of herds of cattle. Waterford, Cork, Limerick, and Galway were walled and isolated cities. The ultimate settlement of Ireland commenced under the Tudors. District after district was held to have escheated to the Crown, owing to the rebellion of the inhabitants, and grants were made to English or Scottish tenants with a view to the establishment of what were called plantations, for Ireland was thought of almost precisely as the American plantations of New England and Virginia. Of these settlements, whose foundation was continued into the time of Cromwell, the most remarkable were (1) those which extended the English Pale westward almost to the Shannon, comprising the districts that were formed into the King's and Queen's counties, so named after Queen Mary and her husband, Philip of Spain ; (2) the Scots' plantation in the counties Antrim and Down ; and (3) the plantations established at Derry, in the reign of James I., by the twelve Livery Companies of London. The final division into counties, achieved under the direction of Cromwell, exhibits a uniformity of areas and nomenclature which suggests a comparison with the Mercian counties of England, also formed in the process of conquest.

Lastly, there are two fragments of Britain which fall outside the county organisation. The Isle of Man was long a separate lordship under the mere suzerainty of the English king. It still has a separate legislature, and is not affected by the Acts of Imperial Parliament unless expressly named. The same is true of the Channel Islands, divided into the separate and rival Bailiwicks of Jersey and Guernsey, which are remnants of the old Norman Duchy of the English kings.

Such in slightest outline is the complex of events which has fixed the racial and historical geography of Britain. The details are innumerable and heterogeneous, but a broad view of their tendency suggests the recurrent influence of a few potent physical conditions. The Wealden uplift has been of crucial importance in determining the lie both of the Kentish promontory and of the Kennet-Thames valley, the one offering a landway, the other a waterway to the interior of the island. The Wealden forest, by imparting an almost peninsular circumscription to the chalk plateau of Kent, has caused the withdrawal from Dover to inland London of the focus whence the roads from the continent radiate into further Britain. London was placed where the land way necessarily bridged the water way. Five trunk roads spread thence—north-eastward into the East Anglian promontory, northward to the Vale of York, north-westward to the Chester Gap, westward to the Bristol Gap, and south-westward to the Solent harbours. But in the time of the Anglo-Saxon invasions a fortified London barred the direct ways both by land and river, compelling the Saxons to enter by Southampton Water, and the Angles by the Humber and the Wash. As a result the Thames, normally one of the lines of communication radiating from the metropolis, became for a while the frontier between competing forces acting from the

15

south coast and the east. At a later time when the West Saxon was warring with the Dane, Watling Street underwent a similar change of relations.

The Bristol and Chester Gaps have had a dual effect, for they have not only admitted the roads from the continental angle into the recesses of the oceanic border, but have also severed the western and central uplands of South Britain into Devonian, Welsh, and Pennine masses. South Britain may be regarded, therefore, as comprising three zones, ranged concentrically with reference to the continental angle. The first consists of the promontories of Kent and East Anglia, set apart by their fens and forests, and sundered by the estuary of the Thames; the second is the midland plain, continuous from the Solent to the Humber; the third is the belt of uplands, broken into three sections by arms of sea and lowland. It was the conquest of the second zone which determined the essentially Teutonic character of mediæval and modern England, for the invaders had made little impression when they had only seized the south-eastern promontories, London still being held against them; and, on the other hand, the Celts were fatally defeated when the Teutonic conquest had been pushed through to the Severn and the Dee, and they had been divided into three separate communities inhabiting three uplands in the ends of the land. Nor could the advance cease even with the occupation of the great plain, for Wales, by reason of the eastward tilt of its drainage, was unable to maintain for long the independence which would otherwise have pertained to its upland character. By the open valley of the upper Severn, invaders from the plain, at first the Brythons, and afterwards the Normans, were able to drive a wedge of conquest between north and south. The Normans also penetrated by the coastal sill of the south to the extreme promontory of Pembroke, and the natural citadel of Gwyneth, in rear of Snowdon, was thus the last district of South Britain to be reduced to subjection.

The Chester Gap, affording an exit from the English

Plain, may be correlated with the Dublin Gap opposite, which gives wide entrance to the Irish plain of Meath. It was by this way that the Goidels, and afterwards the English, succeeded in thrusting a colony into the midst of Ireland, whence their influence could spread northward, westward, and southward through the intervals between the mountain groups. The marginal position and fragmental nature of the Irish uplands, and the open aspect of the heart of the island, rendered conquest comparatively easy, while the sea in rear, by detaching the conquerors from their base, caused them, in successive epochs, to become identified with their new possession. As a result, the Irish population, judged by physical standards, exhibits a striking uniformity, notwithstanding the differences of language and religion (Figs. 92, 94, 95). The estuary of the great river Shannon, being westward, has proved an additional cause of isolation.

What the Chester Gap was with reference to Ireland, that the Vale of York has been with reference to Scotland. The Brythons first, and at a later time the Angles, penetrated northward to the Firth of Forth, each in turn driving their predecessors to take refuge behind the upland in the west. At the opening of recorded history the Pictish aborigines had thus been forced by the Brythons into the promontory of Galloway, and the Brythons themselves were afterwards confined by the Angles to the median belt of Strathclyde. The northward salient of the county of Northumberland, in the interval between Bamborough Castle and the Cheviot, gives yet a third expression of the strategical advantage conferred, by the unimpeded way along the Vale of York and the coastal sill of Durham and Northumberland, upon forces acting from the south. But as the St. George's Channel, separating Ireland from England, has prevented racial and political fusion, despite the facilities for communication offered by the Chester and Dublin Gaps, so the southern uplands of Scotland, extending through to the cliffs of St. Abb's Head, long prevented the union of North and South Britain, notwithstanding the open pathway through York and Newcastle. In the case both of the Romans and the English, power based on a single line of communications became attenuated to the north of the Peak and Humber, and a border had to be established across the isthmus of mid-Britain. In each instance, however, the frontier was so drawn as to obtain the advantage of lateral communication, through the Tyne Gap, with the subsidiary (because much impeded) west coast road.

The Highlands lying beyond the Scottish midland plain, present on a larger scale the characteristics of Wales in relation to the English plain. The valley of Glenmore, as a central feature of the clan-country, corresponded in some sort to the Menai Strait in the principality of Gwyneth ; and Strathmore and the sill round the Buchan promontory afforded entry for the Teutonic lowlanders as far as Inverness, answering in a degree to the coastal pathway of South Wales, through Gwent and Glamorgan, to English Pembroke. The glen of the Tay might be thought of as analogous to the Severn valley, but that it is constricted in consequent reaches, where gorges, as at Killiecrankie, have protected the wider longitudinal valleys within.

The Shetlands and the Orkneys, the plain of Caithness in the extremity of the mainland, and the great archipelago of the Hebrides, together with the North Channel (admitting to the Irish Sea and the Isle of Man), have afforded appropriate sea ways and insular or peninsular bases for the boatmen of the Norwegian fiords. As a consequence, the Norsemen from the west and the Danes from the east were able to join hands, through the Aire Gap, across the isthmus of mid-Britain, a fact which found expression in the extension of Domesday Yorkshire, and the ancient diocese of York, from the east coast to the west.

On the whole, then, human movement in Britain have been of two orders—from the continental angle radially towards the oceanic border, and on the other hand, from the eastern and from the southern coast tangentially inward. The radial line from Kent, through London and the Chester Gap, to the Isle of Man and the North Channel, roughly bisects the continental angle, and indicates the belt of conflict between the westward and the northward tangential pressures. Instances of such pressure and conflict are to be found in (1) the westward entry of the blonde race at the expense of the brunette (southern) aborigines; (2) the midland warfare of the Angle with the Saxon; (3) the conquest of the Danelaw by Wessex; (4) the invasion of Argyll by the Irish Scots; and (5) the immigration of the later Scots into Ulster. On the other hand, the Goidels, the Brythons, the Belgians, the Romans, and the Normans seem in the main to have moved radially outward. The same conception may even be applicable, in a general way, to the advance of ideas across Britain. Three religions, for instance, entered successively from the southeast—Romano-Celtic Christianity, Anglo-Saxon Paganism, and the Christianity of Augustine. Rebounding from the oceanic edge, like a wave from a cliff, the earlier Christianity returned from Ireland and Scotland upon northern England, to encounter there the second advance of missionary effort, and as entering and returning waves throw up a crest where they meet, so the Celtic and the Roman Christianity struggled in the crisis which culminated in the Synod of Whitby in A.D. 664.

If the oceanic borderland of Britain be regarded as connected with the Scandinavian upland, for racial as for physical purposes, we shall still find essentially the same contrast between the south and the east; for Ireland has a dark population, of comparatively uniform character, both physical and mental, and Norway a blonde population of even more striking uniformity; whereas the two strains appear to have met along the great divide of Scotland, so that the population of Argyll and Galloway has Irish affinities, and that of Caithness and Buchan Scandinavian tendencies.

It is, therefore, clear that the salient geographical attributes of Britain are identical, whether tested by the physical or the historical geographer. They consist of a fundamental relation with Scandinavia, a balance along radial lines between the plain of the continental angle and the uplands of the oceanic border, an opposition between the leeward and windward slopes of the median belt of uplands, and a certain antithesis between the eastern (Baltic-ward) and southern (Mediterranean-ward) shores. The geography of Britain is in fact the intricate product of a continuous history, geological and human.

Note on Authorities.—On Roman Britain Haverfield's map in the *Oxford Historical Atlas* should be consulted, also a paper by Haverfield in the *Archæologia Oxoniensis,* June 1894. An authoritative general article will be found in the *Edinburgh Review,* April 1899.

On the Teutonic settlements J. R. Green's *Making of England* and *Conquest of England* are essential and contain many references.

On the whole subject the *Oxford Historical Atlas* is indispensable. The execution of the maps leaves much to be desired, but the notes which accompany them are of scholarly accuracy. Pearson's *Historical Maps of England,* although now superseded as a general authority, may still be referred to with advantage.

Note on the word "impenetrable" at p. 195.—Exception has been taken to the use of this epithet as applied to a forest. It must be remembered, however, that a part of the resistance offered to an invader by a physical barrier is due to human opposition. A small number of aborigines may, in fact, render a close forest impenetrable for a conqueror, just as a few piratic fishermen may heighten the resistance of a marsh, or a few Bedawin that of a desert.

CHAPTER XIV

METROPOLITAN ENGLAND

In the past chapters Britain has been described from the standpoints of its relation to the surrounding lands and seas, of the moulding of its surface and the system of its rivers, of the climatic conditions which it presents for animal and vegetable life, and of those settlements and organisations of human society in the early, only half-conscious periods of which the French historian Michelet has written that in the beginning history is all geography. At the risk of some repetition, it is desirable, in order to obtain the full effect of the composite environment, to attempt the correlation of these various factors, as exhibited in the topography of the several divisions of the country. With this object it is necessary to part the land into county groups, corresponding as nearly as may be to important differences of physical structure, and to broad historical and economic distinctions. Of major divisions answering to this requirement it is obvious that Scotland and Ireland must be two. Two more may be based on the fundamental contrast between south-eastern and north-western England, Wales being counted as a portion of the latter.

The south-east of England is in the main a fertile undulating lowland, richly cultivated, and at present devoid of coal-mines. Its life is so far concentrated in the vast metropolis, which has nearly seven million people, that of other towns only two, Portsmouth and Plymouth-Devonport, have as many as 200,000 inhabitants ; and there are only three more, Brighton, Southampton, and Norwich, of 100,000. The north-west, on the other hand, has two wide uplands, the Cambrian and the Pennine, whose higher

levels are fit only for sheep-walks and grouse-moors, but
the lower slopes, together with the plains around, contain
the visible coal, and bear the chief industrial life of England.
There is here no one predominant centre of population, but
two cities, Liverpool-Birkenhead and Manchester-Salford,
of near a million inhabitants each; three, Birmingham,
Leeds, and Sheffield, of half a million ; and six of a quarter
of a million, Newcastle-Gateshead, Hull, Bradford, Nottingham, Leicester, and Bristol.   There are probably not
fewer than a dozen more of at least 100,000.   These
two regions of alien aspect may be distinguished as
Metropolitan England and Industrial England.   They
merge along a line drawn diagonally from the mouth of
the Severn to the Wash.   Northamptonshire belongs on
the whole to the Metropolitan section, but Gloucestershire is a debatable county, whose life consists for some
purposes with the one division and for some with the other.
Roughly, the great Jurassic escarpment, locally known as
the Edge,[1] is to be regarded as the delimiting barrier.

   The life of Metropolitan England is chiefly conditioned
by three circumstances : (1) nearly all the main roads
and railways converge upon London ; (2) the coast-line,
extended from Norfolk to Cornwall, everywhere looks
across the Narrow Seas to the neighbouring continent ;
and (3) there are no considerable sources of mechanical
motive power.   As a consequence nine-tenths of the army
in Great Britain is stationed within Metropolitan England :
the three great naval ports are there : the commercial as
opposed to the industrial control is there : and the whole
region has more or less of a residential character.   Industrial England, on the other hand, has several important
cross roads, but a less immediate connection with the
continent.   It has but a small population of the leisured
classes, for rich and poor alike are workers, and as a result
the prevalent opinions both in politics and religion differ
not infrequently from those of the metropolis.   Moreover,
the social life of Metropolitan England is old and aristo-
cratic, whereas that of Industrial England is new and

---

[1] As in Edgehill and Wotton-under-Edge.

more democratic, for Industrial England, as a great community, is even more recent than the New England of America.

Outside London, Metropolitan England falls naturally into four quadrants, south-eastern, north-eastern, north-western, and south-western, and of these the last named must be subdivided into a nearer and a further section, for it extends to the remote Land's End (Plate III.).

The South-Eastern Quadrant, consisting of the three counties of Kent, Surrey, and Sussex, is one of the most naturally compact sub-divisions of all Britain. Almost every detail of the topography is dependent upon two fundamental events in the physical history of the land, the uplift of the Wealden dome along an axis striking east and west, and the intersection of this diagonally from south-west to north-east by the erosion of Dover Strait. The core of the district, lying along the axis of the upfold from Horsham to Hastings, consists of the sandstone hills of the Forest Range which, with the surrounding clay bottoms, were formerly clothed with the dense Wealden Forest. The remaining features are, necessarily, bi-lateral, the Chalk Downs of the north being balanced by those of the south, and the clay flats along the Thames by those of the Sussex coast westward of Brighton. From the divide the drainage is carried northward to the Thames through gaps in the Downs of Surrey and Kent, and southward to the Channel through similar gaps in the Sussex Downs. At Beachy Head, at Hastings, and at the South Foreland, where the two belts of chalk and the sandstone range have been cut back by the Channel waves, the land is fronted by cliffs; but the relatively recent origin of the Strait of Dover is marked by the lack of any considerable subsequent streams [1] draining directly to the sea. On the other hand, the relative antiquity of the denudation of the Weald is evidenced by the development of long subsequent tributaries from several of the consequents which breach the ranges of Down. This is notably the case with the Medway,

[1] The Rother is the largest.

which has thus become the largest river of the district (*cf.* pp. 87–92, 96, 113).

Of minor elements in the topography, the most striking is the change in the direction of the North Downs from east-north-east in Surrey and west Kent, to south-east through eastern Kent. The accessory features of the north coast of Kent may be correlated with these separate limbs of the Downs. The Isle of Grain and the Isle of Sheppey are the terminal coastal expression of the lie of the Surrey and west Kent Downs from the Hog's Back to Rochester, while the Isle of Thanet, beyond the marsh belt which represents the former channel of Wantsum, is connected with the east Kentish range. The chalk expands terminally so as to occupy all the eastern promontory of the county, from Folkestone to Deal and from Dover to Canterbury, and further to south, emergent from under the chalk, is a greensand ledge, which bears Folkestone and the old Cinque Port of Hythe. Beyond this again is Romney Marsh, an alluvial flat at the mouth of the Rother, due to the deposit of silt in the lagoon behind a shingle bar, which formerly bent evenly from Hastings past Romney to Hythe, and has now been cusped seaward into Dungeness by the combined action of the waves and tidal currents (*cf.* p. 42).

The county divisions, Surrey and Kent in the north and Sussex in the south, are expressive of the conditions under which the Jutes and Saxons took possession of the country. Having first occupied the two ranges of open chalk upland, the invaders ultimately met in the heart of the Wealden Forest, where the frontier line has ever since been drawn. The word weald is equivalent to the German word " wald," a forest, and there are here many other place-names, ending in " hurst," " den," and " field," which betoken a closely-wooded country. By closing the westward road to the Jutes of Kent, the Roman Provincials of London reserved the occupation of Surrey to be effected by the East and Middle Saxons, thereby originating the frontier between Surrey and Kent. Where Surrey marches with Berkshire is a great heath, now much planted with pine woods, due to the largest patch of the Bagshot sands. To-day the population of south-eastern England is no longer chiefly gathered about the Downs, but is densest in the valley of the Thames, along the north coast of Kent, and upon the coastal flats of Sussex (Fig. 111).

Outside the metropolitan area the life of south-eastern England is based mainly upon four activities—the traffic from the continent, the defence of the continental angle, the cultivation of the land, and the pleasuring of London. The first of the four is of most ancient significance. It has been chiefly concentrated upon the natural roadway leading from Flanders and Picardy over the Strait of Dover, and from the Kentish promontory westward across the Stour, the Medway, and the Thames, between the marshes of the estuary on the right hand, and the chalk heights, backed by the Wealden forest, on the left hand. Canterbury and Rochester, at the river passages, had already risen to a local importance when the missionaries from Rome established in them the stools of the first English bishops. There were at least five available landings from the Channel, whence the roads gathered to the Canterbury crossing. In succession southward they were (1) Roman Richborough, followed by Sandwich, in the mouth of the Wantsum strait ; (2) Deal, with the anchorage of the Downs under the lee of the Goodwin Sands ; (3) Dover, where the little stream of the Dour cut a notch to the level of the foreshore between two lofty cliff-shoulders, now crowned by the castle and the citadel ; (4) Folkestone, where the ledge of greensand comes down to the sea between the chalk cliffs and Romney Marsh ; and (5) Hythe, preceded by Roman Lymne, at the former mouth of the Rother. Sandwich, Dover, and Hythe were among the mediæval Cinque Ports which had the duty of defending the threatened angle of the land. Romney and Hastings, completing the federal corporation of five, were placed the one on the shingle bar north of Dungeness, the other at the end of the Forest Range. The harbours of most of the Cinque

Ports have been silted up, or closed by drifting shingle, and the traffic is now concentrated at Dover, where a

FIG. 111.—The Density of Population in Eastern and South-eastern England in 1891.—*After* BOSSE, *by permission of* BARTHOLOMEW.

harbour has been maintained at great cost, and to a less degree at Folkestone (*cf.* pp. 42, 198).

The Thames is usually regarded as opening to the sea where the Nore lightship is anchored between Shoe-

buryness and Sheerness, and here the lateral estuary of
the Medway offers a convenient flank retreat and a basis
for the defence of the metropolitan water.   The dockyard
of Chatham, beside Rochester bridge, is the more defen-

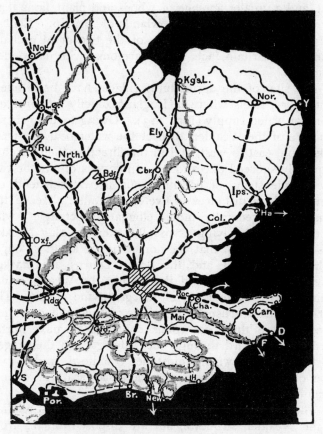

FIG. 112.—The Chief Railways of Eastern and South-eastern
England.

sible because situated on the land-road between Dover
and London.   A great naval harbour is being constructed
at Dover for the easier barring of the Channel and for
the protection of the Thames.

Notwithstanding the neighbourhood of an immense market, and the prevalence of a climate in which continental and channel influences[1] are happily blended, south-eastern England exhibits, because of the composition of its rocks, a wider spread of heath and common land, and a greater acreage of woods and plantations than any other equal area in the lowlands of Britain. Kent is the chief hop country and one of the two great orchard countries of Britain, facts which harmonise with its wooded character.

The sites of the agricultural villages have been determined here, as elsewhere in England, chiefly by considerations of water supply (Fig. 113). Owing to the general structure of the Wealden district the water-bearing strata strike from east to west, and in this direction the churches frequently succeed one another at intervals of one or two miles, while strips of country poor in water extend on either hand for distances of five or six miles. Hence the parishes are generally much elongated rectangles, with their longer sides lying across the water-bearing streaks. It is for this reason that the northern and southern edges both of the North and the South Downs are marked by chains of villages, and that within the Weald similar chains follow the margins of the greensand ridges. The market towns are usually members of these village series, placed where the local roads converge to pass northward or southward through the water gaps in the ranges. Of these gap towns, Maidstone, Guildford, and Lewes have obtained an added importance as seats of county administration.

The coastal pleasure resorts bear no essential relation to the Wealden structure, but are disposed radially from London in the quadrant of a circle. Brighton, Eastbourne, Hastings, Ramsgate, and Margate are large towns almost wholly dependent on the business of pleasure, the first-named having with its suburbs a population of not less than 150,000. To the same category belongs the inland town of Tunbridge Wells, on the sandy heights of

[1] See p. 175.

the Forest Range. Other sandy areas at high level are becoming discontinuous suburbs of London. In the extreme south-west of Sussex is Chichester, an ancient cathedral city embodying the traditions both of the Romans and the South Saxons.

The main railway lines of the district, belonging to the South-Eastern and Chatham, and the Brighton Companies, spread, as might be expected, radially to the continental entries and the pleasure resorts, to 'Dover and Folkestone, to Hastings, to Brighton, and by way of Chichester to Portsmouth (Fig. 112). Apart from the dockyard of Chatham, the most noteworthy seats of industry are the railway works of Brighton and Ashford.

The North-Eastern Quadrant of Metropolitan England includes the three counties of Norfolk, Suffolk, and Essex. Essentially they are formed of the most eastern of the series of curved belts which between the lower Thames and Chester constitute the midland plain (Figs. 48, 101). The western margin of the district nearly coincides with the chalk escarpment, except in west Norfolk, where a considerable area of the greensand has been unsheathed along the obsequent course of the Little Ouse. Here too a strip of Fen is included, lying beyond the Great Ouse at King's Lynn. The flow of the river system is eastward and south-eastward, down the consequent slope which has been detached from the Pennine-Cambrian divide by the development of the subsequent basin of the Wash. The counties of Hertford and Middlesex, together with the southern ends of Buckinghamshire and Oxfordshire, belong to the same drainage belt, but apart from practical considerations, there are real physical contrasts to be drawn between the three counties of the east and the district immediately to the north-west of London. Not only is the range of the Chilterns both higher and narrower than the broad spread of the chalk in Suffolk and Norfolk, but also the rivers Colne and Lea exhibit a definitely southward trend to the Thames, whereas the rivers of the three eastern counties, even as far south as the Chelmer and Crouch of Essex, have a markedly eastward flow to the sea (Plate III.). In fact, the channel of the Thames in the neighbourhood of Tilbury and Gravesend has been cut through a small chalk upfold, connected with the stretch of the North Downs from the Hog's Back east-north-eastward, and there is a minor divide striking northward with perfect clearness from Tilbury to Saffron Walden, in the north-western corner of Essex. The chief characteristic of the eastern counties when compared with those of the Wealden group is a certain breadth and monotony of topography, due to the fact that they are formed of a single structural slope, not of opposed slopes from an axial line, and that the rises on their surface, perhaps owing to the effect of glacial erosion, which did not reach to south of the Thames, have an elevation less by one-half than that of the fragments of the Wealden uplift (*cf.* pp. 112, 118, 121).

Westward of the north and south divide of Essex are the remains of Epping Forest, and beyond these again the broad alluvial strip which, from Ware southward to the Thames, has replaced the marshes of the Lea. Hence the Middle Saxons of London were able to maintain a partial independence of East Saxon rule at Colchester and Chelmsford. Further to the north the Fens severed East Anglia from the midlands. Thus the three counties of the east exhibit almost as marked a severance of position and structure as do the Wealden counties of the south-east. Being placed opposite to the mainland they have always had continental relations; indeed Colchester was a Roman, and apparently a British port of earlier date than London. One of the great Roman roads, known in after times as Ermine Street, struck inland from Colchester, round the edge of the Fens, by Cambridge to Lincoln (Fig. 98). Perhaps the Great-Eastern line from the West Riding and Lancashire, through Doncaster, Lincoln, and Ely, to Harwich and the continent, may be considered as the modern equivalent of Ermine Street (Fig. 112).

The three counties of the group have been shaped round the estuaries upon which the original settlements were founded. Norwich is at the head of the former sea navigation of the Yare. Ipswich, Colchester, and Chelmsford are at the points where the road from Norwich to London, now replaced as an artery by the Great Eastern Railway, crossed the lower reaches of the Orwell, Colne, and Chelmer. Harwich marks the entry of the one considerable natural harbour in all the interval between the Thames and the Humber. Yarmouth resembles Deal in having an open roadstead under the lee of a sandbank, and Yarmouth and Lowestoft are conveniently placed bases for the great fisheries on the banks of the North Sea. Pleasure is one of the minor industries of the east, although Cromer, Felixstowe, and Southend have a less importance than the range of large pleasure towns along the Wealden shore. Thus the chief part of the population of this quadrant is drawn by various circumstances to the seaward edge.

The agriculture of the East Anglian counties exhibits the arable character that might be expected of their broad structural monotony and of their half continental climate. Moreover the till, or mixed clay deposited over great areas by the glacial sheet, is specially appropriate for the plough. Of the fenward towns, Bury St. Edmunds, upon an obsequent westerly stream, is the chief market, and King's Lynn, at the mouth of the Great Ouse, is a small port, hampered by the uncertainties of navigation amid the shoals of the Wash.

The North-Western Quadrant, spreading from the angle between the Lea and the Thames over the counties of Middlesex, Hertford, Cambridge, Huntingdon, Bedford, Buckingham, Oxford, Northampton, and Rutland, differs from the other divisions of Metropolitan England in that it is wholly removed from the coast, and that it is therefore devoid of any clear physical definition. Thus it will be necessary in treating of it occasionally to extend our view at least to Berkshire and North Wilts, and sometimes into

the lowland portion of Industrial England.   None the less,
it has specific characteristics which obviously differentiate
it from all the surrounding regions.   It consists essentially
of portions of the two great south-eastward slopes of the
midlands, Cretaceous and Jurassic, together with a section
of the clay belts between them.   Three groups of streams
discharge the surface drainage :—(1) a consequent group
from the Cotswolds into the Oxford Thames ; (2) a consequent group from the Chilterns into the lower Thames ;
and (3) a great subsequent and longitudinal group into
the Wash.   One of the fundamental features is, therefore,
a north-westerly watershed, coinciding approximately with
the line from London to Chester.   To the south-west,
in the basin of the Thames, the Chiltern and Cotswold
ranges are comparatively high, whereas their north-eastward continuations through Northamptonshire and East
Anglia are low.   Since the draining of the Fens, the basin
of the Wash rivers has, as a consequence of the
lack of barriers, acquired somewhat intimate connections with East Anglia and Lincolnshire (cf. pp. 61,
85, 112).

In harmony with this structure the topographical
details trend in two directions—north-eastward and south-
westward with the grain of the rocks, and radially from
the metropolis across the grain.   In the first direction are
the chains of villages along the water-bearing strips at the
foot of the Chilterns, comparable to the similar chains
disposed eastward and westward in the Wealden country,
and also the Icknield way, by which the mediæval traffic
passed from the west of England along the front of the
Chilterns into East Anglia.   The raids of the West Saxons
from beyond the Thames, and of the Angles from the
Wash, were clearly guided by similar influences, nor can
we fail to bring into the same category the spread of
the great diocese of Lincoln from the Witham through
the Wash into the rivers of the Fens, and from the
minsters of Ely and Peterborough, by the longitudinal
ways, to the ecclesiastical outposts of Oxford and Dorchester, on the Thames boundary of Mercia (cf. p. 211).

But that which gives a fundamental unity to the quadrant under consideration is the radial spread of the roads leading from the metropolis to the west and north of England, and to Ireland and Scotland beyond. Watling Street was constructed along the line of least resistance, where the river crossings were fewest, near the divide between the Wash-ward and the Thames-ward drainage. The chief western roads crossed the Thames at Maidenhead and Staines. These were based, in parts at any rate, upon the work of the Roman engineers. There were subsequently added the north road, and the road to Oxford and Worcester. Of the water ways, the Thames was the most frequented, and Oxford grew to importance near the head of its navigation. Bedford and Northampton hold corresponding positions upon the Ouse and the Nen, but these subsequent rivers belong rather to the longitudinal system of communications, and tended to divert the life of the Fen country north-eastward, and therefore away from the metropolis. The canal system, which preceded the railways, exhibited to the full the radial tendency. The Grand Junction Canal followed the same general direction as Watling Street, and three several canals branched from the Thames, connecting the Kennet with the Bath Avon, the upper Thames with the Gloucester Severn, and the Cherwell with the Warwick Avon. It was not, however, until railways were introduced that the radiation of many ways from the metropolis to Industrial England imparted its present unique character to the region. It is now crossed by no fewer than nine express lines of railroad diverging from London—the Great Eastern (to Doncaster), the Great Northern, the Midland, the North-Western, the Great Central, and four branches of the Great Western system, diverging from Reading, Oxford, and Swindon. But it may be questioned whether the whole region is not now further removed from the full tide of national life than it was in earlier generations, for the greater part of the traffic is carried through it with little stoppage, and has no more influence upon the rural districts traversed than has the shipping of the Suez Canal upon Cairene Egypt.

Many of the towns rose, under the older conditions of slow traffic, at points where the radial ways crossed the rivers. Of such are St. Albans, Hertford, and Ware on the hither side of the Chilterns, and Bedford and Huntingdon beyond them. But some of the industries of the north-west and of the metropolis, gradually driven afield by the rise of rents in the populous areas, are finding convenient location upon the main lines of railway, as at Northampton and Bedford. The largest of the modern railway towns, whose position is obviously determined by low rent and central position rather than by considerations of economy in the freight of heavy coal and iron, has been established at Swindon.

The proper activities of the region are chiefly agricultural, but without any such marked characteristics as in the case of East Anglia or the Weald. Of late the rich alluvium of the Fens has been utilised for the growing of roots on a great scale, the heavy produce being transported upon the light railways recently constructed. There are small industries, appropriate to an agricultural region, as, for instance, the straw-plaiting of Luton, and the chair-making of Wycombe, but a majority of the towns are merely market centres. The ancient universities of Oxford and Cambridge, based in the main upon agricultural endowments, are naturally placed within this quadrant, the one in the Thames basin towards the west and south, the other looking to the north and east, in the basin of the Wash.

The South-Western Quadrant extends from the metropolis to the remote Land's End, and must, therefore, be divided into hither and further sections. The former, consisting of the four counties of Hants, Wilts, Berks, and Dorset, coincides with the earlier Wessex, and is known locally as the South of England. It is composed of the later rocks, and is, therefore, a part of the English plain. The further division, containing the three counties of Somerset, Devon, and Cornwall, is described as the West of England, and is built chiefly of the ancient rock of the uplands. It was delimited eastward by the forest belt of Selwood, which formerly curved along the frontier of Somerset beneath the chalk upland of Wilts, affording such refuge to the aborigines that the West Saxons invaded Somerset by a circuitous route from the north. This at least is the inference drawn from the fact that the percentage of Celtic place-names increases from the north south-westward.

The four counties of the South have a corrugated structure, whose principal parts are the western end of the Wealden uplift, forming the chalk plateau of North Hants and South Wilts, and two parallel downfolds, the one dipping beneath the Kennet valley, and rising beyond into the Marlborough and Ilsley Downs, the other underlying the Frome valley and the Solent, and reappearing in the range of the Dorset Downs and the Isle of Wight. The drainage system corresponds to this structure. There are two eastward streams, the Kennet and the Frome, following the axes of the downfolds, the one into the lower Thames, the other into that part of the sea where Poole Harbour and the Solent and Spithead appear to indicate a sunken valley. In addition, there is a series of consequent streams originating along the northern edge of the Hants and Wilts plateau—where the chalk is sharply up-flexed—and flowing southward into the Frome-Solent depression. These consequents are gathered into two groups, the one consisting of the Test and Itchen of Hampshire, whose combined estuary is Southampton Water, the other of the Salisbury Avon and Dorset Stour, which converge at Christ Church. In three directions border strips of the district extend beyond the Cretaceous area : along the eastern edge of Hampshire is included a small portion of the Weald ; along the south shore of Dorset a strip of the Jurassic rocks rises from under the chalk range, and is prolonged seaward by the detached limestone block of Portland, connected with the mainland only by the shingle of the Chesil beach ;

while in the north and north-west of Wilts, clays of Jurassic date emerge from under the chalk escarpment, forming a lowland belt, which is drained by longitudinal reaches of the upper Bristol Avon and upper Thames. A remarkable feature is the Vale of Pewsey, an east and west depression lying to the south of the upper Kennet valley, due to the denudation of a small dome of chalk, and to the resulting exposure of the underlying less resistant rocks. This little Weald is drained, not by any longitudinal stream, but by the headwaters of the consequent Avon of Salisbury, and the similarity to the larger Weald is further enforced by the analogous chaining of the village centres along the water-bearing outcrops near Devizes (Fig. 113; cf. pp. 89, 92, 113, 114).

Along the south shore are the insular or peninsular Isles of Wight, Purbeck, and Portland, corresponding roughly to the Isles of Thanet, Sheppey, and Grain along the north coast of Kent, and betokening a rough correspondence of parts as between the Wealden and Southern districts, but with a transposition from north to south. This reversed similarity of features becomes very evident when we consider the modern distribution of population and social activities. The earlier settlements of the south-east were on the chalk uplands of the North and South Downs, and the settlements, first of the Belgians, and afterwards of the West Saxons, were placed on the central upland of Hants and Wilts, whence colonies appear to have crossed the axial valleys to the chalk ranges of Dorset and Berks. The earthworks and stone circles of the vanished races are frequent all over the tree-less upland, as at Stonehenge and Avebury. In modern times, however, the population is most concentrated along the lowland strips of the north and south (Fig. 111). In the north, the thickly peopled belt which extends from Thanet and Dover to London is prolonged westward past Windsor and Reading to Newbury. In the south, the populous coastal sill, which commences with Brighton and Worthing, is continued past Chichester and Portsmouth to Ryde, Southampton, Bournemouth, Poole, and

Dorchester. Thus, while the greater population is in the north of the Wealden county group, it is in the south of the Southern county group. In fact, but for their different relations to the metropolis, the south and the south-east of England would form a single natural region, symmetrical in structure, in system of drainage, and in conditions of settlement. There is a relative sparsity of

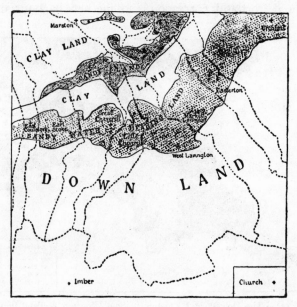

FIG. 113.—The Relation of Parish Boundaries and Parish Centres to Water-bearing Rock-strips near Devizes.

modern population along the whole of the upfold from Wilts into Kent, whereas each of the downfolds has an axial seam of dense peopling. In each case, too, there is a central broadening, so that the dense area is spindle-shaped, London bisecting the length of the one spindle, Southampton that of the other (Fig. 111). In the details, moreover, of the grouping there are striking similarities, allowance being made for the vast preponderance of the Imperial metropolis. Winchester, the old capital of

Wessex, and Southampton, the port, may be taken to
correspond respectively to the west and east ends of
London ; while Portsmouth, placed on a lateral harbour,
has the same position relatively to Southampton Water and
Spithead that Chatham on the Medway holds with regard
to the estuary of the Thames.   Bournemouth, under the
lee of the Isle of Purbeck, and Weymouth, under that
of Portland, are the pleasure towns, while the harbour of
refuge at Portland corresponds to the new harbour under

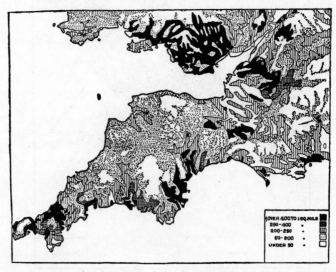

FIG. 114.—The Density of Population in South-Western England in 1891.
After BOSSE, *by permission of* BARTHOLOMEW.

construction at Dover.   The ancient cities of Salisbury
and Winchester are placed at the exit of the valleys
from the chalk plateau, Salisbury at the point where
five tributary valleys converge, and Winchester immediately below the turn in the Itchen valley which directs
the through road from Southampton north-eastward to
the source stream of the Wey, and thence past Farnham
and Aldershot, over the Bagshot sands, to the Thames
bridge at Staines, and to London.   The spread of the
diocese of Winchester through the counties of Hants and

Surrey is thus expressive of a certain physical unity, and the boundaries of the old diocese of Salisbury coinciding with those of the county of Wilts and its two colonies of Dorset and Berks, were equally significant (Fig. 104). Only the westward expansion of Southern Hampshire beyond the lower Avon requires the explanation of some unknown event in history, but it is noteworthy that the northward limit of the New Forest, which was the chase of the kings at Winchester, here coincides with the boundaries of the counties of Hants and Wilts. The New Forest corre-

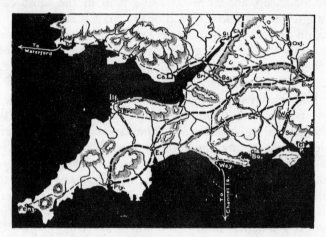

FIG. 115.—The Railways of South-Western England.

sponds, alike in its structural position and its relative sterility, to the great waste of Bagshot sands, spreading between Aldershot and Windsor.

The economic activities of the area are based on the same foundations as those of the south-east. Southampton is the port towards the continent, Weymouth having a minor function in this respect. But Southampton is more than a southern Dover,[1] for it presents to ocean traffic, especially as a port of call, the advantage of the shortest land line to London; indeed, in this respect, the modern South-ampton constitutes a new factor in the British commercial

[1] But see note on Dover at p. 258.

system, for London, Bristol, Liverpool, and Glasgow are essentially termini of the ocean routes. Portsmouth, almost wholly dependent on the expenditure of the national revenue, is yet the largest town of the Southern counties. The railway town of Swindon, and the group of little cloth towns about the Bristol Avon, although lying within Wiltshire, belong by their function rather to the North-Western Quadrant, where it marches with the industrial half of England.

The unenclosed areas of thin upland pasturage, fit only for sheep, are more extensive than in the south-east, owing to the unbroken spread of the chalk plateau. Therefore, on account of the relatively small value of the ground, but partly also for strategical reasons, both the main stations of the field army in Great Britain are within the southern county group, at Aldershot and on Salisbury Plain.

For various reasons the railroads have no such obvious meaning upon the map as in the case of the three preceding quadrants. The Great Western system, which winds round the foot of the uplands, utilises for one of its lines the Thames gap above Reading, and for another the Kennet valley, and thus contrasts with the South-Western which strikes diagonally across the chalk upland almost without deviation, necessarily presenting steeper gradients than its competitor (Fig. 115). On the other hand, it has the compensation of a shorter mileage to Exeter.

The Further Section of the South-Western Quadrant is a long peninsula, rooted in the mainland between the westward projections of the counties Gloucester and Dorset. Rocks of ancient make compose the whole of Cornwall, most of Devon, and much even of Somerset ; so that the Devonian peninsula may be regarded as a portion of the buried floor emergent from beneath the plain, and rising into a series of upland masses, as it were the vertebrae of a spine. Owing to the disposition of these uplands, the low grounds are divided in a chain of compartments. Of these, the first is the valley of the Bristol Avon, delimited southward by the transverse upfold of the Mendips, at each end of which, towards the sea on the one hand, and towards the Jurassic scarp on the other, are entries to the second compartment. This in turn occupies the centre of Somerset, and consists largely of the drained marshes of the Parret and neighbour rivers, where the historic site of Athelney suggests a comparison with the refuge of Here-ward at Ely in the midst of the eastern fenland. Beyond are the Blackdown Hills and the Quantocks, with a gap between them, in which stands Taunton, at the gate of Devonshire. The third of the compartments spreads from Taunton southward, between the Blackdowns and Dart-moor to Exmouth and Torquay, and westward to Barnstaple Bay, between the lofty treeless uplands of Dartmoor and Exmoor, where the red deer still runs wild. This lowland is the Devon of green pasture, sunken lanes, and red cattle. To a small extent it is drained northward to the Bristol Channel, but in the main southward by the apparently consequent Exe.[1] On a bluff, looking westward, at the head of the estuary is built the city of Exeter. The fourth compartment lies to the south of Dartmoor and the Bodmin Moors, between which flows the Tamar to "the three towns" of Plymouth, Devonport, and Stonehouse; while the fifth, although smaller and less coherent, may be regarded as occupying the end of Cornwall, where tin and copper mines, pilchard fisheries, Celtic words, place-names, and traditions, and the prevalence of dark, aboriginal people impart to a group of small towns a marked individuality (*cf.* pp. 59, 80, 125).

Throughout the whole length of the district run the two competing lines of the Great Western and South-Western Railways, which cross one another at Exeter, and present the same contrast of engineering as in the Southern counties, for the Great Western winds through the coastal gap at the end of the Mendips, through the depression beyond Taunton, and round the south of Dartmoor, whereas the South-Western traverses the hilly borderland between Somerset and Dorset, climbs the high shoulders

---

[1] See note on the rivers of Devon at p. 258.

of the Blackdowns, and surmounts the watershed north of Dartmoor (Fig. 115). From the point of view of human activities, the West of England must be considered according to its several compartments, although in the days of sailing-ships it had a significance as a whole, owing to its position between the two great lanes of water traffic, leading to Bristol on the one hand, and to Southampton and London on the other. Throughout its length agriculture is conducted under the conditions of an oceanic climate. Cheese and cider were formerly, and to some extent still are, the staples of food, at any rate for the rural population. The mines and industries of Bristol, and the pleasure towns of Bath and Weston-super-Mare stand apart from the local life of the region, having connections chiefly with the metropolis and with Industrial England ; but much wholesale distribution into the west is organised from Bristol. The mid-Somerset and mid-Devon compartments are in the main agricultural, although the latter possesses two ranges of pleasure towns, with contrasted characteristics, of which Ilfracombe is the chief in the north, and Torquay in the south. Plymouth-Devonport resembles Portsmouth, and has nearly as great a population, but as a mercantile port of call corresponds also in some degree to Southampton. Dartmouth and Falmouth, to east and to west, are similar calling points, but of third and fourth rate significance. In the days of fast-sailing clippers, especially in time of war, Falmouth had a special function of its own, being the harbour nearest to the Land's End, and readiest, therefore, for the receipt of news from the ocean. In addition to Falmouth, the group of Cornish towns consists of Truro, Camborne, Redruth, St. Ives, Penzance, and, somewhat apart, Bodmin. Their metal mines and fisheries are less important than formerly, but granite, of which, as already stated, a series of bosses stand in chain down the core of the peninsula, has become an increasing source of wealth. In its decay it supplies the kaolin, which is transported by sea to the Mersey, and thence by canal to the Staffordshire potteries, for the manufacture of china. Twenty-five miles beyond the Land's End is the little group of the Scilly Isles, whose oceanic climate is of such equability that subtropical vegetation will grow, and the islanders make their chief living by the supply of early flowers to the London market.

At the focus of the four quadrants is the Great City which has grown with each addition to the territory ruled from it, each increase of the population for which it is a distributing centre, each bettering of the means of communication enabling it to outbid the local sub-centres. London is the one community of Britain whose long continued importance places it in the category of the great historic cities of Europe, beside Rome, Paris, Vienna, Bruges, Ghent, Florence, Venice, Lubeck, and Augsburg. In the Middle Ages, when Britain was a pastoral country and wool the staple export, London was a large town, and all the other centres of the land, as measured by modern standards, merely villages. The metropolis, in fact, occupied in mediæval England a position equivalent to that now held by Melbourne in the colony of Victoria, Sydney in New South Wales, and Buenos Ayres in Argentina.

London has had two lives. It first rose to greatness during the latter part of the Roman dominion in Britain, so that the city walls denied the Thames road to the Saxon barbarians. Afterwards it lay vacant, with ruined walls, and the Danes made the Thames one of their chief lines of invasion. But the second life of London had already commenced when the Conqueror crossed the Channel, and the campaign which followed the Battle of Hastings hinged almost entirely on the reserved power of the great city (Fig. 125). The Mayor of London took his place along with the Peers of the Realm among the signatories of Magna Charta. In subsequent generations London played a decisive part in the wars of Stephen, of Simon de Montfort, and of the Roses. In the great civil war the wealth and power of London was one of the ultimate causes of the overthrow of Charles the First. At the accession of James the Second the population

amounted to half a million, while Bristol, the next largest
city in England, had but thirty thousand. Within the
last hundred years, for the first time in her long history,
London has had rivals in Britain, for though her people
have now reached within the police area a total of more
than six millions, there are three other cities, Glasgow,
Manchester, and Liverpool, each of which, with its suburbs,
has a million inhabitants. Until within the last two cen-

FIG. 116.—The Position of London : Larger Considerations.

turies north-western England was poor and thinly peopled;
now it has become Industrial England, balancing Metropolitan England.

London is placed where the road from the Continent
through Kent, confined between the Thames marshes and
the Wealden forest, emerges on the banks of the river
at the head of the estuary (Fig. 116). London Bridge
is the pith and cause of London. Below, either on the
north side or the south, and often on both, are flats of

alluvium, with a breadth of at least three miles. In the earlier centuries high tide converted these into an arm of the sea, replaced at low water by a reedy fen, through which the river wound with uncertain course. The tributary flow of the Lea was through a similar though narrower marsh bottom, and the Isle of Dogs was the Lea delta, compelling the Thames to cut a bluff into the Greenwich rise on the southern shore (Fig. 117). Thus London stood

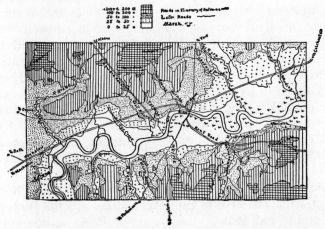

FIG. 117.—The Position of London : Smaller Considerations.

on an angle of solid ground, with tidal marsh to east and south of it, across which roads were afterwards brought on the Hackney and Newington causeways.

Once north of the Bridge the traffic was free to spread along the great fan of roads north-eastward into East Anglia, northward to Scotland, north-westward to Chester and Ireland, westward to Bristol, and south-westward to Southampton. Moreover, by the impediment which it presented to water traffic London Bridge came to mark the limit between sea and river navigation. Thus London arose on a commercial foundation. It was a bridge place, a place of transhipment from water to land and from river to sea, and a centre for the distribution of passengers and goods down the several roads.

The country ways which have guided its growth are still discernible in the maze of streets registered upon the plan. The Kent Road, heading from Rochester, crosses the Darent at Dartford, the Cray at Crayford, and the Beverly at Deptford, and appears to aim at an old ford which must once have existed at Westminster. The Edgware Road strikes directly south-eastward from the Midlands upon the same point, and there can be little doubt that the early crossing of the Thames was at Westminster, and that in pre-Roman times the Watling Street of Kent was already continued north-westward, with a slight bend only, into the track now marked by the Edgware Road and the Watling Street of the Midlands. At a later time London was built on a bluff, cut into the clay by the rush of the river, at a point where the ground is firmer than at Westminster, and the road was diverted so as to pass through it. There is a way in the City, close to St. Paul's Cathedral, still known as Watling Street, although turned from the original direction. The remainder of the ancient trunk-roads out of London radiate from the City. The Mile End Road crosses the Lea at Bow (in other words, at "the bridge" or arch), and fording the rivers of Essex at Romford, Ilford, and Chelmsford, runs ultimately to Norwich. Bishopsgate and the Kingsland Road pass northward on a gravel terrace, which extends for twenty miles between the marsh strip of the Lea and the Forest Hills of Highgate and Enfield. This becomes the North Road, leading to York and Edinburgh. Oxford Street, crossing the line of the Edgware Road and Park Lane, which are directed upon Westminster, runs westward over the Colne at Uxbridge to Oxford and Worcester. Piccadilly is part of a way which splits at Hounslow, the more northern branch bridging the Thames at Maidenhead and continuing to Bath and Bristol, the more southern making use of an ancient ford, now replaced by a bridge, at Staines (that is to say, "the stones"), and running thence over Bagshot Heath to Winchester and Southampton. South of the Thames, roads of comparatively recent construction lead through the

Wealden forests in the directions of Portsmouth and Brighton.

The City, the place of business, is the nucleus of London. London Bridge, St. Paul's Cathedral, the Mansion House, the Royal Exchange, and the Bank of England are its significant monuments. West of the City were the ancient palaces of Westminster and White-hall, for the rule of the country was necessarily drawn —in Roman times from York, in Norman times from Win-chester—to the neighbourhood of the great centre to which all news came and whence all roads led. The relative complexity of modern government is indicated by the Houses of Parliament, and by the Public Offices erected beside the Royal Palaces. Between the City and Westminster are the Law Courts and the Temple, the seats of justice and of the study of the law; to northward and westward have arisen large residential quarters dependent on West-minster, the City, and the Temple. Here are the chief artistic, literary, and scientific circles of Britain, and here, therefore, the imperial treasure houses, the British Museum and the National Gallery. Eastward of the City is the Port of London, with its great series of docks and its outports for shipping of heavy burden at Tilbury and Gravesend. North-eastward of the City, and south of the river, are the industrial quarters, which together constitute London the largest manufacturing town of the land. They have no single characteristic industry, but are employed for the most part in the miscellaneous trades which wait upon the necessities and the luxuries of a great capital.

Outside all is a vast ring of suburbs, of which Green-wich and Woolwich, Kingston and Richmond are historic. Even Windsor is a royal suburb dependent upon West-minster. The life of the great metropolis at the beginning of the twentieth century exhibits a daily throb as of a huge pulsating heart. Every evening half a million men are sent in quick streams, like corpuscles of blood in the arteries, along the railways and the trunk roads outward to the suburbs. Every morning they return, crowding into the

17

square mile or two wherein the exchanges of the world
are finally adjusted. Perhaps London Bridge is still the
most thronged of the ducts through which the humanity
of London ebbs and flows.

In a manner all south-eastern England is a single
urban community ; for steam and electricity are changing
our geographical conceptions. A city in an economic
sense is no longer an area covered continuously with
streets and houses. The wives and children of the merchants, even of the more prosperous of the artisans, live
without—beyond green fields—where the men only sleep
and pass the Sabbath. The metropolis in its largest
meaning includes all the counties for whose inhabitants
London is "Town," whose men do habitual business
there, whose women buy and spend there, whose
morning paper is printed there, whose standard of
thought is determined there. East Anglia and the West
of England possess a certain independence by virtue of
their comparatively remote position, but, for various
reasons, even they belong effectively to Metropolitan
England. Birmingham, in Industrial England, is the
nearest independent community, with its own heart-
beat, with subject boroughs which call it "Town," with
its own daily newspapers guiding opinion along lines
not wholly dictated from London.

Note on Dover.—It is not unlikely that with the completion of the
great harbour some years hence, Dover may become one of the chief
ports of England, competing with Southampton and Plymouth. Should
coal be found in the neighbourhood in paying quantities, it might grow
to be a great city.

Notes on the rivers of Devon.—A very significant clue to the origin
of the Devonian drainage is probably to be found in the relation of the
Taw to its tributary the Mole. The Taw, apparently an obsequent river,
flowing NNW., intercepts the southward Mole at an acute back angle (*cf.*
the Clyde, p. 131). The Mole seems to have been one of the consequent
heads of the Exe (*cf.* p. 125).

Note on authorities.—For the topographical detail of Britain consult
the great series of county handbooks issued by Murray, with maps by
Bartholomew. To these, for the more hilly portions of the land, should
be added Baddeley's "Thorough" Guides. Some of the handbooks

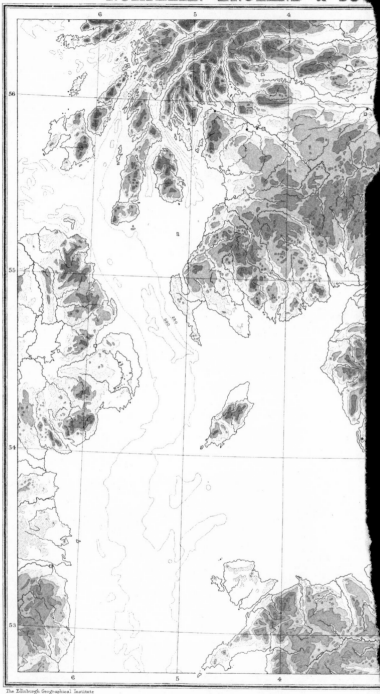

Scale = 1: 2,250,000
English Miles

Kilometres

REFERENCE
TO COLOURING

FEET		METRES
3000		914
2000		610
1000		305
500		152
250		76
SEA LEVEL		SEA LEVEL
250		76
500		152

HEIGHT OF LAND

DEPTH OF SEA

POPULATION
OF TOWNS

500,000
100,000
50,000
20,000

J.G.Bartholomew.

published in connection with the meetings of the British Association are of considerable value, especially for the neighbourhood of the great provincial towns. "The Book of British Topography" (1881), by J. P. Anderson, is an elaborate bibliography of topography and topographical history. On the railways, see Ackworth's "Railways of England" and "Railways of Scotland." One of the later editions of Paterson's "Roads" may be referred to for the highways.

There are valuable papers by Mr. G. G. Chisholm on "The Distribution of Towns and Villages in England" in the *Geog. Jour.*, vol. ix. p. 76, and vol. x. p. 511. No exhaustive analytical account, however, of the details of British geography will be possible until the results of the various surveys have been co-ordinated and supplemented in the manner suggested by Dr. H. R. Mill in his "Fragment of the Geography of England," *Geog. Jour.*, vol. xv. pp. 205 and 353.

For London and Westminster, see Sir W. Besant's volumes, especially his "South London" and "Westminster." Also from an antiquarian standpoint, Hare's "Walks in London." And from an economic standpoint, Booth's "Life and Labour of the People of London" (9 vols.).

CHAPTER XV

INDUSTRIAL ENGLAND

INDUSTRIAL England is built on a broader scale than Metropolitan England. It consists of fewer and larger natural elements, but has no obvious topographical centre. Essentially it is formed of two great upland blocks, the Cambrian and the Pennine, and of the plain of New Red sand and clay, which, commencing in the Cheshire gap, spreads on the one hand southward to the Bristol C and on the other northward through the Vale o the coast of Durham. From the Pennine-Camb transverse streams descend eastward and sou to be gathered up by the longitudinal Ouse, T Avon-Severn, and to be cast into the sea by t of the Humber and the Bristol Channel. North of the divide a large part of the drainage is car the south-eastern corner of the Irish Sea by t of the Mersey and Dee, while the valley of lies apart in Cumbria, behind the group of mountains. The coal basins, which have im specific character to the region, are disposed areas. In the centre they envelop the souther the Pennine range, and edge the Cambrian upland its north-eastern border : in the south they spread from Glamorgan across the lower Severn to Bristol : in the north they underlie the Northumbrian and Cumbrian coastal sills. A triple correspondence is discernible in the location of the denser populations (Fig. 118). The Cambrian and Pennine Uplands, together with the Southern Uplands of Scotland, are, for the most part, given over to the pasturage of sheep, while dairying has long been productive in the clay bottoms, once choked with forest, of

Cheshire, of the Trent valley, and of the Avon and Severn valleys. To all of these the Bristol and Cheshire gaps admit something of the oceanic climate (*cf.* pp. 83, 111, 176).

From the point of view of communications it is clear that three trunk-ways must always have entered the region from the direction of the metropolis, one running westward to the lower Severn and South Wales, another northward through the Vale of York to the east coast of Scotland, and a third north-westward through the Cheshire gap, there branching, on the one hand, along the west of the Pennines to Cumberland and the west of Scotland, and, on the other hand, through the north of Wales towards Ireland. But modern industrial conditions, no less than Roman military necessities, demand a series of lateral connecting roads. In each case the points of critical importance are to the north-east, the north-west, and the south-west; at the ports of Hull, Liverpool, and Bristol in the later period; and at the legionary stations of York, Chester, and Caerleon in the earlier. Thus the chief lateral ways, whether modern railways or Roman roads, have traversed the southern end of the Pennines from east to west, skirted the eastern border of Wales from north to south, and struck diagonally across the plain in a direction generally parallel to the Jurassic edge, as in the case of the Midland railroad and the Roman Fossway.

Despite its massive structure, the subdivision of Industrial England for the purposes of more detailed description presents certain difficulties. These are principally due to the fact that the original organisation of society, based on the waterways, has been masked to a far greater extent than in Metropolitan England by growth under later conditions. The development of the coalfields has led to the settlement of vast populations upon the high ground near the watersheds rather than upon the banks of the navigable rivers. Especially is this the case with the district round Birmingham, in the very heart of the land (Fig. 62). On the whole, it

appears best to accept a division into five districts, four
of them ranged from north to south-west chiefly upon
the consequent slope from the Pennine-Cambrian divide,
and one to include most of the slope towards the Irish
Sea. Named in the order convenient for their description,
they are—(1) The four counties of the western midlands,
Warwick, Worcester, Stafford, and Shropshire; (2) the
counties of the lower Severn and South Wales, that is
to say, Gloucester, Hereford, Monmouth, Glamorgan,
Brecknock, Radnor, Cardigan, Carmarthen, and Pembroke; (3) the counties of the Cheshire gap and North
Wales, that is to say, Lancashire, Cheshire, Flint, Denbigh, Carnarvon, Anglesea, Merioneth, and Montgomery;
(4) the five counties of the Humber basin, York, Derby,
Nottingham, Leicester, and Lincoln ; and (5) the counties
of the far north, Northumberland, Durham, Cumberland,
and Westmorland.

Although the four counties of the Western Midlands
present an outline roughly quadrangular, the arrangement
of the essential features of the district is markedly triangular. The abrupt southern end of the Pennine upland
and the eastern edge of the Cambrian upland determine
the lie of two sides, while the third consists of the Jurassic
edge, placed diagonally from south-west to north-east
(Fig. 119). Within this framework, and lying parallel
to it, are the three valleys of the eastward Trent, the
southward Severn, and the south-westward Avon ; and
almost precisely in the midst of the triangle of rivers,
on the parting between the Severn and the Trent waters,
is the elevated tract known as the Black Country, rising
above the New Red lowlands (Fig. 62). As a whole, the
west midlands differ in aspect from the east midlands and
from East Anglia, and resemble the south-east and the
south of England, for a number of detached hill groups
have a nearly uniform elevation of between 800 and 1000
feet, a height which is exceeded only towards the Welsh
border in the Wrekin and Malvern peaks (cf. p. 61). Of
the more centrally placed features a belt of short ranges

is conspicuous, consisting of Cannock Chase, the Dudley and Lickey Hills, and the Alcester Hills, which together form the median of the five axes of carboniferous uplift radiating from the Peak end of the Pennine range (*cf.* p. 95). In its middle portion this ridge constitutes the divide between the Stour, which is tributary to the Severn, and the Tame, which flows into the Trent, and here, immediately below the crest line, on one of the head-waters of the Tame, stands Birmingham. But the older life of the region lay almost wholly along the river courses, and the centre of the triangle must have been nearly vacant. North-eastward, among the low-lying meadows where the Tame joins the Trent, are Lichfield and Tamworth, the centres of the Mercian kingdom and of the great diocese which extended to the Ribble. It was in this neighbourhood, also, that Watling Street, trending north-westward along the frontier of Warwickshire and Leicestershire, was diverted westward to pass through the gap between the heights of Cannock Chase and Dudley, and to strike the Severn at Wroxeter, beside the Wrekin. Further to the north are the old county towns of Stafford, near the Trent, and Shrewsbury, on the Severn. The cathedral city of Worcester is placed lower down the Severn. Some of the most celebrated sites of English history lie ranged along and about the historic stream of the Avon—Naseby, Lutterworth, Coventry, Kenilworth, Warwick, Stratford, Evesham, and Tewkesbury ; although the first two and the last are just beyond the boundaries of the four counties. The people of Stratford, in the midst of a practical community, have rested the prosperity of their town upon a literary memory. In the Middle Ages, before the development of the industries of the north-west, the Avon was like a moat in front of the Jurassic edge, the massive bulwark of Metropolitan England. When the traveller crossed its stream he entered a wilderness of lowland forests and upland moors, occupying most of the further part of South Britain. The passenger by train may now be said to enter Industrial England when he has crossed the

Warwick Avon by the Great-Western Railway at Evesham or Leamington, or by the North-Western or Great Central Railways at Rugby (Fig. 119).

The life of the Black Country is based upon a coalfield

FIG. 118.—The Density of Population of Industrial England in 1891.
After BOSSE, *by permission of* BARTHOLOMEW.

which strikes north and south for twenty miles, from Cannock Chase to the Clent Hills. The Great Western and North-Western lines, having converged upon Birmingham from Leamington and Rugby, traverse the coalfield side by side for twelve miles to Wolverhampton. Midway between Birmingham and Wolverhampton stands Wednesbury, with Walsall to the right, and Dudley to the left. The whole district is one great workshop, both above ground and below. At night it is lurid with the flames of the iron furnaces ; by day it appears one vast, loosely-knit town of humble homes, amid cinder heaps

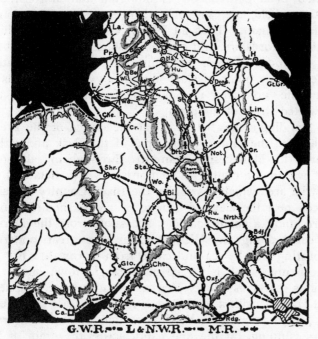

G.W.R.⌒ L & N.W.R. ⌒ M.R. ✚✚

FIG. 119.—The Railways of the Midland Plains of England.

and fields stripped of vegetation by smoke and fumes. Birmingham, with more than half a million inhabitants, is estimated just beyond the south-eastern border of the coalfield. As in the case of the other great urban communities of Britain, the core of the city has lately been reconstructed. All around are dependent industrial towns, for which Birmingham is the market. Northeastward on the Trent is the brewing town of Burton ;

eastward on a small detached coalfield are Tamworth and
Nuneaton ; south-eastward is the cycle town of Coventry ;
south-westward are the nail-making centres, Bromsgrove
and Redditch, and beyond them Worcester with its potteries ;
westward is carpet-making Kidderminster ; north-westward,
near the Severn, upon another little coalfield, are the iron
towns of Wellington and Coalbrookdale, while northward
is boot-making Stafford. Leamington and Malvern, still
further afield, are, in some degree, residential suburbs
of Birmingham. Thus all Warwickshire, Worcestershire,
south Staffordshire, and mid-Shropshire have Birmingham
for the focus of their economic life, which is ultimately
based on the block of Coal Measures, with rich bands of
ironstone, upheaved in South Staffordshire through the
New Red strata of the plain.

Standing somewhat apart, at the source of the Trent,
high upon the south-western spur of the Peak and rather
nearer to Manchester than to Birmingham, although
just within the county of Staffordshire, is a detached industrial area which resembles the Black Country in being
placed near the elevated ground of a watershed (Fig. 62).
Here, upon a small coalfield, accessible from the Mersey
by canal along the Weaver valley, are great potteries,
importing clay by sea and canal from Cornwall. For six
miles runs what is in effect a single town known in
various parts as Stoke, Newcastle-under-Lyne, Burslem,
and Hanley, with a joint population of at least 200,000.

Birmingham is at the intersection of important railways running, on the one hand, across the grain of the
country from London to the Cheshire gap, and, on the
other hand, with the grain from the Trent to the Severn
(Fig. 119). The main line of the North-Western Company,
seeking the most level way from London to the Cheshire
gap, passes along the Tame and Trent valleys, by Nuneaton,
Tamworth, Lichfield, and Stafford, and leaves the high
ground of the Black Country to the left ; but there are a
series of loops in connection with this line, of which the
first is to the right hand, through Northampton to Rugby ;
the second to the left hand, from Rugby, through Birming-

ham and Wolverhampton, to Stafford ; and the third from junctions north and south of Stafford, through the Potteries, to Stockport and Manchester. The Great Western line has a trend corresponding to the North-Western, from Oxford and Leamington, through Birmingham and Wolverhampton, to Shrewsbury and Chester. Of the cross country lines, the most important belongs to the Midland system, and passes from Lincoln and Newark, through Nottingham, Derby, Burton, and Birmingham, to Gloucester and Bristol, while an express route of the Great Western runs from Birmingham, through Worcester and Hereford, to Cardiff. Birmingham is about equally distant by rail from Liverpool and Bristol, and only a little more remote from London and Hull. It thus profits by the competition of four rival ports.

Notwithstanding the proud sentiment of nationality, and the possession in common of an independent mother tongue (Fig. 93), North and South Wales are now for many purposes more intimately connected with the adjoining parts of England than with each other. Wales was the massive upland refuge (Fig. 32) of the Britons when driven from the English plain, but the growth of a Welsh state has always been hindered by the transverse lie— east and west—of the chief valleys and coast roads. As early as the eleventh century alien strongholds were planted along the upper Severn, and a wedge of Englishry forced between the north and south Welsh (*cf.* p. 211). In modern times the tendency has been accentuated by the increase of coastwise traffic to Liverpool and to Bristol, the construction of trunk railways from London to Holyhead and to Milford, and the development of the coalfields of Flint and Denbigh, o.. the one hand, and of Glamorgan on the other. The relative difficulty of access between north and south is such, that when of late the Federal University of Wales was being organised, and men from Cardiff, Aberystwith, and Bangor wished to confer, Shrewsbury, lying beyond the Welsh border, was the most available place of meeting. There is no town in Wales whose site has "nodality" enough to raise it to the position of capital of the Principality.[1]

The counties of the lower Severn and South Wales may therefore be regarded as constituting a single group by virtue of their physical and economic relations. From Worcester to Gloucester the Severn flows southward parallel to the Malvern ridge, but from Gloucester it turns south-westward, and gradually broadens into a trumpet-shaped estuary. This is sharply constricted where islets in mid-channel, the Steep and Flat Holms, indicate the lie of the denuded Mendip upfold. Thence the waterway turns westward, broadening into the Bristol Channel. To north of the first reach of the Channel proper is a rectangular salient formed of a plain of soft Jurassic rocks adherent to Wales, though no part of its structure. This plain, which was the original Morganwg, must formerly have spread across to the shore of Somerset (*cf.* pp. 86, 102).

Within the Holms the Severn estuary receives three rivers from the north, the Wye, the Usk, and the Taff, and one from the east, the Bath Avon. It flows through a broad alley, floored with New Red clay, the high escarpment of the Cotswolds being to the left hand, and the faulted edge (*cf.* p. 87) of the Malvern Hills and of the Forest of Dean to the right (Fig. 47). Two small Carboniferous uplands pierce the New Red floor, the one bearing the Bristol coalfield, the other that of the Forest of Dean. The Avon and the Wye intersect these uplands, making picturesque gorges through the Carboniferous limestone at Clifton, on the one hand, and on the other between Monmouth and Chepstow (Figs. 64, 65).

West of the Malverns, and north of Monmouth, spreads the fertile Herefordshire plain, formed of Old Red sandstone, and differing, therefore, in nature from all other portions of the English lowland, although resembling certain parts of Scotland (*cf.* p. 87). From its western margin rises the dark edge of the Cambrian

[1] On nodality, see page 239.

upland, through which emerge, by deep-cut notches, the eastward valleys of the upper Wye and upper Usk. Immediately to the south of the Usk valley, in the Brecknock Beacons, are heights of nearly 3000 feet, and from these a series of parallel streams, of which the chief is the Taff, descend south-eastward into the Severn estuary.

Apart from the great trough-formed vale of the lower Severn, apart too from the little plain of Morganwg, all the structure of the region, as well in the English borderland of Hereford and Monmouth, as in South Wales proper, is of Old Red and Carboniferous date. A watershed strikes through it southward from the Silurian country of Plinlimmon, throwing the rivers Wye and Usk *eastward* and southward in great consequent and subsequent reaches, and the Towy and Teifi *westward* and southward in symmetrical bends. The Towy finds a mouth at Carmarthen, to south of the Pembroke peninsula, and the Teifi at Cardigan, to north. The same eastward and westward trend of the country, which is evident in the lie of the Brecknock Beacons and of the upper valleys of the Wye, Usk, Towy, and Teifi, is also indicated in the coastal features of St. David's Head, St. Bride's Bay, Milford Haven, the peninsula of Gower, the plain of Glamorgan, and the Bristol Channel. But the Malvern ridge runs southward in a direction parallel to the lower reaches of the Wye and Usk ; the Cotswold edge south-westward parallel to the Severn estuary ; and the Mendip upfold, continued in the Holm islets, west-north-westward parallel to the Bath Avon.

Thus the whole district may be regarded as consisting of five natural elements—(1) the western promontory of South Wales, where it slopes through Cardiganshire and Carmarthenshire into the comparatively low-lying county of Pembroke ; (2) the upland counties of Radnor and Brecknock, delimited steeply towards the east ; (3) the lowland plain of Herefordshire, between the edge of the Welsh upland and the Malvern ridge ; (4) the coastal sill of Monmouth, with the plain of Morganwg west of Cardiff ;

and (5) the vale of the lower Severn in Gloucestershire and north Somerset, as far as the transverse Mendip ridge.

Twice at least in the early history of Britain must conquerors from the narrow seas have crossed the limestone upland of the Cotswolds and looked down from its brink upon the vale of Berkeley and Gloucester. (1) From Silchester the Romans advanced to a base at Cirencester, where the ascent to the upland begins, and thence to the Severn, founding a great colony at Gloucester, where they bridged the river. But establishing themselves also at Bath, and among the lead mines of the Mendips, they had occasion to institute ferries lower down the Severn, at points subsequently known as the Old and the New Passages, the former now marked by the Midland Railway bridge to the Dean collieries, and the latter by the Severn Tunnel. The New Passage, being placed below the mouth of the Wye, gave direct access to the great legionary centre of Caerleon on the Usk, thus avoiding the traverse at Chepstow. From Gloucester to Caerleon, and along the coastal sill into Pembroke beyond, the road leads across the lower reaches of a series of rivers, and here, in consequence, have sprung up since Roman times a succession of towns, each a bridge place and a port, Chepstow, Newport, Cardiff, Neath, Swansea, and Carmarthen. Similarly, the way from Gloucester towards Exeter crosses the Bath Avon at a point immediately above the Clifton gorge, and here Bristol has been built, beside a bridge and at the head of a navigation. (2) The West Saxon Hwiccas, when they had overthrown the Britons in the battle of Deorham, near Bath, descended to the waters of the Severn, and thence seized the Roman settlements of Gloucester and Worcester. Being impeded, however, by the rapids upon the lower Wye, they must have marched overland to Hereford either from Gloucester or Worcester ; for the lower Wye became the boundary of England towards Wales, not the approach to Hereford, although that city was from the earliest times attached to England. The three allied dioceses of

Gloucester, Worcester, and Hereford record the Hwiccan realm. In the coastal entry, Glamorgan and Monmouth became the land of Gwent and the diocese of Llandaff ; while the remainder of South Wales, from Pembroke, up the Teifi and the Towy and down the Wye and the Usk to their emergence from the upland, were the land of Dinefawr, and ecclesiastically the diocese of St. David's (Figs. 99, 104).

The industry of the region now centres in the two great towns of Bristol and Cardiff. Bristol grew to importance in connection with the trade to Ireland, incidentally, no doubt, maintaining the detached English colony in Pembrokeshire, and it still has a great importation of Irish cattle. But after the discovery of America, the merchants of Bristol adapted their resources to the new trade in colonial produce, and still have great commerce in sugar, tobacco, and cocoa. The West Indian fruit trade promises a modern development of the same traffic. In rear of Bristol is a range of small towns, extending from Trowbridge on the Avon, to Stroud in a transverse valley of the Cotswolds. Here the wool of the Cotswolds was woven, and with the aid of Bristol coal, the West of England cloth industry has been maintained even against the competition of the West Riding of Yorkshire. Under the shelter of the Cotswold edge are the two large residential towns of Cheltenham and Bath.

Cardiff, Newport, and Swansea, with inland Merthyr Tydvil, are dependent upon the great coalfield of South Wales, whose coal, largely of anthracitic character, is the chief source of the smokeless fuel employed by the war fleets and the mail steamers of the world. It is the one raw product still exported on a vast scale by Britain. Ores of iron and other metals are imported to South Wales, and, together with such iron ore as is produced locally, are smelted in its furnaces, especially for the making of rails, and in connection with the tinplate industry. At Pembroke, on Milford Haven, is one of the minor dockyards of the British Navy, and a base for the defence both of the Bristol and the St. George's Channels.

Herefordshire presents a singular contrast, both to the barren uplands which border it on the north-west, and to the busy fields of industry which lie around it in other directions. It is one of the most rural districts yet remaining in England, and with its red soil, red cattle, and apple orchards is enriched with many a landscape suggestive of Devonshire. A gulf of oceanic warmth and moisture extends up the valley of the Severn between the Cotswold edge and the Welsh upland (Figs. 85, 90).

The Great Western railroad system repeats in a general way the lie of the Roman roads. From Swindon diverge the lines to Gloucester, to the Severn tunnel, and to Exeter. A more direct line, avoiding Bristol, is being constructed from Swindon to the tunnel (Fig. 119).

North Wales and the Cheshire Gap bear the same relation to each other that do South Wales and the valley of the lower Severn, but the economic importance of the parts is reversed; for in North Wales there is no great coalfield equivalent to that of Glamorgan and Monmouthshire, while the industries of the lower Severn are small when compared with those of the Mersey. On the whole, the structure of the northern Welsh region is simpler than that of the south. The rich meadow-plain of Cheshire spreads over New Red clays, beneath which is coal too deep to be won ; but the coal-beds are uptilted on either margin, against the edge of the Cambrian upland to the west and on the flank of the Pennine moors to the east (Fig. 45). From the heights on the right hand descend the head-streams of the Mersey ; from those of the left hand, through the transverse vale of Llangollen, emerges the Dee ; but the two rivers remain apart, divided by the Wirral peninsula, and there is no general gathering of the waters as in the estuary of the Severn. In North Wales, within the great bend of the Dee, are the valleys, cleft into the upland, of the Clwyd and Conway ; beyond these is the serrate range of Snowdon ; and remotest of all are the meadows of Gwineth, on either bank of

the Menai Strait.   Here are the little cathedral city of Bangor and the English castles of Conway, Carnarvon, and
Beaumaris, tokens respectively of the Celtic principality
and of the Edwardian conquest.   The land of Powys, in
the upper Severn valley, about Montgomery, Welshpool,
and Newtown, belongs physically and historically neither
to North nor to South Wales, nor yet to Chester or Bristol,
but rather to Shrewsbury and the English midland (*cf.*
pp. 124, 125).

Chester was at once the Caerleon, the Gloucester, and
the Bristol of the north, and yet—because the Dee does
not receive the Mersey—at a disadvantage as compared
with each of the three.   It was the centre of the Roman
military border, with roads to York on the one hand, and
to Caerleon on the other.   The Northumbrian conquest
of it marked a critical advance of the Angle settlements,
for the dominion of the Britons was thereby severed into
Wales and Cumberland.   Under the Norman kings, the
Earls Marcher of Chester ruled from the Clwyd to the
Ribble (Fig. 102).   In the later Middle Ages there was
a busy traffic with Dublin, but Chester lost its early
relative importance when the Dee became choked with
deposits.   The great macadamised road from London to
Ireland was constructed, not by the coastway, through
Chester, Rhyl, and Conway, which is followed by the
modern railway, but in a direct line from Shrewsbury,
through the gorge of Llangollen, across the head of the
Conway valley at Bettws-y-Coed, and by a notch in the
Snowdon range to the Menai Bridge and Holyhead.

Cheshire and Anglesea are now among the more
prosperous agricultural districts of Britain, a fact partly
due to the dairy-farms, flourishing under conditions of
oceanic moisture, and partly to the neighbourhood of
insatiable markets.   Along the Weaver valley, in the
midst of rural Cheshire, are the New Red salt mines of
Northwich, Middlewich, and Nantwich.   Slate is quarried
in the Welsh mountains, and coal is raised on their
border, in Flintshire and Denbighshire.

But the chief activities of the region lie beyond the
18

Mersey. Here in south Lancashire—merely an outlying border of Domesday Cheshire—a tongue of moorland is thrust south-westward in the direction of Liverpool, between the Mersey and the Ribble. At the southern foot of this higher ground, where the streams converge from the Lancashire and from the Pennine hills, are Manchester and Salford, a single city for all purposes except that of local government. Manchester is now rather a market than a manufacturing town, and since the construction of the Ship Canal from the Mersey it is becoming a seaport. Around, in a great ring, are the large industrial towns of Warrington, St. Helens, Wigan, Bolton, Bury, Rochdale, Oldham, Stalybridge, and Stockport. Macclesfield, further to the south, belongs to the same trade area. Eccles, to the west of Manchester, and Altrincham and Knutsford in Cheshire, are the residential suburbs. Four thousand masters, drawn from all the neighbour towns, do business twice a week in Manchester Royal Exchange. Because of easy access from America, because of the damp climate —suitable for the working of fibre, at the western foot of the Pennines, and because of the hereditary skill of the population, Lancashire is mainly occupied with the spinning and weaving of cotton. There is a certain division of labour as between town and town; thus Bolton spins the fine counts and Oldham the coarse. There are also many industries more or less incidental to the cotton trade, the making of spinning and weaving machinery, for instance, at Oldham, and of the chemicals used in dyeing at Widnes and St. Helens.

On the north side of the moorlands, in the Ribble valley, are other towns of the same group, Accrington, Darwen, Burnley, Blackburn, and Preston. Although more remote, these too have Manchester for their trade centre. It is at Manchester that the spun yarn and the woven fabrics are sold, but the raw cotton is bought at Liverpool, the port of entry for the whole district. Chester was once the chief port of this region, and Ireland the goal of the trade ; but, as already stated, the Dee was gradually encumbered with silt, while the Mersey has remained open and accessible even to the large vessels employed in the American trade, a fact chiefly due to the shape of the Mersey estuary and to the resultant scour of the tidal water passing to and fro through the narrow passage at the mouth (*cf.* p. 41). On either hand of this passage stand Liverpool-Bootle and Birkenhead, a single commercial organism, bound together by ferries and a railway tunnel. Liverpool is the port not merely of Manchester, or even of the Manchester district, but for many purposes of all the great industrial area which lies between Liverpool, Leeds, and Birmingham. For passengers and mails it serves also London, and to some extent the Continent of Europe. Southport and Blackpool, Llandudno and the north coast of Wales, Douglas and the Isle of Man, Buxton and the Peak of Derbyshire are the playgrounds of Manchester and Liverpool. Even the vacant moorlands of North Wales and Westmorland belong to the same economic province, for Manchester draws its water supply from Thirlmere in the north, and Liverpool has constructed a great reservoir in the Vyrnwy valley, which is tributary to the Severn.

If there be a centre of Industrial England in any sense equivalent to that of Metropolitan England, it lies here beyond the Cheshire gap. Separate lines of railway converge upon Manchester from Chester, Crewe, the Potteries, Derby, Sheffield, Huddersfield, Leeds, Bradford, Burnley, Preston, and Liverpool. From the direction of London the Great-Western line enters the district along the eastern edge of Wales, by Ruabon and Wrexham on the Denbighshire coalfield ; the North-Western comes to Crewe, there dividing to Manchester and to Liverpool ; the Midland makes use of the transverse Wye valley (*cf.* p. 126), in order to surmount the Peak towards Stockport and Manchester ; while the Great Central passes from Sheffield over the Pennine ridge immediately to the north of the Peak (Fig. 119). Parallel railways connect Manchester with Liverpool, and a hundred and twenty expresses cross between the two places each day. It is proposed to bind them together by means of an electric railway with trains running at more than a hundred miles an hour. The magnitude of the facts may be appreciated if it is borne in mind that here, in one small district of England, are twin cities each of nearly a million inhabitants, and that in all the world of white men there are only five other non-metropolitan cities on as great a scale—Glasgow, Hamburg, Moscow, Philadelphia, and Chicago.

By virtue of their single river system, the Humber Counties are perhaps more coherent than any other division of South Britain. Along their western border is the broad Pennine upland, trenched by the dales of eastward streams, which rise near its western margin (*cf.* p. 126). These are gathered together by the subsequent channels of the Ouse and Trent, beyond which are the Jurassic and Cretaceous uplands of the Lincolnshire and Yorkshire Wolds, the Lincoln "Cliff," and the North York Moors. Through these the whole of the Pennine drainage is ultimately carried seaward by a single transverse estuary, the Humber (Fig. 61). As a consequence of this formation there are six successive zones ranged between the Pennine-Cambrian divide and the shore of the North Sea:—(1) the Pennine upland (Fig. 35), mostly of millstone grit; (2) the Pennine slope, consisting, from Leeds to Nottingham, of a single field of Coal Measures, sixty miles in length; (3) the low plain of New Red clay along the courses of the Ouse and Trent, overlaid in its centre, about the head of the Humber, by the alluvium of Hatfield Chase; (4) the belt of Jurassic limestone, with an edge rising above the Trent Valley, and a more lofty extremity in the North York Moors; (5) the belt of Chalk upland extending through East Lincolnshire from the Wash to the Humber, overlapping the Jurassic strata in south-eastern Yorkshire, and curving finally into the cliffs of Flamborough Head; and (6) the marsh belt along the coast of Lincolnshire, and in the Holderness district of Yorkshire. The last three zones belong structurally and by climate to Metropolitan England, but are otherwise inseparable from the Humber basin, and of late the activities of the great coalfield have invaded them, not merely in the Humber ports or the coastal watering-places, but also in the iron-mining district of Lincolnshire. Cleveland, at the sea-foot of the North York Moors, although within Yorkshire, belongs rather to the Northumbrian field of industry.

In addition to the breach made by the Humber, there are three notable gaps through the hill ranges which define the axial lowland of the Ouse-Trent basin. The Trent enters by a depression in the south-west between the salient angle of the Peak and the isolated granitic upland of Charnwood Forest (Fig. 119). Further north the Pennine range is cut transversely in the midst by the Aire valley, offering an easy way into South Lancashire (Fig. 31); while the Vale of Pickering, between the North York Moors and the Yorkshire Wolds where they trend eastward to Flamborough Head, affords access from the plain of the Ouse to the coast at Scarborough (Fig. 61). The shore line consists of two very different stretches; it lies low along the edge of the marshes, from Gibraltar Point to Bridlington, but is broken and steep from Flamborough Head, past Scarborough and Whitby, to Cleveland or the "Cliff Land."

From an agricultural standpoint the Humber basin consists of three belts. (1) On the Pennine uplands are great pastures, the commencement of a sheep run which extends over most of the southern upland of Scotland. It was on the local wool and the number of rapid streams that the industrial activity of the West Riding was originally founded. (2) The Vales of York and Trent, once choked with forest, have been reduced to meadow-land, especially in the south, for in the north moisture is somewhat deficient owing to the rain-shadow cast by the Pennine upland. (3) Prior to the recent general decrease in the cultivation of corn, the Jurassic and Cretaceous upland was one of the great wheat-fields of England. The East Riding is, therefore, grouped with Lincolnshire and Norfolk in the classification of counties adopted for statistical purposes by the Board of Agriculture (Fig. 128).

Throughout recorded history, as well in Roman as in mediæval times, the main road to Scotland lay through the valley of the Trent and Ouse. York, Lincoln, and Leicester were the Roman cities of the district. York was the station of the legion in w'.ose charge was the defence of the provincial frontier against the Caledonians. Lincoln was at the point of convergence of the Fossway from Bath and Leicester, of Ermine Street from Colchester, and of the North Road from York (Fig. 98). But even under the Romans the natural waterway, on the whole the most available in Britain, must have been utilised for heavy traffic. A canal still in use, known as the Foss Dyke, from the Witham at Lincoln to the Trent above Gainsborough, is said to be of Roman construction. The Angles and the Danes entered by the Humber, and their towns were built on the river banks at York, Nottingham, Derby, Leicester, and Lincoln, and at Stamford on the Welland. For convenience of access when the Roman roads had decayed, the diocese of York extended up the Trent to Nottingham, and that of Lincoln spread down the Witham, and up the Wash rivers to beyond Bedford and Northampton (Fig. 104). The land way of a later time crossed the Trent at Newark and the Don at Doncaster. Thus the original settlements lay beside the rivers, and with the exceptions of Lincoln and Nottingham, upon low grounds.

But in the last two centuries a vast population has gathered on the higher land of the Pennine Coal Measures. Owing to the long outline of the coalfield, and to the variety of its industries, no single town has here the importance of a Manchester, or even of a Birmingham ; but there is a constellation of great cities of the third rank. Leeds, Sheffield, Nottingham, and Leicester are ranged northward and southward along the zone of the Pennine slope. In the north the coalfield is broader than in the south, and here, in consequence, to the west of Leeds, is a fifth city, Bradford, and to the south-west the towns of Halifax and Huddersfield. Woollens and iron, in different forms, are the chief products of the industry of the region.

The communications with the outer world are in part through Liverpool, and in part through the Humber ports of Hull, Grimsby, and Goole. Hull is the sixth of the great cities of the Humber area. Scarborough, Whitby, Cleethorpes, and Skegness are the watering-places on the coast, Harrowgate and Buxton those of the uplands.

Two lines of railway from the metropolis to Scotland pass through the length of the Humber counties (Fig. 119). Of these the East Coast line, owned in successive parts by the Great Northern and the North-Eastern Companies, follows the more level way from Peterborough through Newark, Doncaster, and York (Fig. 61), but as a consequence traverses no densely peopled area south of Durham. The Midland Railway, on the other hand, strikes by a difficult road through Leicester, Nottingham, Sheffield, and Leeds, and thence through the Aire gap into Edendale and to Carlisle. The chief cross country lines—the Great Central, the Lancashire and Yorkshire, and the North-Eastern—diverge from the Humber ports to Leeds and Sheffield, and converge again upon Liverpool.

The district contained in the four Northern Counties consists essentially of two form-elements, which express themselves both in the relief and the outline. The East Coast lies nearly parallel to the Pennine axis, and is cleft at right angles by a series of consequent rivers, of which the largest are the Tyne, the Wear, and the Tees. On the other hand, the West Coast is salient at St. Bees Head, and contains the knot of Lake mountains, culminating in Helvellyn and Skiddaw, upon which a radial system of drainage has been developed through long, deep glen-lakes. Were it not for the saddle of Shap Fell, a thousand feet high, the Lake mountains would be severed from the Pennine by the longitudinal valleys of the Lune and the Eden (Fig. 31). Tyneside is connected transversely with Edendale by the deeply trenched Tyne gap, and the activities of the Northumbrian and Cumbrian slopes of the mid-British isthmus are thus in some degree bound together.

Historically, however, as is suggested by the separate

dioceses of Durham and Carlisle (Fig. 104), the two sides of the country have stood more or less apart. Cumbria apparently resisted Northumbrian influence, acting through the Tyne gap, more effectively than the less productive coastland of Lancashire was able to oppose invasion through the Aire gap. But in Roman times, and after the Norman Conquest, the road through the Tyne gap was of inestimable value for the defence of South Britain. The Stuart raid into England in 1745 was by the west coast over Shap Fell.

The counties of Northumberland and Durham, and that district of Yorkshire which is known as Cleveland, constitute a region apart, with more than a million inhabitants. They are surrounded on all sides by the sea or by moorlands, except for three natural gateways. The road from York and the south enters at Northallerton, between the North York and the Pennine Moors ; the road from Scotland enters near Alnwick and Bamburgh, between the sea and the Cheviot Hills ; and the western passway comes from Carlisle through the Tyne valley. Newcastle is thus at the focus of the roads in the heart of the densely peopled area. The lower reaches of the rivers Tyne, Wear, and Tees are the scenes of chief activity. Coal in close proximity to the sea is the origin of the wealth ; engineering and shipbuilding are the principal industries. The towns are really three, each ranged along a water street. The first is known in different parts as Newcastle, Gateshead, Jarrow, South Shields, North Shields, and Tynemouth ; the second is Sunderland and Wearmouth ; the third is Darlington, Stockton, Middlesborough, and Hartlepool. With the exception of Newcastle, which had a trade in coal with London in Tudor times, all the industrial towns of the north are very recent as compared with the fortress-city of Durham, whose cathedral and castle crown a rocky, almost river-girt peninsula on the Wear.

Along the north-western foot of the Cumbrian hills lies a detached coalfield spreading far under Solway Firth, and upon this, along the coast, extends a chain of towns,

Maryport, Workington, and Whitehaven. Further north, where the roads converge from Maryport in the west, Newcastle in the east, Lancaster in the south, and Scotland in the north, in the midst of a fertile plain forming the southern shore of Solway Firth and the delta of the Eden, is the ancient city of Carlisle, which holds the western gateway from Scotland into England. The southern foot of the Lake mountains is fringed by the detached Lancashire district of Furness, rich with hæmatite ore and steel industries.

The Scottish and the English railway-systems connect at Berwick and at Carlisle. The latter, owing to its position midway between Glasgow and the great industrial centres of England, is one of the chief railway junctions in the kingdom (Fig. 121). Thence the lines radiate (1) to Whitehaven and the Cumbrian coalfield; (2) through Lancaster to Liverpool, Manchester, and London; (3) through Leeds to London; (4) to Newcastle; (5) through Galashiels to Edinburgh; (6) through Carstairs to Edinburgh, Aberdeen, and Glasgow; (7) through Kilmarnock to Glasgow; and (8) through Stranraer to Belfast. The course of each of these eight lines is a detailed commentary on the configuration of the country. Each of them belongs to a separate company, but all the lines of Northumberland and Durham, on the other hand, are the property of a single company, the North-Eastern, of which Newcastle is the centre.

Notes on authorities.—For general references, see note on p. 259. There should be added to the list of papers given in Note 4 on p. 145, a prize essay by Mr. Cowper Reed on the "Geological History of the Rivers of East Yorkshire," an epitome of which will be found in the *Geog. Jour.* xviii. p. 209. Mr. Reed discusses more especially the origin of the obsequent drainage of the Vale of Pickering. He assumes successive cycles of denudation, a stage, in the argument of Davis, which has here been neglected, as being somewhat speculative and not essential to the general conception, however pertinent to difficulties of detail.

CHAPTER XVI

SCOTLAND

THE subdivision of Scotland for the purpose of describing the geographical correlations in its several parts may depend upon either of two considerations. On the one hand, is the great structural distinction between the Highlands, the Rift Valley, and the Southern Uplands, upon which rests a difference of productivity, both of degree and kind ; and, on the other hand, the opposition between the east and west coasts, with their respective stream slopes, which has determined the relative accessibility of the various districts and the grouping of the communications.

The diagonal line of fault dividing the Rift Valley from the Highlands, separates Scotland into two roughly equal portions (Figs. 38, 39). The parallel line dividing the Rift Valley from the Southern Uplands is of subordinate value ; nor, for many purposes, is the continuity of the Highlands appreciably broken by the narrow trench of Glenmore. With the exception of their eastern sill (Fig. 30), the counties north of the Highland line are one of the most thinly-peopled regions of all Europe (Fig. 120), and, with the same exception, they contain fewer cattle and sheep, and less tillage than any other portion of the British Isles (Figs. 126, 127). Gaelic is the language of the inhabitants, except along the coastal sill and in a few of the more open straths (Fig. 93). Owing to the north-eastward and south-westward graining of the rocks there are no wide valleys opening to the Rift, for in their consequent reaches even the streams of the Tay system have to pass through gorges, as at Killiecrankie (Fig 66). The Highlands are, therefore, relatively

9   8   7   6

59

4000

3000

2000

1000

500

58

250

57

500

250

1000

500

56

9   8   7   6   5

Scale ~ 1 : 2,250,000
English Miles

Kilometres

REFERENCE
TO COLOURING

FEET	METRES
4000	1220
3000	914
2000	610
1000	305
500	152
250	76
SEA LEVEL	SEA LEVEL
250	76
500	152
1000	305
2000	610
3000	914
4000	1220

HEIGHT OF LAND

DEPTH OF SEA

POPULATION
OF TOWNS

500,000
100,000
50,000
20,000

J.G.Bartholomew.

inaccessible except from the eastern sill and the western sea. But the Southern Uplands are completely intersected by the open Tweed and Nith valleys (Figs. 121, 122). They constitute one of the great sheep runs of Britain, a fact betokened by the trade term of "Tweed" cloths. Their population is proportionately larger than that of the Highlands, although small indeed when the comparison is with the Rift Valley or the Northumbrian and Cumbrian coalfields.[1] Their inhabitants speak English, even in Galloway. Therefore Scotland may be regarded as falling naturally into two halves, of which the "Highlands" contain the Grampian and Northern Uplands, together with the eastern sill, while the "Lowlands" consist of the Rift Valley and the Southern Uplands.

From the point of view, however, of the drainage slopes, North Britain presents no similar bi-symmetry, for quite three-quarters of the country are drained into the eastern sea. Moreover, the Rift Valley cannot in any sense be regarded as harmonising with the river system, whether the rivers be classified according to origin or destination (*cf.* p. 143). It is traversed by waters from two sources, which flow into two seas, in such manner as to divide it into three sections. In Clydesdale and Ayrshire the streams descend from the Southern Uplands to the western sea ; in Lothian they come down from the Southern Uplands into the eastern sea ; and they flow into the eastern sea across Strathmore from the Highlands. With the first section is intimately connected, by natural ways, the Solway and Galloway slope of the Southern Uplands ; with the second, the valley system of the Tweed ; with the third, that portion of the Highlands, for the most part drained by the river Tay, which lies to the east of Drumalban and to the south of the Mounth.

On a balance of considerations, then, it appears that Scotland falls most naturally into four great divisions— (1) Lothian and the Tweed borderland ; (2) the West of Scotland, consisting of the Solway dales, Galloway, the

---

[1] Along the Solway shores and in the valley of the Tweed there is a density of population about equivalent to that of Buchan and the Moray coast.

coastal plain of Ayrshire and Clydesdale, and—grouped
with these by reason of the sea communications—the
peninsulas of Argyll and the Hebridean Isles ; (3) Strathmore, the peninsula of Fife, and that portion of the
Highlands which lies to the east of Drumalban and to
the south of the Mounth ; and (4) the remainder of the
Highlands, with the low coastal strip which ranges through
Buchan, Moray, the Black Isle, Caithness, and the Orkneys.
Each of these divisions contains one of the four large
towns of Scotland, and each has also a secondary town
at an important centre of communications.   In the first
is the great combined city of **Edinburgh** and Leith, and
Berwick, although technically in England, must be regarded as belonging to the same division, because of its
position at the parting of the ways leading, on the one
hand, up the Tweed valley, and on the other, by the coastal
defile to Dunbar and Edinburgh.   **Glasgow** is situated in
the midst of Clydesdale, and *Dumfries* is at the parting of
ways leading northward through Nithsdale to Kilmarnock
and Glasgow, and westward through Galloway towards
Ireland.   **Dundee** is the largest town of the Tay basin, but
Perth is at the centre of the ways in Strathmore.   **Aberdeen**, a city on the same scale as Dundee, stands at the
entry to Buchan, while *Inverness* is at the convergence of
the road (1) along the Moray coast from Buchan, (2)
over Drumochter from the Tay valley, (3) through Glenmore from Argyll, (4) through Glencarron from Skye and
the Western Isles, and (5) along the coast of Sutherland
from Caithness and the Orkneys (Fig. 121).   The first
of the divisions corresponds to the Scottish extremity
of the old Angle kingdom of Bernicia ; the second
to Pictish Galloway, British Strathclyde, Scottish Argyll,
and the Norse Lordship of the Isles ; the third, with the
addition of Buchan, to Pictish Alban ; the fourth, with
the exception of Buchan, to Pictish Moray and Norse
Caithness (Fig. 106).   The second division, including all
the western coasts, coincides with the pre-Reformation
Archbishopric of Glasgow, and the other three divisions,
including all the eastern coasts, to the Archbishopric **of**

St. Andrews ; for the mediæval organisation of the Church in Scotland was based, as in other lands (*cf.* pp. 242, 278), on water communications.

South-Eastern Scotland spreads from the English border to the Firth of Forth (Fig. 122). It consists of two groups of counties—(1) Berwick, Roxburgh, Selkirk, and Peebles in the basin of the Tweed, and (2) Haddington, Edinburgh, and Linlithgow in Lothian. The lines of its structure are drawn from south-west to north-east in alternate ridges and furrows. In succession from the English border they are—(1) the Cheviot range ; (2) the valley of the Teviot and lower Tweed from Hawick to Berwick; (3) the plateau of the Southern Upland, ending north-westward in a scarped edge ; (4) the strip of low ground, partly inland, partly coastal, which is drained north-eastward by two little subsequent rivers, the Dalkeith Esk and the Haddington Tyne ; and (5) the Pentland ridge, with the subsequent streams of the Water of Leith and the Almond along its north-western foot. The Firth of Forth, entering from the west, makes a north-eastward bend beyond the constriction at Queensferry, and spreads to a great width in prolongation of the lie of the Esk, Leith, and Almond valleys. Between the end of the Pentlands and the coast of the Firth there is a gap, in the midst of which is set the Castle rock, and around this, in the gateway leading to inner Scotland, has grown up the capital city of Edinburgh. The Tweed traverses the Southern Uplands diagonally from west to east, and then bends north-eastward in conformity with the general grain of the land. Its tributaries fall, therefore, into two series, the one consequent, descending from the north-west to its lower left bank, the other subsequent, from the south-west to its upper right bank. In each of these series there is one stream of exceptional significance. Gala Water, from the north-west, has so notched the edge of the plateau which overlooks the Lothian coastland, as to sunder it into two masses, known as Moorfoot to the south-west, between the Gala Dale and Tweeddale, and

Lammermoor to the north-east, between Gala Dale and
the cliffs of Dunbar and St. Abb's Head (Fig. 121). The
Teviot, on the other hand, follows the northern foot of
the Cheviot range, bearing in the direction of its flow and
the breadth of its valley the same relation to the lower
Tweed that the Kennet bears to the lower Thames.

FIG. 120.—The Density of Population in Scotland in 1891.

The tracks followed by the railways to Edinburgh
supply an excellent commentary on the physical configuration (Fig. 121). The East Coast line crosses the Tweed at
Berwick, surmounts the cliffs of St. Abb's Head by a little
valley, and descends into Lothian at Dunbar, whence it
turns up the Haddington Tyne and, crossing to the coast
of the Firth, enters Edinburgh from the east. The so-called
"Waverley" route from Carlisle and the head of Solway

Firth, runs up Liddesdale to the ridge which connects the Cheviots with the Southern Uplands, and descends into the Teviot valley at Hawick; thence it traverses the "Scott" country, past Abbotsford and the ruin of Melrose; finally it strikes up Gala Dale, through the Southern Uplands, and descending to the Esk at Dalkeith, enters Edinburgh in company with the East Coast line. The West Coast line extends from Carlisle up Annandale, crosses the Southern Uplands into the head of Clydesdale, and descending to Carstairs Junction, turns northeastward along the foot of the Pentland Hills, and so enters Edinburgh from the west. Certain details in the county boundaries

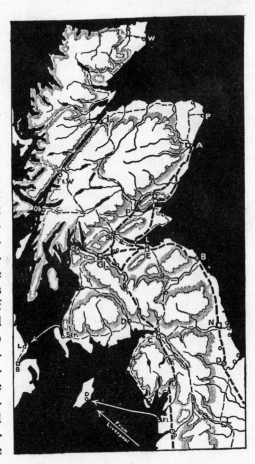

FIG. 121.—The Railways of Scotland.

point to the importance of former communications along the same lines. Roxburghshire includes the upper part of Liddesdale, although this is on the Solway slope, and Edinburghshire includes the upper portion of

Gala Dale, although this belongs to the basin of the Tweed.[1] A larger fact of similar meaning is the northward extension to the Tweed of that part of Northumberland which is grasped between the end of the Cheviot Hills and the sea coast. In the days before railways nine out of ten travellers entered Scotland along the east coast, and the expression "beyond the Tweed," as an equivalent for Scotland, is therefore precise, notwithstanding the fact that the Tweed constitutes only one-sixth of the whole boundary.

Every topographical detail of the borderland is clothed with historic and legendary interest (Fig. 122). The boundary between Scotland and England coincides for forty miles with the water-parting of the Cheviot Hills, which rise north-eastward into a great terminal dome 2600 feet high, a conspicuous landmark as seen from vessels on the North Sea, especially when snow-capped in the spring-time. Between the foot of this hill and the coast is the undulating plain, some ten miles broad, which constitutes the eastern gateway to Scotland. It is traversed by two roads, the one along the shore, the other in the valley of the Till which falls into the Tweed near Coldstream. Here, by the sea, is Bamborough Castle, and within sight of it Holy Island and Lindisfarne, the centres respectively of Northumbrian power and of Irish missionary effort. The battlefields of Flodden and Homildon Hill lie near the inner road. Three considerable streams, the North Tyne, the Otter, and the Coquet, descend from the Cheviot ridge transversely into Northumberland. At the head of the Otter is a historic pass, Carter Bar, leading into England from the longitudinal valley of the Teviot. The battlefield of Otterburn is ten miles below the Bar on the English side. Between the western end of the Cheviots and the head of Solway Firth is another passage into Scotland, through a bog or moss, now drained, which is traversed by the mouths of

---

[1] On the other hand, the valley of the Lyne, flowing to the Tweed, is included within the county of Peebles, although it rises in the Pentland Hills, well beyond the front of the Southern Uplands.

the Liddel and Esk.   At low-water there was a way across the Solway sands, dangerous on account of the rapid inrush of the tide.

Nearly two-thirds of the population of the seven south-eastern counties is concentrated in the city of Edinburgh and the adjacent port of Leith (Fig. 120).   With their suburbs they together form a city of half a million inhabitants.   Galashiels and Hawick, seats of the Tweed wool industry, are towns of less than twenty thousand people, and Berwick is of like size.   The whole county of Peebles,

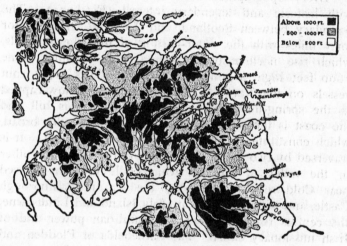

FIG. 122.—The Border.

occupying the moorland saddle between Tweeddale and Clydesdale, contains fewer than twenty thousand human beings, fewer, that is to say, than twenty to the square mile.   Even the three Lothian counties, renowned for skilful tillage, have towns that are no more than large villages.   In close neighbourhood to Edinburgh, tending to swell its relative importance, is a small coalfield, with dependent industries, about Dalkeith in the Esk Valley.

The natural features of western Scotland are disposed along two series of parallel belts intersecting one another.

19

The first series strike north-eastward, as in Solway Firth, the Southern Uplands, and the Highland edge ; the second cross from south-east to north-west, as in Clydesdale, and along the moorland divide between Lanarkshire and Ayrshire. Most of the population is settled in three lowlands delimited by these intersecting belts, the first being along the Solway shore beneath the Southern Uplands, the second in Clydesdale, and the third in the coastal plain of Ayrshire. Two well-defined gap-ways connect the three lowlands, the one along Nithsdale, from Solway Firth into Ayrshire, and the second through the moorlands, from the north of Ayrshire into the lower valley of the Clyde. A broad swell in the floor of the Rift Valley, projecting from the foot of the Pentlands, divides the coastal plain of Lothian from the valley of the Clyde, but a depression, denuded almost to sea-level, runs between this and the Campsie Fells (Fig. 28). Through this depression, from the neighbourhood of Glasgow to that of Falkirk and Grangemouth, run side by side the most important canal of mid-Scotland, and the so-called Grame's Dyke of Roman construction.

As in the case of Edinburgh, the lie of the chief railways comments on the configuration of the country (Fig. 121). Three lines enter Glasgow from South Britain : one comes directly westward from Edinburgh, having approached Scotland by the east coast ; the second crosses from Carlisle, up Annandale and down Clydesdale, and parting from the Edinburgh branch at Carstairs, runs along the valley of the Clyde into Glasgow from the south-east ; the third also comes from Carlisle, but by way of Dumfries, through Nithsdale to Kilmarnock in the Ayrshire plain, and thence by the gap in the moorlands to Paisley, and so into Glasgow from the west.

No isolated crag, crowned by a castle, formed the centre of Glasgow. Its first growth was due to the convergence of many lines of communication. The road which comes down the Clyde from Tweeddale and Annandale here divides, and passes by the right bank to Dumbarton, and by the left to Greenock ; while a second way crosses the island from Edinburgh and Stirling, through Falkirk, and thence along the southern foot of the Campsie Fells over Glasgow Bridge, and by Paisley, through the gap between the Largs and Loudoun Hills, into the lowland of Ayrshire. As is commemorated by its ancient University and Cathedral, Glasgow was important even in the days when Edinburgh was the court of kings and still indisputably the Metropolis of Scotland.

Perhaps the most remarkable aspect of the industrial development of the northern kingdom is the degree to which it has been centralised in Glasgow. With its suburbs Glasgow has now nearly a million inhabitants, and is the second city of the United Kingdom. As a port it almost ranks with Liverpool ; as a seat of industry it rivals Manchester. But around is no ring of great towns comparable to the secondary towns of Lancashire. Paisley, Greenock, and Coatbridge-Airdrie are the largest places in the Clyde field of industry, and none of them has more than a hundred thousand inhabitants. Of the third rank are Dumbarton, Hamilton, and Falkirk, and with these may be counted Kilmarnock and Ayr on the Ayrshire coalfield, and Dumfries in the Solway land at the parting of the ways to Glasgow and Belfast.

The portion of the Highlands which may be counted as tributary to Glasgow is that which lies opposite to the mouth of the Clyde at Greenock. It consists of a series of south-south-westward ridges, with longitudinal glens and lochs, some containing fresh and some salt water. Of these the chief are Loch Long, Loch Fyne, and Loch Awe. Transverse depressions, probably eroded by former consequent streams, strike in a south-easterly direction, affording opportunities for shortening the long circuit of the promontories (*cf.* p. 132). Thus the islands of Bute and Arran were detached from the mainland by intersecting consequent and subsequent valleys, drowned by the inflow of the sea. A depression at the Crinan isthmus has permitted of the construction of a canal across the root of the peninsula of Kintyre. Islay and Jura must also be supposed to have owed their insulation to the intersection of sunken consequent and subsequent valleys. Yet another transverse notch, through the pass of Brander to Loch Etive, gives exit to the obsequent, westward drainage of Loch Awe: it is by this way that the West Highland railway approaches Oban. Northward of the peninsulas and isles of Argyll are the volcanic masses of Mull and Skye, and the long gneissic ridge of the outer Hebrides. These too belong to the Glasgow sphere of influence, rather than to that of Edinburgh, by virtue of the inevitable water communications. Oban is at the point of intersection of the west Scottish ways, where the water road through the Crinan Canal, which leads up the Firth of Lorne, and through the Caledonian Canal to Inverness, is crossed by the rail and steamer route from Callander and Stirling, through the Sound of Mull to Tobermory, and round Ardnamurchan Point to Portree in Skye and to Stornoway in the Lewis. But even Oban has a population of not more than five or six thousand, a circumstance very significant of the small economic resources of the Western Highlands.

The essential feature of the third division of Scotland is Strathmore, the broad belt of fertile lowland along the outcrop of the Old Red sandstone, which extends northeastward between the edge of the Highlands and the Ochil-Sidlaw ridge. Both the edge and the ridge are cleft at intervals by rivers emerging from the Highland glens on the one hand, and on the other penetrating to the sea (Fig. 66). Strictly speaking, the name Strathmore applies only to that portion of the Old Red belt which is crossed by the rivers of the Tay system concentrating at Perth, but for the purpose of general description it is convenient to extend it over the low saddle which bears the divide between the Tay and the Forth, and along the belt of plain which continues in the same south-westward direction to the shores of Loch Lomond. The great road to Buchan and Inverness, now followed by the Caledonian railway, enters Strathmore past the castle-crag of Stirling, set in the gap between the Campsie and Ochil ranges. Turning north-eastward through Perth and Forfar, it strikes the coast again at Montrose, and thence runs to Aberdeen through the defile of Stonehaven, between the Highlands and the sea. From this trunk-road a series of glen-ways branch to the left into the Highland portions of the counties of Stirling and Perth ; and of these, two are now followed by the railways from Callander over Drumalban to Oban, and from Dunkeld over Drumochter to Inverness.[1] To the right of Strathmore are two outlying districts, the peninsula of Fife and the Carse of Gowrie, lying the one beyond the Ochils and the other beyond the Sidlaws, along whose shores are disposed a series of small ports, calling places for the coastwise traffic between Leith and Aberdeen. Of these the principal are Kirkcaldy, St. Andrews, Arbroath, Montrose, and Stonehaven. Dundee, standing on the Firth of Tay, in the Carse of Gowrie, has grown to a size four times as great as that of any other town within this county group, a fact now due to the jute industry rather than to the whale fishery, which in its more prosperous days had one of its chief bases at this port. Since the rise of Dundee, a direct railway has been constructed from Edinburgh, which crosses the Firths of Forth and Tay by bridges ranking among the great engineering achievements of the last century. Of the inland places of Fife, only Dunfermline is entitled to count among Scottish towns of the third order. At Clackmannan, and again near Kirkcaldy, are small ends of the coalfields of Lanarkshire and Midlothian re-emergent to northward of the Firth of Forth (Fig. 39).

The fourth division of Scotland lies beyond the Mounth, which strikes east and west through the Grampian Highlands, obliquely to the grain of the land (cf. p. 62). The Mounth forms the boundary between the counties of Perth and Forfar on the south, and Inverness and Aberdeen on the north. It constitutes the nearest approach to a mountain range in Scotland, and for nearly fifty miles has no pass lower than 1500 feet. The highest summit is

[1] Drum is a back, a "neck," a pass of the kind known as a "col."

Lochnagar, but immediately above the sea at Stonehaven it rises in Mount Battock to no less than 2500 feet. The summits of Ben Alder and Ben Nevis may perhaps indicate a westward prolongation, but in this part it is deeply cleft by Loch Ericht and Loch Treig. In the more restricted sense it constitutes the southern boundary of the portion of the Highlands whose drainage is north-eastward and eastward to Inverness and Buchan. Two natural entries, each now traversed by a railway, lead into the terminal section of Britain, the one by Stonehaven beside the sea, the other over Drumochter near Loch Ericht, but the new West Highland Railway has been carried along Drum-alban, and through the cleft of Loch Treig to Fort William.

Beyond the Mounth the country has two characters. From the summit of Lochnagar, on a clear September day, the golden harvest of lowland Buchan is visible on the one hand, and on the other the purple heather of high, far-spreading grouse moors. Nine-tenths of the people of all the counties north of Perth and Argyll are con-centrated in the plains of Buchan and Caithness, and along the coastal sill round Moray Firth. By far the greater number are collected in Aberdeenshire and Banff-shire, and especially in the triangular area demarked by the coastal towns of Banff, Peterhead, and Aberdeen. This is a region well populated and well cultivated, with its own port and university of Aberdeen, which is the head of the land road from the south, and the distributing centre northward to Peterhead, north-westward to Banff, and westward up the valleys of the Don and the Dee. The valley of the Dee is incised along the northern foot of the Mounth, and constitutes the ancient division of Mar, within which are three villages of celebrity, Braemar, Balmoral, and Ballater. Northward of Braemar, round the sources of the Dee and the Deveron, is the largest mass of lofty ground in the British islands. It contains Ben Macdhui, Braeriach, Cairntoul, and Cairn-gorm, the highest mountains in Scotland with the exception of Ben Nevis, all rising above 4000 feet. Great bosses of granite are exposed, both in the eastern Highlands and in Buchan, and granite quarries are a source of wealth to Aberdeen and Peterhead, additional to the arable and pasture lands and to the fisheries.

Westward of Banff, the coast road runs to Inverness over a sill of Old Red sandstone, in places as much as ten miles broad, which is intersected by the lower reaches of the rivers Spey and Findhorn. The broad strath of the Spey is almost of comparable importance to' Deeside, and contains the health-resort of Grantown. The Highland Railway from Drumochter was originally carried to the Spey mouth, but of late the main line has been diverted, by a series of works transverse to the rock grain of a rugged district, from Aviemore directly to Inverness (Fig. 121). Beyond Inverness the coastal sill turns northeastward to Tarbatt Ness, and is cut by the three Firths of Beauly, Cromarty, and Dornoch into two peninsulas, of which the more southern is known as the Black Isle. Into the heads of these three firths flow the torrents of the greater part of the Northern Highlands.

Inverness was long merely a garrison town in an alien country, comparable to Waterford and Wexford in mediæval Ireland, but the sheriff of Inverness claimed jurisdiction over Glenmore and all the Northern Highlands (Fig. 108). The clans were not effectively reduced to order, however, until about a century and a half ago, when the road was constructed over Drumochter which branches on the one hand through Glen Spean to Fort William, and on the other over the Pass of Corryarrick, at a height of 2500 feet, to Fort Augustus in the midst of Glen More.

On the borders of Sutherland and Caithness, visible across the firth from the Moray shore, is the great mountain mass of Morven, which compels the railway from Inverness to strike inland, and to enter Caithness from the west rather than from the south. Beyond Morven, on the shore of Pentland Firth, is the plain of Caithness, by the speech of its peasants not Celtic and Highland, but English and originally Scandinavian. Here are the little

fishing towns of Thurso and Wick. Beyond Pentland Firth
are the Orkney Islands, cliff-edged plains for the most part,
fragments of Caithness, but with a hill in the Island of
Hoy some 1500 feet in height. Sixty miles again farther
to the north-east, with the small Fair Island to mark the
mid passage, are the Shetland Isles, geologically a fragment of the Highlands proper, rather than of Orkney
and Caithness, but by the race and history of their inhabitants equally Scandinavian.

The west coast of Sutherland, Ross, and Inverness is
a series of lofty, storm-beaten forelands projecting between
a score of sea lochs and fiords, each of which is headed
by a short glen with a torrent descending from the water-
parting, here but a little way inland. A few fishing villages,
and a few hotels and country houses, are the only centres
of population along this remote shore.

Aberdeen is a city of 150,000 inhabitants; Inverness
has about 20,000; Peterhead at the extremity of Buchan,
and Elgin midway along the Moray sill, are towns on
the scale of about 10,000; Wick and Thurso have less
than 10,000; and beside these, in all the spacious country
to north of the Highland line, measuring in area more
than the six northern counties of England, there is nothing
greater than a large village.

Note on Authorities.—For general indications see the note at the end
of Chapter XIV. The volumes of the *Scottish Geographical Magazine*
contain many detailed papers on the home country. Bartholomew's
Atlas of Scotland is better than anything of like nature available for
South Britain.

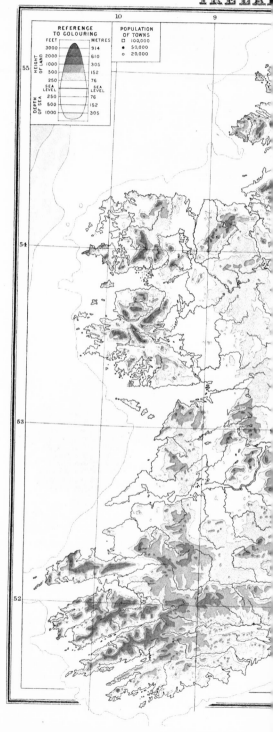

REFERENCE
TO COLOURING

FEET		METRES
3000		914
2000		610
1000		305
500		152
250		76
SEA LEVEL		SEA LEVEL
250		76
500		152
1000		305

HEIGHT OF LAND

DEPTH OF SEA

POPULATION
OF TOWNS
□ 100,000
● 50,000
○ 20,000

Plate 6.

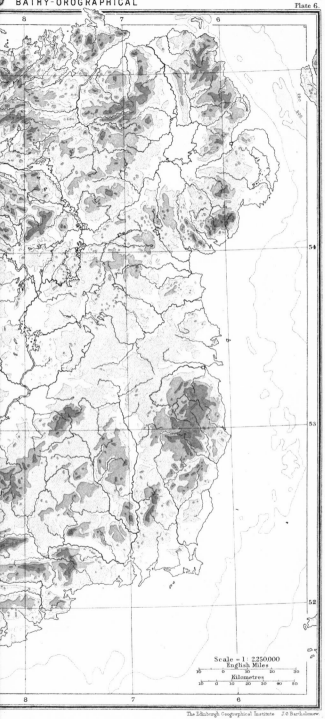

Scale = 1 : 2,250,000
English Miles

Kilometres

CHAPTER XVII

IRELAND

THE largest single feature in the configuration of Ireland is the central plain, which with a breadth of 50 miles spreads from the east coast for 100 miles westward, dividing the northern from the southern mountains. The edges of the level ground are approximately marked by straight lines drawn from Dundalk to Ballina, and from Dublin to Galway. Except, however, at the heads of Killala, Clew, and Galway Bays, the plain does not penetrate to the Atlantic Ocean, for a broken rim of peaks is ranged along its Connaught border (Fig. 33).

Midway through the island, the Shannon, the longest river of the British Isles, flows completely across this plain from a source in the northern mountains, within twenty miles of the sea, to a gorge in the southern mountains at Killaloe, and thence past Limerick into a great westward estuary. From Lough Allen where the source streams gather, to Killaloe at the entry of the gorge, the river descends less than 60 feet in 80 miles ; but between Killaloe and Limerick it falls 100 feet in 20 miles to the head of the tideway. Above Killaloe, therefore, the flow of the river is not rapid, although the volume of water carried seaward is relatively great. The Shannon, everywhere broad, here spreads to lake breadth along quite half its course, forming Loughs Ree and Derg, and from time immemorial it has proved a sufficient barrier to divide the plain into two portions, Connaught to the west and Meath to the east (Fig. 68).

Although the central plain of Ireland occupies but a third of its surface, it must not be supposed that the remainder of the island consists of uplands comparable to

the Scottish and Welsh Highlands, or even to the Southern
Uplands of Scotland or the Pennine Moors of England.
The Irish hills resemble rather those of the Rift Valley of
Scotland or of the Devonian peninsula of England ; for
Ireland, more compact in outline than Great Britain,
presents internally no such natural divisions as are produced in the greater island by the elevated watersheds and
the more or less symmetrical disposition of the rivers.
The high grounds of Ireland are for the most part insular
masses rising out of a coherent plain, upon which the
divides are so ill determined that in some portions the
river courses present no intelligible system. Perhaps the
general character of the land-relief may best be realised
from the statement that no fewer than twenty-three out
of the thirty-three Irish counties contain peaks of more
than 1000 feet, and twelve of them have peaks of more
than 2000 feet, and yet it is possible to ride from the
central plain to the sea, without exceeding an elevation
of 300 feet, by no fewer than twelve intervals through the
hills :—(1) by the Erne to Donegal Bay : (2) by Lough
Neagh and the Bann to the Giants' Causeway : (3) by the
Lagan to Belfast Lough : (4) by Newry to Carlingford
Lough : (5) down the Slaney to Wexford : (6) down the
Barrow to Waterford : (7) down the Shannon to Limerick :
(8) through the median depression of County Clare to the
estuary of the Shannon : (9) to Galway Bay : (10) to
Clew Bay : (11) to Killala Bay : and (12) to Sligo Bay.
And these are additional to the broad entry of Meath.

The plain is chiefly floored with almost undisturbed
strata of Carboniferous limestone, but the gorge of the
Shannon at Killaloe is a clear indication that vast series
of deposits, probably of the Coal Measures, were once
accumulated above the existing limestone horizon (Fig. 46).
Within these deposits the now emergent uplands were
buried, and it is the long process of denudation, carried
almost to maturity, which has deprived many of the central
Irish streams of all indication of their consequent or subsequent origin. Often flowing over an almost imperceptible
slope, their courses have been easily diverted by such local

changes as the growth of a bog, or the removal of a bar of soluble limestone. Only in the south of Ireland do we find definite topographical method, and clearly articulated systems of drainage.

The historical divisions of Ireland are obviously related to these physical contrasts (Fig. 109). Invaders, first of Goidelic and later of English race, entered from the Cheshire gap by the defenceless coast of Meath, and spreading inward over the plain, dispersed the older inhabitants to right and left, into the Ulster and the Munster mountains, or drove them beyond the Shannon into the mountainous limit of Connaught. Leinster, consisting essentially of an upland of exceptional massiveness, connected by structure with the neighbouring Wales, was left somewhat apart; indeed at one time it appears to have been held by tribes of Brythonic speech, kin to the modern Welsh rather than to the Goidelic Irish (Fig. 96). But the symmetry of the divisions resulting from the mode of settlement was obscured by the annexation of Meath to Leinster, in order to form a province with Dublin for a focus. It is convenient, therefore, to substitute for the traditional division into four provinces—Ulster, Connaught, Munster, and Leinster—an arrangement into three belts in harmony with the physical and historical generalisations. They are equivalent (1) to Ulster in the north ; (2) to Munster and ancient Leinster, which excluded Meath, in the south ; and (3) to Meath and Connaught in the centre. Each of these belts contains one of the principal cities of Ireland—Belfast, Cork, and Dublin.

Ulster consists of the nine counties, Antrim, Down, Armagh, Monaghan, Cavan, Fermanagh, Tyrone, Derry, and Donegal. Of these Antrim is of exceptional structure and configuration. It is a plateau of volcanic basalt rising from the valley of the lower Bann and Lough Neagh to an elevation of 1800 feet in the summit of Trostan, whence it falls almost precipitously to the sea (cf. p. 73). Fair Head, a sheer cliff at the north-eastern angle, is distant only thirteen miles from the Mull of Kintyre in Scotland,

and the North Channel flows through the strait to the inner
seas of Britain. Nearer to the mouth of the Bann, at the
Giant's Causeway, the columnar structure of the basalt is
very impressive. To the rear of the Antrim plateau is
Lough Neagh, as large as the county of Rutland, and nearly
as large as the Lake of Geneva, but with a maximum depth
of only fifty-six feet. It is a quadrilateral sheet of water,
twenty miles in length, and fifteen miles in breadth, produced by the fracture and collapse of a portion of the
basaltic beds. Beyond Lough Neagh is the central valley
of Ulster, which although narrower than the Rift Valley
of Scotland, strikes south-westward along the same axis.
Through it has been constructed the Ulster Canal, from
Belfast Lough to the Shannon. On either hand rise
parallel mountain belts prolonging respectively the Southern
Uplands and the Grampian Highlands of Scotland (Fig.
45). In the centre is Portadown, the principal junction
of the Ulster railways, where meet four lines traversing
gaps in the bordering uplands—from Dublin and Newry,
from Belfast and Lisburn, from Cavan and Monaghan, and
from Londonderry and Omagh. Considered with reference
to the lie of the central valley, the Bann and the Erne
must be regarded as transverse rivers. They rise in the
south-eastern upland, cross the central valley, the one
through Lough Neagh, the other through the upper and
lower Loughs Erne, and enter the sea at either end of the
north-western upland of Donegal. They correspond, therefore, in type to the Clyde. The Lagan has a source in the
Mourne mountains, beside that of the Bann, but bends
north-eastward into the longitudinal Belfast Lough.

The north-western uplands of Ulster occupy the
counties Donegal, Tyrone, and Derry, with the exception
of the south-eastern portions of the two latter. They
have a south-westward graining like that of the Scottish
Highlands, and are drained chiefly by the north-eastward, longitudinal Foyle, which descends past Londonderry to a broad sea lough, half closed near its exit by a
tongue of alluvium. West of Lough Foyle is a second
more fiord-like inlet, Lough Swilly, and between the two

the peninsula known as Inishowen, that is to say, Owen's Island, which projects to the cliffs of Malin Head, the northernmost point of Ireland. The mountains of Inishowen rise to more than 2000 feet, although the isthmus between Loughs Swilly and Foyle which connects the peninsula to the mainland, is less than 300 feet high. Donegal consists of many rolling, parallel ridges striking south-westward. In Errigal it rises to 2400 feet, and in the south-western point, Slieve League, sheer from the sea to 1900 feet. Ridges and valleys alike are devoid of trees, and clad almost everywhere with peat-bog. The natural entries to the Foyle basin, the only fertile portion of the district, are from the mouth of the Bann by the north coast, and by a low pass from the south-east into the head of the valley at Omagh.

The south-eastern uplands of Ulster constitute a well-defined belt which ranges through the counties Down, Armagh, and Monaghan, and subsides gently into the central plain in Longford and south-eastern Cavan. This belt is pierced transversely by clefts which contain the Strangford and Carlingford sea-loughs, corresponding to Wigtown and Luce Bays along the southern uplands of Scotland. About midway in its length, the granitic mass of the Mourne mountains emerges from the surrounding schists and slates, and rises in Slieve Donard, beside the shore of the Irish Sea, to an elevation of 2800 feet.

That part of the Ulster coast which contains the cities of Londonderry and Belfast, together with the Lagan and Bann valleys, is distinct from all the remainder of Ireland, by virtue of agricultural, industrial, and racial peculiarities. In the six counties, Antrim, Down, Armagh, Tyrone, Derry, and Donegal, although they measure only about one-sixth of the surface, are grown more than a third of the oats, more than a third of the potatoes, and all the flax of Ireland (Fig. 128). Linen-weaving is the characteristic industry, but Belfast, importing coal and iron from Great Britain, has become one of the great centres of British shipbuilding. It has now a population amounting to some 350,000, among whom Protestants of Scottish origin are the dominant section. A group of small dependent towns stud the district around, the chief being Lisburn, Lurgan, Newry, and Carrickfergus. On the margin of the Belfast neighbourhood stands the ancient city of Armagh, the ecclesiastical capital of Ireland both for Catholics and Protestants. The Bann is navigable through Lough

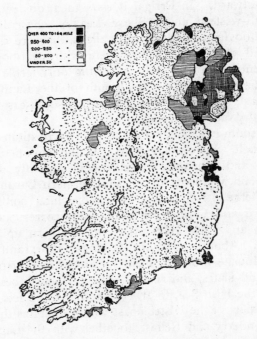

FIG. 123.—The Density of Population in Ireland in 1891.

Neagh as high as Portadown, and a small industrial area, marked by the towns Coleraine and Portrush, lies about its mouth. Enniskillen is at the point where a bridge spans the short length of river connecting the upper to the lower Lough Erne.

The south of Ireland, consisting of Munster and Leinster proper, exhibits a delicacy and simplicity of build such as occurs in no other part of Britain. The Counties Waterford, Cork, and Kerry, roughly equivalent to the ancient region of Desmond, are formed of a series of parallel rock-folds, upon which rests a surface of ridges and furrows almost as expressive of the supporting structure as the roof of a Gothic cathedral (*cf.* pp. 80, 135). The

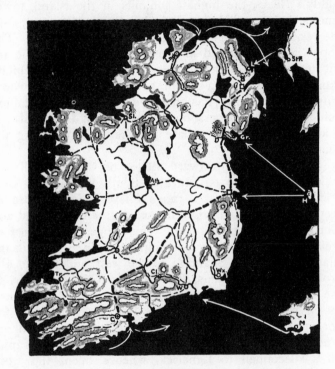

Fig. 124.—The Chief Railways of Ireland.

lower Suir, and the upper Blackwater, Lee, and Bandon flow eastward along the axes of downfolds. Bending in succession, they breach southward gorges through the limiting upfolds, and emerge on the obliquely cut coastline between Carnsore Point and Cape Clear. Where their estuaries cross the last downfolds they expand a little to right and left, and constitute the almost land-locked harbours of Waterford, Youghal, Cork, and Kinsale. In the ends of Kerry and Cork, the sea has invaded the longitudinal valleys, here inclined to the south of west, and formed the ria-sounds (*cf.* p. 82) known as Dingle Bay, Kenmare River, and Bantry Bay, thus imparting the familiar fringed outline to the extremity of Ireland. Where the slender promontories merge with the mainland, Macgillycuddy's Reeks, the highest summits in the island, tower among the oceanic mists to a height of 3400 feet, with the wood-girt Lakes of Killarney at their foot. The population is gathered in the valleys and along the intricate coastline. The produce of the pastures is chiefly exported from Cork, a city of 100,000 inhabitants, whose outport, Queenstown, has an added significance as a calling point for mail steamers bound to or from Liverpool. It is also a supplementary base for the fleets watching the channel entries.

North of the westward ridges of Cork and Kerry, which prolong the structure of South Wales, is a conspicuous south-westward range, Slieve Bloom, whose lie seems to indicate an origin in common with Scotland and North Wales (Figs. 68, 69). This range, in the heart of Ireland, divides the two most important river basins in the island, that of the Shannon to the west, and that of the group of sister streams, the Barrow, Nore, and Suir, to the east. The Shannon follows the foot of Slieve Bloom in the slow expanse of Lough Derg, and traverses the gorge of Killaloe through mountain masses which are hinged to Slieve Bloom. It then descends the rapids of Castleconnell to Limerick, whence opens the westward estuary. There, on either hand, are plains of the Munster counties Clare and Limerick, which together formed the ancient division of Thomond. They contain some of the richest pasture in the land, and have for their market and port of exit the considerable town of Limerick. Eastward from Limerick the Golden Vale extends to the Suir, between Slieve Bloom and the mountains of Cork, thus offering a lowland way, followed by the Waterford and Limerick railroad, from the Shannon to Waterford (Fig. 124).

Originating side by side in Slieve Bloom the Barrow, Nore, and Suir have middle courses so far apart that the lower Barrow flows southward along the foot of the Wicklow mountains, and the Suir eastward beside the ridges of County Waterford. Yet all three gather to a common estuary known as Waterford Harbour.[1] The basin of the Slaney, with its estuarine harbour at Wexford, may be counted as an element in the same drainage area, the richest agricultural district in Ireland. The four conjoint basins are equivalent to the Leinster counties, Wexford, Carlow, Kilkenny, Queen's County, and southern Kildare, together with the Munster county of Tipperary. Where crossed by the railway from Dublin to Cork, they have an elevation of about 400 feet, which is higher than the average of the Irish plains. With this fact may be correlated the unusual absence of lakes.

Five-eighths of the barley of Ireland is produced in the basins of the rivers which drain into the harbours of Wexford and Waterford, a fact partly explained by the northward loop of the July isotherm of 60° Fahrenheit (Fig. 86). A fifth of all the barley of Ireland is produced in the single county of Wexford, and here alone is there an acreage under barley nearly equivalent to that under oats. A natural consequence of the favoured character of this district is that the only inland towns of Ireland of any considerable size are placed here, Kilkenny upon the Nore, and Clonmel upon the Suir.

Eastward of the Barrow and northward of the Slaney is the mountain mass of County Wicklow, the nucleus of the ancient Leinster. It culminates at a height of over 3000 feet in Lugnaquella, sister peak to Snowdon, for Wicklow is to be thought of as a fragment of North Wales, visible across the sea. On either side the same south-westward graining and a like mineralogical structure result in similar landscapes. To the north of Dublin Bay is the peninsular rock of Howth Head, a detached fragment of the Wicklow axis, analogous to the Great

[1] c.f. Spenser, " Faerie Queene," Book IV., Canto xi. 43.

Orme's Head, detached from the range of Snowdon by the mouth of the Conway river. The rapid torrent Avoca, and the Liffey, encircling the northern foot, bear away the mountain rains. On a sill between the Wicklow mountains and the sea is the pleasure resort of Bray, the Irish Brighton, in the dry rain-shadow of the steep upland.

The central plain of Meath and Connaught forms three basins separated almost imperceptibly by boggy divides. In the centre occupying the King's, Westmeath, and Longford counties of Leinster, and the County Roscommon of Connaught, is the fertile plain of the middle Shannon, with Athlone in its midst at the chief crossing of the river, in the interval between Loughs Ree and Derg. Westward of the Shannon basin in Counties Galway and Mayo are the streams which wander over the slightly undulating slope to the lake chain of Con, Mask, and Corrib, and so to exits in Killala and Galway Bays. Eastward of the Shannon basin is the Boyne, flowing from low-lying sources through County Meath to Drogheda. The bogs of the plain, with the exception of the great bog of Allen, in King's County and Kildare, have been largely drained, but communications across the lowland must formerly have presented no small difficulties. Thus while Dublin, and the coast-land to north of it, constituted the English base within the "pale," and the mountain edge of Connaught was the final retreat of the native Irish, the great plain between, intersected by the Shannon, was the scene of incessant contention. Except for the small ports of Dundalk and Drogheda in County Louth, and the little cattle-markets of Mullingar, Athlone, and Ballinasloe, there are no towns within an area larger than Yorkshire and Lancashire combined. Clew Bay cuts the western rim into two portions, the Nephin mountains to the north, and the peaks of Connemara to the south, while Lakes Con, Mask, and Corrib, at an elevation of less than 80 feet, nearly connect Killala Bay with Galway Bay, and form a moat between the mountains and the plain, which almost insulates the rocky fortress of western Connaught. Galway and Sligo, the chief towns of Connaught, are ports engaged in fishing and the exportation of agricultural produce.

Dublin is placed in the midst of the east coast, where the plain of Meath and the mountains of Leinster adjoin. It was originally founded as a bridge-town on the Liffey, and the bay is a harbour of inferior character, although the best available along the monotonous coast of the plain. The mail steamers from Great Britain make use of the outport of Kingstown at the southern point of the entry.

Dublin is the nucleus of communications throughout Ireland, whether by canal or railroad. The Royal and Grand Canals radiate from the Liffey, the one westward, the other north-westward to the Shannon, and a great through line of navigation extends from Belfast Lough by the Lagan and the Ulster Canal to Leitrim, and thence down the Shannon to its mouth. A southward branch of the Grand Canal is carried to the head of the navigation of the Barrow. Dublin is therefore connected by waterways with Belfast, Limerick, and Waterford.

The three trunk railways are the Great Southern and Western, striking south-westward from Dublin, through Kildare, Queen's County, and Tipperary, to Limerick Junction, and thence to Limerick and to Cork : the Great Midland and Western runs through Athlone to Galway, and the Great Northern of Ireland through Drogheda, Dundalk, and Portadown, and thence, on the one hand, to Belfast, and on the other, to Londonderry.

To an extraordinary extent, therefore, the life of Ireland is centralised in Dublin. Cork, Waterford, and Limerick export the cattle of the south, and Londonderry and Belfast the manufactured products of the north, but Dublin, opposite to Chester, Liverpool, and Holyhead, is the centre of distribution for the whole island. Were it not for the industrial activities in and about Belfast, the grouping of the population in Ireland at the present day would strikingly resemble that of England in the Middle Ages. Dublin corresponds to mediæval London and Cork to mediæval Bristol, and the remainder of the people are spread evenly over the rural districts.   There is no inland town of as many as 20,000 inhabitants.   No greater contrast could be imagined than that presented by the maps (Figs. 120, 123) indicative of the density of population in Scotland and in Ireland.

Note on authorities.—For general authorities see note at end of Chapter XIV.   Bartholomew's contoured map in colours is perhaps the most graphic representation of the form of the land.

CHAPTER XVIII

STRATEGIC GEOGRAPHY

THERE now remain for consideration what we may describe as the dynamical aspects of British geography. Every civilised nation is related in two ways to the land which it occupies. Whatever the exchanges effected by trading, it is (1) ultimately dependent upon the past and present produce of its own territory, and (2) it must be prepared to defend that territory against the intrusion of covetous neighbours. The two groups of ideas involved may be roughly indexed under the terms economic and strategic. We may describe economic geography as concerned with the raising and distribution of commodities, and strategic geography as dealing with the larger topographical conditions of offence and defence.[1] But the problems to be solved are closely inter-related, for defence is essentially the protection of the means of economic subsistence ; and the distribution of products, being conducted in chief measure along lines of least resistance, follows and prepares the paths of strategic opportunity. Nor can the two studies be made applicable respectively to peace and to war, for never are economic resources more anxiously reviewed than when war is impending, while the pressure of strategical considerations is urgent upon governments at all times, since diplomacy has been well described as the banking system of sovereigns, whereby they draw upon their respective potentialities of offence and defence, and adjust differences without unsheathing the sword.

The defence of Britain rests fundamentally upon the theory implied in the command of the sea. This expression

[1] See note on p. 314.

is not meant to convey any claim of sovereignty on the high seas beyond the gunshot zone along the coast. Such a claim was formerly made by England, and at times was acquiesced in by other states, probably with a view to the easier suppression of piracy.[1] In a military sense, however, a Power has command of the sea, as against another Power with which it is at war, when it has destroyed the enemy's fleet or securely blockaded it, and has thus carried the national frontier for the purpose of the war, and for that purpose only, to the enemy's coast. Had Britain obtained command of the sea in a war, say, with France, the effect would be to carry the British frontier to the coast of France, and to add the Channel to Britain as a part of the globe within which the commanding Power could prepare attack against the enemy. This command, even when complete as against the enemy, would be limited by the rights of neutrals. But it is clear that under such circumstances England would be safe from invasion by sea, and France would be liable to it ; hence the expression that the navy is Britain's shield, and the army her spear. The enemy's coasts are the utmost limit of sea power, whose final office is to give freedom in the selection of the point at which to deliver an attack with land forces. Had France, on the other hand, obtained command of the sea, the conditions would be reversed. France would move freely in the Channel, and would deliberately choose her anchorage for the invasion of Britain.

Viewed from this standpoint, the defence of Britain resolves itself into three problems : (1) the retention of the command of the sea, or rather, of the power of taking that command should occasion demand it ; (2) the defence of Great Britain should the command of the sea be temporarily lost ; and (3) the separate defence of Ireland in the same contingency, for under such a condition the prompt and certain reinforcement of the army in Ireland would not be practicable.

If the enemy's command of the sea were complete,

[1] See note on p. 24.

all the shores of Britain would in theory be threatened equally, and the task of their defence against a raid almost hopeless. Practically, however, owing to the limited radius of action of modern fleets, which must periodically replenish their supplies of fuel, the regions of Britain most threatened are those about the continental angle and the Channel entries. The position of the Metropolis, and the paralysing blow which its seizure would imply, give added importance to the defence of the former region. As regards the latter, it must be observed that the isolation of Ireland, although

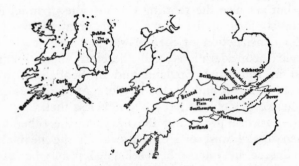

FIG. 125.—The Military Centres of Britain. – – – – – The March of the Conqueror from Hastings to Berkhampstead, where London surrendered.

weakening the United Kingdom by an additional problem of defence, allows of an alternative approach from the Western Ocean to Liverpool and Glasgow, in a quarter remote from Brest and Corunna. The great traffic passing from the south-west up the English, the Bristol, and the St. George's Channels might be diverted to the North Channel, should circumstances make that course desirable.

All the chief bases of naval action lie within Metropolitan England, near the shores, that is to say, of the Narrow Seas. Chatham, Sheerness, Portsmouth, and Devonport are the dockyards; they stand opposite to the Rhine mouths, to Cherbourg, and to Brest. Harbours of refuge lie between them at Portland, at Dover, and at

Harwich. The great naval arsenal is at Woolwich ; the naval schools are at Dartmouth, Portsmouth, and Greenwich. Walmer, on the coast of Kent, is the depôt of the marines, and the three divisions of the marines ashore are stationed at Chatham, Portsmouth, and Devonport. The dockyards of Pembroke in Wales, and Queenstown in the south of Ireland, are the only important naval stations beyond the limits of Metropolitan England, and their position has an obvious bearing on the defence of the ocean roads where they enter the St. George's and the Bristol Channels. The four English dockyards serve not merely for the construction of new ships and for repairs, but are also the refitting bases of the Channel Fleet and the stations of the reserve. The great private yards for the construction of men-of-war are free from these strategical considerations, and therefore more naturally placed in Industrial England and in Scotland—on the Tyne, at Barrow, and on the Clyde. At Cardiff is available the world's chief supply of smokeless fuel.

The exercise ground of the navy, on the other hand, is often to the west of Ireland, clear of the steam lanes of commerce, in waters where seamanship may be learned in oceanic weather. Here a remarkable series of havens gives abundant shelter—Loughs Foyle and Swilly, Blacksod and Clew Bays, Dingle Bay, Kenmare River, and Bantry Bay (Berehaven). If Britain were for a time to lose the command of the seas, these harbours on the remote edge of the land, away from all the great centres of population, might become nests of hostile cruisers.

As with the navy, so with the army, the preparations for the defence of Great Britain are chiefly concentrated within Metropolitan England, for the purpose of protecting from sudden descents London, the brain of the Empire, and the naval bases. To some extent, also, military force is present in the Metropolis as an ultimate sanction of the power of the government and for the reinforcement of the police.

The centres of the mobile army in England are at

Aldershot and on Salisbury Plain, on the flank of an enemy's line of march from the south coast to London, and in a position to relieve Portsmouth and to repel attack either from the Devonian Peninsula or the Bristol Channel. They are convenient, moreover, for the shipment of an army going over seas from Southampton, London, and Bristol.

Colchester is the prepared basis for the defence of the Metropolis from attack on the east. Dover, Chatham, Portsmouth, and Devonport have garrisons, but Portsmouth is probably the only first-class British fortress, as the expression would be understood on the Continent. There is a small garrison at Portland, and there are large depôts at Winchester and Canterbury. There are Guards at Windsor, and Cavalry at Hounslow, in the western outskirts of London. Woolwich is the chief station of the Artillery, and Chatham of the Engineers. At Woolwich, Sandhurst, and Camberley are the institutions for military education. At Waltham and Enfield on the Lea are the factories of explosives and small arms, and at Pimlico the clothing factory.

In Industrial England and in Scotland there are military centres at York and at Edinburgh; but the troops stationed in these districts remote from the Continent are but a few thousand for recruiting purposes and for the support of the police. They consist usually of regiments lately returned from foreign service, whereas those preparing to go abroad are concentrated at Aldershot and on Salisbury Plain. As in the case of the Navy, there are private works in Industrial England which form an ultimate reserve for the manufacture of weapons.

In Ireland the location of the military forces is analogous to that in the greater island, and for somewhat similar reasons. Strategy in Ireland turns necessarily on Dublin, and on the roads in rear of the Wicklow mountains which communicate between Dublin, on the one hand, and Waterford and Cork on the other. The chief military station, apart from Dublin, is the Curragh, the Irish Aldershot, near Kildare on the Liffey, where the roadways branch which lead down the valley of the Barrow to Waterford, and across the plains of Queen's County and Tipperary to Cork and Limerick. Most of the remaining troops are distributed among a number of small stations within and about the triangle Waterford—Limerick—Cork. In the north and west are but a few scattered units, comparable to those commanded from York and Edinburgh, which are utilised for recruiting purposes, and occasionally for the reinforcement of the constabulary.

Thus the same contrast between the south-east and the north-west which characterises almost every other aspect of British geography is to be found also in its strategic geography, except in so far as this is modified by the separate insularity of Ireland and the importance of the oceanic antechamber to the south-west. The effective forces are within and about the continental angle, but the reserves of men and constructive power, both military and naval, are distributed through Industrial England, Scotland, and Ireland.

Note on "strategical geography."—Military geography is a somewhat ambiguous expression. As commonly employed it includes two separate studies, the one connected with tactics, or the conduct of battles, the other with strategy, or the conduct of campaigns. The former is chiefly of professional interest, and is closely associated with military surveying and sketching ; but the latter, in that it enters into certain aspects of the problem of the advisability of declaring any given war, is a subject for the consideration of statesmen no less than of generals and admirals.

Note on authorities.—The peculiarities of naval mobility, which give meaning to the idea of the command of the sea, may best be studied in Captain Mahan's books, especially his "Influence of Sea Power upon History."

CHAPTER XIX

ECONOMIC GEOGRAPHY

THE most generally distributed element of the British environment is the moist equable climate, and as a consequence the most characteristic enrichment of the surface is a widespread verdure. This is expressed agriculturally in the prevalence of pasture, one-half of England, and at least three-quarters of Ireland, Scotland, and Wales being green with grass of some sort.[1] Yet this is an artificial condition, for there can be no doubt that in primitive historical times Britain was clothed almost from end to end with continuous forest. Therefore timber was the natural material for building, and the earliest industries were the tanning of hide with the bark of trees, and the smelting of iron with charcoal. Two centuries ago the chief centres of iron-making were still in the Forests of Arden and the Weald.

One of the first, and, at the time, one of the most significant improvements effected in Britain was the introduction of the beech tree by the Romans. The result was to add the beech nut to the acorn as mast for swine, in early times by far the most frequent of British domestic animals. Great droves of them were attended by swineherds in the glades, as they are to-day in Servia and the neighbouring forest lands of the Balkan Peninsula. The agricultural statistics prove that there are now nearly ten times as many pigs in Ireland as in Scotland, although the two countries are approximately equal both in area and population. We may perhaps correlate this circum-

---

[1] For a summary of the statistics on which the statements in this chapter are based, see the table printed at p. 322, and the notes on p. 340.

stance with the relatively late prevalence in Ireland of wild
forest conditions, even though the pig has now become a
household parasite, and in some districts almost a domestic
companion. The total number of pigs in England is
greater than in Ireland, yet in England there is only one
head of swine to about fifteen people, whereas in Ireland
there is one to three. The degree to which forest has
now been cleared from Ireland is indicated by the general
employment of peat for fuel.

Although only small and doubtful remnants of the
primeval forests remain to us, yet several of the more
recently wooded districts still have many trees. A quarter
of the timber plantations of England are concentrated in
the region to the east of Wiltshire and to the south of
the Thames, principally in the three counties of Hants,
Sussex, and Kent. Two-thirds of all the orchards of Great
Britain lie in Kent, and in the belt of counties extending
from Hereford through west Gloucester and Somerset to
Devonshire. Hop gardens are confined to portions of
the same two districts.

With the gradual removal of the forests came other
significant changes in the landscape. Stone and brick
were substituted for timber, at first in public buildings,
and afterwards in private. The half-timbered houses
common in the Weald of Kent are an interesting survival
of the period of transition. Speaking broadly, the north
and west may now be pictured as a region of stone building, and the English plain as one of brick building.
The aspect of the open country exhibits an analogous
contrast in the stone walls which divide the western
and northern fields, and the hedgerows of the English
plain.

The early progress of the clearance is made evident by
the fact that, according to the Royal Commission which
investigated the coal question in 1870, the average production of coal for fuel in the hundred and fifty years
between 1500 and 1660 was about a million tons a year.
London was already notorious for the darkening of its
atmosphere with Newcastle coal.

Many of the higher districts, now deforested, have been overgrown with heath and bracken, and mountain pasture has spread over much of their surface, but in the damp climate of Ireland entire hills have become cloaked with peat, so that the upland bogs are even more extensive than those which in the plain have cumbered not a few of the lake basins. In the lowlands, however, it is meadow that now takes the part in rural economy formerly occupied by forest. The effect of the watery lowland meadows of Ireland, where frosts and droughts seldom arrest the herbage, is to be seen in the statement, that although Ireland has an area only five-eighths that of England, it has very nearly as many horned cattle. There are, indeed, as many head of cattle in Ireland as of human beings.

In Wales, also, cattle are very numerous, especially in the lowland county of Anglesea and the adjacent portion of Carnarvonshire in the north, and Carmarthenshire and Pembrokeshire in the south. England bears nearly four times as many cattle to the square mile in Cheshire as in Kent, and generally it may be said that the south British districts with most cattle are, on the one hand, the three south-westward peninsulas of North Wales, South Wales, and the west of England, and, on the other hand, the region of wet clays of the New Red series in Cheshire, Staffordshire, Derbyshire, and Leicestershire. In Scotland, despite a considerable number of cattle in the peninsula of Fife and in the Wigtown promontory, there are only half as many again as in Wales, and not more than about a quarter of the number in Ireland. As a result of these facts, and of the development of a large industrial population in Great Britain, the chief export from Ireland to the greater island is now of cattle and butter.

But the characteristic wealth of Britain in the Middle Ages, and so far as agriculture is concerned even at the present time, is to be found in its vast flocks of sheep, fed for the most part upon the uplands. In the early centuries, when the valleys were choked with forest and

morass, some of these uplands were tilled, for they were
the chief residence of the scanty population when the
southern counties were being formed about the chalk
downs of Kent, Surrey, Sussex, Hants, Wilts, Dorset, and
Berks.   But after the Norman Conquest England became
the mediæval Australia, raw wool being her "staple"
export wherewith to buy a share of the spices and other

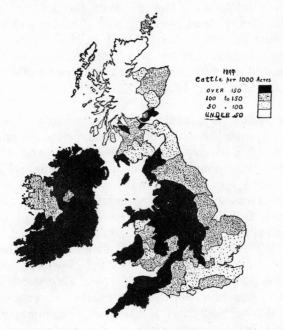

FIG. 126.—The Proportion of Horned Cattle in different parts
of Britain.

luxuries of the East.   The wool went chiefly to Flanders,
whence cloth was imported to England, and an export
duty was one of the chief sources of the revenues of the
Crown ; and in token of this the Lord Chancellor still
presides in the House of Lords seated upon a woolsack.
To-day there are in Great Britain more than twenty-
six million sheep, or approximately one sheep for each

human being.   In Ireland, although the area is one-third
that of Great Britain, there are only about four million
sheep or one-sixth as many as in the sister island.   The
significance of these figures becomes evident when we consider that in all the great colony of New South Wales, one
of the chief sources of the raw wool of the world, upon an
area nearly three times that of Britain, there are only some

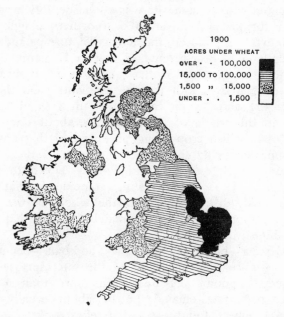

FIG. 127.—The Proportion of Land under Wheat in different parts
of Britain.   For note on index, see p. 340.

forty million sheep, or in other words, an excess of little
more than a third as compared with the United Kingdom.
The flocks are most numerous upon the central hills
of Britain—in Wales, on the Pennine range, and on the
southern uplands of Scotland.   In the Welsh county of
Brecon, and in the Scottish Border counties of Roxburgh,
Selkirk, and Berwick, there is upon the average one sheep
to each acre.

A notable addition was made to the agricultural wealth of the country when the cultivation of roots and clover was introduced in the time of the Stuarts from the Netherlands. In the United Kingdom as much land is now sown with clover, turnips, and other similar crops—being winter foods for cattle and sheep—as is ploughed for wheat, barley, and oats. As might be expected from the greater difficulty of feeding animals for the market in Scotland as compared with Ireland, there is a considerably larger area under turnips and clover in the northern kingdom than in the western ; indeed, the acreage of turnips and swedes in Scotland is nearly one-half that in England, although the total surface of Scotland capable of cultivation is not more than a fifth that of England. On the other hand, the acreage under potatoes in Ireland is larger than in the whole of Great Britain, about one-sixth of the total British crop being produced in that portion of Ireland, measuring about one-nineteenth of the whole of Britain, which extends from County Down to County Donegal. It is an interesting coincidence that in the same small district is grown the whole of the flax of Britain, upon an area approximately equal to that planted with hops in England.

Cereals—chiefly wheat, barley, and oats—occupy only a little more than one-tenth of the total surface of the United Kingdom. Of this tenth more than a half is under oats, the remainder being about equally divided between wheat and barley. Therefore only one-fortieth of the land of the United Kingdom, equivalent to the joint area of Lincolnshire and Nottinghamshire, is given to the production of wheat, and the home-grown crop amounts to not more than a fifth of the quantity consumed. Fully nine-tenths of the British wheat fields are concentrated in eastern England, since to yield abundantly wheat demands a hot dry summer, a condition which on an average of years is adequately satisfied only in a portion of Great Britain, and in a very small part of Ireland. A small but important area of wheat production is in Scottish Lothian and the Merse of Berwick, where owing to intensive cultivation the number of bushels to the acre is the largest in the kingdom. Barley is a little less exacting of climatic favours, but the greater portion of the crop is, none the less, grown in the plain of England and along the east coast of Scotland. Oats, on the other hand, can ripen where the summers are cooler and more moist, and they are in consequence the most widely spread of all British crops, being raised in all parts of both islands which lie below the level of about a thousand feet. In most of Ireland and in the Highland glens of Scotland they supply the only cereal harvest.

The position of the chief markets for English-grown corn reveals the very local character of predominant cereal cultivation in Britain. Norwich usually heads the list in the quantity sold of both wheat and barley. Next in importance are London, Chelmsford, Ipswich, Peterborough, Lincoln, Hull, and Berwick.

The principal contrasts of the agricultural topography of Britain are roughly demarked by the divisions into which the counties of Great Britain have been grouped for statistical purposes by the Board of Agriculture, a method which is here tentatively extended to Ireland. England proper has been divided into two belts, of which the western is a little larger than the eastern, and each of these has been further divided into four sections, in such manner that the forty counties constitute eight sections of approximately equal acreage (Fig. 128). The western belt, extending from Cornwall and Dorset to Northumberland, is distinctively a pastoral country. It possesses ten times as much space in rough mountain grazings as the eastern belt, in addition to an area of permanent pasture covering nearly one-half of its surface. Thus the four sections of the west together hold more than ten million acres of grass of one sort or another, as against five million in the eastern sections. A similar contrast, although less emphatic, is to be observed as between western and eastern Scotland. The characteristics of the several sections are expressed in the following table, compiled from the Agricultural Statistics of 1900 :—

Section.	Total Acreage.	Woods.	Hill Pasture and Heath.	Permanent Pasture.	Arable.
I. . . .	3,647	118	33	972	2,026
II. . . .	3,765	114	38	1,016	2,249
III. . . .	3,882	439	115	1,380	1,416
IV. . . .	3,345	154	5	1,719	1,160
V. . . .	3,899	255	81	2,018	1,203
VI. . . .	4,205	200	254	1,840	1,325
VII. . . .	5,072	202	1,029	2,102	1,112
VIII. . . .	4,729	184	584	2,307	986
IX. . . .	4,774	182	1,128	1,977	858
X. . . .	6,545	457	2,121	519	2,174
XI. . . .	12,909	421	7,295	876	1,327
XII. . . .	4,118	XII.— Contains an acreage under Potatoes of 209 out of 654 for all Ireland, and under Flax of 43 out of 47 for all Ireland. XIV.—Contains an acreage under Barley of 125 out of 174 for all Ireland.			
XIII. . . .	12,019				
XIV. . . .	4,196				

Each number in this table must be multiplied by 1000 to obtain the acreage. The numbers of the sections correspond to those shown in Fig. 128 opposite.

On the whole, then, we may summarise the present condition of the surface of Britain as follows. The Highlands of Scotland are wild heaths devoted to grouse and deer. The Southern Scottish, the Pennine, and the Cambrian Uplands are mountain pastures supporting great flocks of sheep. The promontories of Galloway, North Wales, South Wales, and Devon, together with the Irish plain and the north-western Midlands of England, are largely given over to cattle-raising and dairying. Oats are grown on the lower grounds of all parts, but wheat, and to a less degree barley, are almost confined to the east of England, and to certain small portions of eastern Scotland and south-eastern Ireland. Roots and clover are characteristic of the highly farmed districts of the east of England and of Scotland, while potatoes and pigs are characteristic in Ireland. Flax is practically limited to Ulster, and hops to the four counties of Kent, Sussex, Hereford, and Worcester. Finally, Kent, Devon, and the lower Severn valley have many orchards, and the Wealden district and Scotland extensive plantations of timber.

Fisheries are pursued off all the coasts of Britain, but are four times more productive off the east than off

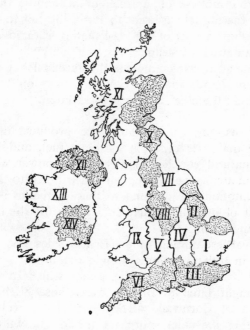

FIG. 128.—The Agricultural Divisions of Britain.—*After the Board of Agriculture* (Craigie). For note, see p. 340.

the west, chiefly owing to the great shoals of the North Sea, whose bottoms supply appropriate food. Grimsby and Hull, conveniently placed alike for the London and the Midland markets, are the chief landing ports in England, while Aberdeen has a similar relation to the Scottish markets. The Atlantic fisheries are at a disadvantage by reason of their remoteness from the great centres of consumption, and railways, aided by government subsidies, have lately, therefore, been constructed through the Scottish Highlands with the object of bringing the Hebridean fish to Glasgow. The harvest of the Orkney and Shetland fisheries, being chiefly intended for salting, and not a little of it for export to Germany and to the Latin countries, suffers less from its outlying position. A curious circumstance in connection with the Cornish red mullet fishery, dependent doubtless on a freak of fashion, is that nine-tenths of the mullets are sent to Paris and not to London. But the whole aspect of the sea-fisheries is rapidly changing, for hundreds of steam "trawlers" and "drifters" now visit fishing grounds as remote as the Faroe Isles and Iceland on the one hand, and the Bay of Biscay on the other. In the rivers the chief fishery is for salmon.

Only less important among the products of a land than the materials of food, clothing, fuel, and building, are the natural supplies of mechanical power wherewith the raw matter is worked up and distributed to the points of consumption. Incidental to these activities is the employment of metallic implements, made for the most part of iron and steel.

The earliest mining in the British Isles was probably for gold in Ireland. Some minute amount of gold is still obtained in Wales. But the mines which in antiquity first brought fame to Britain were those of tin in the peninsula of Cornwall. They have been worked ever since, being the cnief source of tin for the whole world, until in late years rich deposits were found in the Malay peninsula, and in Banca and Billiton, islands in the Malay Sea. Cornish mining has suffered as a result of the competition, but the value of the ore raised is half a million pounds a year, and tin is still, after iron, the most important of British metals. Lead is now of third consequence. Formerly, the Romans, who valued Britain chiefly for its metals, and thought of it much as we to-day think of South Africa, obtained it in the Mendips.

Iron ore, of one kind or another, occurs in many

places widely scattered over the land, and the position of the iron mines has, therefore, been chiefly determined by the accessibility of fuel for the purpose of smelting. In the old days the iron-producing districts were in the forests —in the Weald of Kent and Sussex, in the Forest of Dean near Gloucester, and in the Forest of Arden near Birmingham. It was not until the eighteenth century that coal was largely applied to iron smelting, and in the first instance, very naturally, around Birmingham, where a considerable iron industry was already established. The great deposits of ore in Cleveland and Furness lie away from coal, and were not worked until much later.

It is chiefly, however, by virtue of her great wealth of mechanical power that Britain has attained to her present influence in the world. The sources of power first utilised on any considerable scale were wind and moving water. A water mill was attached to almost every mediæval castle and abbey, and the dues received from it amounted to an appreciable part of the feudal revenues. The position of the cutlery industry at Sheffield, to take only a single later example, was determined by the presence of rapid streams for driving the local grindstones, together with facilities for obtaining by direct water channels a supply of Swedish iron, which was specially adapted to the older methods of making steel.

Only in a comparatively late period of English history was horse power utilised on a great scale for traction, for it was not until after the time of Queen Anne that a system of paved roads was gradually extended over the whole island. In the generation before the introduction of railways, the employment of horses was markedly increased by the new system of canals. To-day, although other and more rapid methods of progression have been introduced, the number of horses in the country is probably greater than it ever was. It undoubtedly exceeds three million, although precise accuracy on this subject is inaccessible, for the statistics do not indicate the number of horses maintained in towns. Of late there has been curious evidence of the manner in which the new inventions of civilisation while adding to the old facilities do not supplant them, in the fact that the parcel post between many important towns has come to be conducted by road, with the object, no doubt, of avoiding the cost of a double handling of the packets at each terminus. Much of the fodder of London horses is hay imported from Ireland, and as Irish hay is grown under the influence of heat and moisture brought by the great currents from the tropical ocean, we may truly describe the power by which the London omnibus is drawn as derived, at two removes, from the tropical sun.

But the great industrial revolution and expansion of a hundred years ago was accomplished with the aid of coal, within which is treasured the solar energy of past geological ages. Coal seems to have been first mined on the large scale at Newcastle-on-Tyne, whence it was carried by sea for domestic consumption in London. More than two hundred million tons are now annually raised in Britain. Of this amount nearly one-half is produced in the great central area which includes Manchester, Leeds, and Birmingham. Most of it is consumed on the spot or sent by rail to London. The South Wales and Monmouth coalfield produces rather less than a fifth, much of which is used for the purposes of steam shipping, no small part being exported to foreign countries. Nearly a quarter is raised in Northumberland and Durham, and of this again the greater part is sent by sea either to London or to foreign countries. Scotland produces a little less than South Wales, a portion being sent by sea from Glasgow and from Grangemouth, but the exports are more especially from the smaller coalfield of Fife through the port of Kirkcaldy.

Coal being bulky and heavy, the raw materials of manufacture were at first carried as near as might be to the pit mouth, and the workers were gathered into towns round the collieries. Cotton could be brought to the coal with much greater ease than coal could be taken to the cotton, and therefore in the first quarter of the past century the great textile industry of South Lancashire was developed upon the coalfield of the west Pennine slope, where the moist climate to windward of the range permitted of the working of the longer staple of cotton. With the rise of the industrial population and the increased demand for food came the extension of tillage and pasture in the less favoured region of the north, the advantage of a market at hand compensating for the smaller fertility of the soil and a more rigorous climate.

At the same time the woollen industries which had grown up on the rapid streams of the West Riding, amid the great sheep runs of the upland, were developed by the utilisation of the coalfield of the east Pennine slope, and there gradually came about a decay of the wool industry in other parts of the country. Only in the little group of West of England towns, near the Bristol coalfield, and to some extent in Norfolk, where Newcastle coal was obtainable by water, were small centres of the old industry continued. At Sheffield and at Birmingham, in like manner, pre-existing iron works were developed with the aid of coal, at the expense of the Wealden forges, where the charcoal from the forest was failing.

Glasgow came to be the chief seat of all the industries of the northern kingdom, so that the fertile zone of the Carboniferous Rift valley, in that it combined agriculture with cotton, woollen, and iron manufactures, was transformed into the Scottish equivalent of no less than four English districts—the South-Eastern plain, the Black Country, South Lancashire, and the West Riding.

The difficulty of feeding these increasing aggregations of workers early compelled the construction of canals and paved roads, more especially as the coalfields were in several instances, as in Staffordshire, removed from the immediate neighbourhood of navigable water. The trade of Lancashire depended largely on the Bridgewater Canal, as great an enterprise for the resources of the eighteenth century as the Manchester Ship Canal for those of the nineteenth. Glasgow canalised the Clyde, and the opening of a canal from the Weaver to the North Staffordshire coalfield permitted of the transportation of kaolin from Cornwall, and thus led to the concentration of the potteries round Stoke. But the opening in the year 1825 of the Erie Canal, connecting New York Harbour with the great lakes of North America, produced the vastest results, for it rendered available the great wheat fields of the west, and while developing new markets for manufactured goods, placed new supplies of food at the disposal of the British population.

In the course of the past half century a fundamental change has taken place in the nature of the British industries. Fifty years ago the trade in textiles was all important ; now that in the metals has grown to be equivalent. The present stage of our civilisation is specially characterised by the magnitude and complexity of its implements of steel, whether domestic utensils, tools of husbandry, factory machinery, weapons of warfare, or means of communication. Railways have been built across whole continents ; wooden ships and stone bridges have been replaced by iron, and these in turn by steel ; and paddles have given place to twin screws driven by quadruple expansion engines. Incident to this change has been the growth of the latest centres of population, at Middlesborough in Cleveland and at Barrow-in-Furness, beside great iron deposits, whence half of the British ore is obtained. But the iron of Britain does not suffice for the demand, and the mines of the Biscayan provinces of Spain have been laid under contribution. As these, however, are already approaching exhaustion, a new supply is being sought in Scandinavia. More than half the steel shipbuilding of Britain is now concentrated on the lower reaches of the three Northumbrian rivers, the Tyne, the Wear, and the Tees, the remainder being for the most part divided between the Clyde and Belfast.

Thus while the first effect of the Industrial revolution was to segregate the manufactures upon the several coalfields, withdrawing them from the remainder of the country, the ultimate result has been less conclusive ; for neither Middlesborough, nor Barrow, nor Belfast stand upon the Coal Measures, or even closely adjoin them as do Leeds and Birmingham. New systems of carriage permit of the conveyance of coal either to the site of the raw materials or to the less crowded districts where land and food are cheaper. But the decentralisation of the industries is now in progress on an international scale, as is evidenced by the growing export of coal from the Tyne and South Wales. Coal is now the one great ballast cargo which Britain sends to the outer world in return for such massive imports as wheat, timber, and iron ore.

The map indicative of the varying density of the population may be compared to that which depicts the contrasts of vegetation. The one is a subtle index of the combined effect of all the several elements which go to make climate, the other embodies the summation for the given epoch of complicated economic forces. In each case, however, there is involved an element of momentum, for as forest will often continue to clothe a surface when the conditions have passed which could reproduce forest, so by a parallel process of geographical inertia societies of men will often continue to reside in the accustomed localities when the causes which drew them together have ceased to act. It is only by a composition of such statical and dynamical considerations that we can explain the influence of the environment upon the distribution of a people.

The grouping of the population of Britain was, in the first instance, determined by the relatively slender wants of an agricultural community. The villages and hamlets tend to be ranged in chains, along the outcropping edges of water-bearing strata, or on the courses of brooks (Fig. 113). Country roads, or streams navigable by boats, usually thread these chains, and other similar ways leading to bridges or harbours cross them at points which may be described as *nodal*. The simplest *node* is the " four ways," the Quatre Bras or Carfax, where the publican and the blacksmith set up their signs. But a spot upon which more numerous land and water roads converge, as in a defile past some natural obstacle, may be said to have a higher degree of *nodality*. In proportion to the increase of traffic upon the roads does the nodality of a town at their point of intersection signify. A change in the methods of communication will often reveal fresh nodal properties in an old site. Hence certain places tend to increase in population more rapidly than others by virtue of a process of *geographical selection*. The gap-towns of the North and South Downs are nodal for their several districts, while London and Glasgow have nodality of a more far-reaching value.

It is obvious that modern industrial towns, based on local supplies of mechanical power or of metals, may grow large although lacking much nodality. Barrow and Middlesborough are recent cases in point. But if such communities endure they tend to create a kind of artificial nodality, as has notably happened with the great railway centre of Birmingham. Even London-Westminster, twice made capital because naturally nodal in a high degree, has accumulated from its subsequent momentum a vast added nodality, as the focus of a radial system of paved roads and railways.

Should the significance of a town's nodality decrease, because, for instance, of mechanical inventions, or of new customs barriers, it does not necessarily follow that the town will forthwith degenerate. Much capital expenditure has been irrevocably fixed in it, or in connection with its trade, and great efforts may be put forth to improve its artificial nodality. Thus it may persist by *geographical inertia*, analogous to the mechanical inertia or momentum of a moving object. It is a "going concern" with a goodwill based on the custom of trade, and is worth saving. So, for example, merchants with interests pledged at Bristol, the effect of whose nodality had been lessened by the employment of larger vessels in modern commerce, constructed an outport at Avonmouth that Bristol might still compete with more accessible harbours.

All the more important towns of mediæval Britain had a certain degree of natural nodality. Usually they were of the kind for which Bristol may stand as type. It was the Bricg-stow or "bridge-place" at the head of a navigation available for small sea-going craft. Lincoln, Norwich, and Canterbury were then bridge-seaports, no less than London, York, Rochester, Southampton, Exeter, Gloucester, and Chester ; for the removal of the forests, by permitting of the more violent denudation of the surface, appears to have caused the silting up of the broad channels which, according to historical evidence, once admitted tide-borne shipping to these now inland cities. Even the smaller towns in the heart of the country were seated upon navigable waters, as in the case of the Danish boroughs, Nottingham, Derby, Leicester, and Stamford, and of Oxford, where the London lithsmen, or boatmen, are mentioned in the reign of Canute.[1] The precise position of some towns was no doubt chosen for reasons of defence ; as, for instance, Shrewsbury and Durham built in river-loops closed by castles. London, the city of highest nodality, was the one great centre for the distribution over England of Oriental spices and Flemish cloths. Dublin would to-day hold a comparable position in agricultural Ireland but for the adventitious development of Belfast, based on imported coal.

As evidenced by the great importance of its Trade Guilds, London, owing to its exceptional nodality, was naturally the most convenient residence for the skilled handicraftsmen, who provided the miscellaneous manufactures required for domestic use throughout the land. But in Edwardian times a number of small industrial communities for the manufacture of cloth were founded in subordinate centres, and many of the fine Decorated and Perpendicular churches of our country towns were built with the wealth of clothiers, more particularly in Somerset, and in Norfolk and Suffolk. The almshouses and other charities of such places as Newbury and Reading frequently originated from the same source.

[1] See J. R. Green's "Conquest of England."

A new motive of urban growth was developed with the trade to the Indies and the American plantations. Tea, sugar, and tobacco were introduced under the Stuarts, and gradually came to be counted among the necessities of life. At this time, therefore, the importance of London as a centre of distribution increased, there being com-

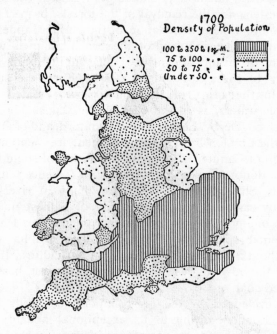

FIG. 129.—The Distribution of Population in South Britain prior to the Industrial Revolution. *From the Census Report of* 1831.

petition only from Bristol, where the Severn offered an estuary open to the west winds, and penetrating, like the Thames, into the zone of maximum density of population (Fig. 129).

With the use of coal for industrial purposes came the rise of a number of large towns whose natural nodality was merely local. Birmingham, Manchester, Leeds, and Sheffield were the first to attain to a relative importance,

and to these must now be added Bradford. In other
cases, however, the new forces merely increased the significance of pre-existing nodal towns. Thus Newcastle, the
bridge-seaport on the Tyne, with a trade in domestic coal
to London, belonged essentially to an earlier period. In
Scotland, where Edinburgh had played the same part of

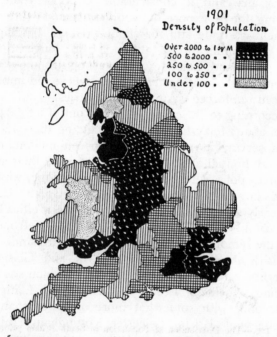

FIG. 130.—The Distribution of Population in South Britain after
the Industrial Revolution.

distributional, administrative, and industrial centre, as had
London in South Britain, Glasgow now developed on the
western ocean ways. Liverpool became rival to Bristol as
the place of import, at first of cotton and then of wheat,
not merely for Manchester, but for all the industrial fields
centred at Manchester, Leeds, Sheffield, and Birmingham
(Fig. 130). Hull, on the other hand, was chiefly engaged

in the export of surplus textiles to the shores of the opposite continent. Even to-day the traffic of Britain to Europe north-eastward of Calais amounts to one-fifth of her total trade. But textiles are now sent to the continent of Europe only in small quantity. London, having been the central market and chief gate of export for the wool of Britain, came naturally to be the market for the wool of Australia, and a considerable entrepot trade arose, involving the re-export of wool for manufacture on the continent—a trade still maintained notwithstanding direct steam communications, although no longer growing. Nottingham and Leicester are striking instances of distributing and administrative centres whose old importance has been reinforced by modern industries.

According to the census of 1901, out of a total population of about forty-two million, including the soldiers and sailors serving abroad, nearly fourteen million, or one-third, are housed in sixteen great cities and their suburbs. The Metropolis with its new outermost zone, which now spreads beyond the Registrar-General's " Greater London," has nearly seven million. The other fifteen cities lie clustered round the Irish Sea, away from the Metropolis and from the remoter belt of the oceanic borderland. Liverpool-Birkenhead, Manchester-Salford, and Glasgow are of the first rank, each having nearly a million souls; Birmingham, Sheffield, Leeds, and Edinburgh-Leith are of the second, with somewhat more or fewer than half a million; while Bristol, Leicester, Nottingham, Hull, Bradford, Newcastle-Gateshead, Dublin, and Belfast are of the third, being of the quarter-million type. Of the four and a half million people in Scotland nearly one-third, or the normal proportion for all Britain, live in the two great urban areas, but in Ireland out of an almost precisely equal population only three-quarters of a million, or approximately one-sixth, are concentrated in the two equivalent areas. A decrease of population appears to be in progress in nearly all the purely rural portions of Britain. In Ireland, which is preponderantly rural, there is a considerable net annual loss notwithstanding the steady growth of Dublin and Belfast, accounted for chiefly by emigration to Great Britain and to America. In Great Britain, however, owing to the rapid develop-. ment of the vast urban population, the net growth has been so large that, despite the shrinkage in Ireland, the increment of the British people has amounted in the last ten years to three and a half million, or half the total of all London.

But two complementary changes, revealed by a comparison of this with the previous census, indicate a tendency which in the course of the next half century may perhaps fundamentally alter the grouping of the population. On the one hand, a zonal disposition of the people is evident in the larger urban communities ; on the other hand, a number of considerable towns, many of them ancient local centres transformed by new industrial activities, are rapidly growing not merely round the coalfields, but scattered over the whole land. Owing to the concentration of affairs towards the heart of each of the great cities, rents have there risen, and it is no longer remunerative to manufacture in the immediate neighbourhood of the exchanges where business is arranged. Southeastern Lancashire is now a single economic unit, of which Manchester is the commercial centre within a vast ring of factory-groups (Fig. 131). In London the conditions are essentially analogous, for the City, nearly co-terminous with the walled London of the Middle Ages, is now inhabited at night time by less than 30,000 people, and in a broad belt of surrounding streets the population is steadily diminishing (Fig. 132). Beyond this, in what were country villages not two centuries ago, is the zone of maximum density of population. Outside again, exhibiting the most rapid increase of population, are the suburbs. Even the coastal pleasure resorts, extending from Southend and Margate to Brighton and Worthing, with an aggregate of several hundred thousand inhabitants, may be considered as a more or less detached rim of the Metropolitan area.

Of the other change, the industrial transformation of

towns, evidence lies in the fact that, except four counties in Wales, and four in England—Westmorland, Rutland, Oxford, and Hereford—every county[1] in South Britain shows an increase of population, although there have been decreases in no fewer than two hundred and fifty out of the six hundred and thirty-five registration districts into which

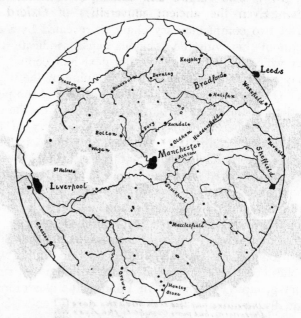

FIG. 131.—The Towns within a radius of thirty-five miles of Manchester. Total Population within the circle, together with Leeds, about eight millions in 1901.

this part of the United Kingdom has been divided. The explanation is to be found in the growth, in the midst of the rural counties, of a number of considerable towns with populations ranging from 30,000 to 200,000 inhabitants. Often the old county towns have been re-energised by industries which might under other conditions have gone to the more densely peopled areas. Instances are Norwich,

[1] *i.e.* Ancient not administrative counties.

Ipswich, Bedford, Reading, and Northampton. Some of the railway towns, such as Swindon and Crewe, essentially inland ports for the building and refitting of trains and for the sorting of passengers and goods, have attained to the same rank. Still larger, however, are Portsmouth, Plymouth - Devonport, and Chatham - Rochester, which have grown with empire and the expenditure on armaments. Even the ancient universities of Oxford and

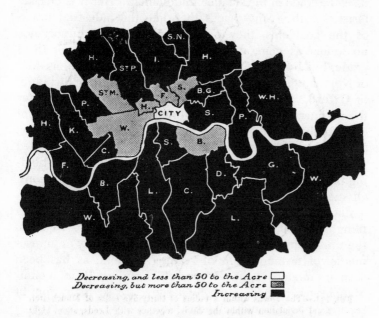

FIG. 132.—The Metropolitan Boroughs and West Ham, showing the small (night) Population of the City, and the Decrease of People in large Areas adjoining, according to the Census of 1901.

Cambridge have attracted to themselves towns of 50,000 inhabitants.

Thus it would appear that the grouping of the British people is entering upon a third stage of development. At first a number of small market-towns, some of them dignified with cathedrals and assize courts, were scattered evenly over all the more fertile parts of the country.

They were local distributive centres at nodal points, subordinate to the great organising focus of London. Then a few of them, placed upon coalfields, grew as though to rival the metropolis, yet possessing no equivalent nodality. And now a certain number of the remainder are being selected for city-growth, while the rest dwindle with the general loss of rural population and the improvement of communication, which tends everywhere to eliminate the trade of the smaller middlemen. But it is characteristic of the rising places that, like the industrial towns of the coalfields, they obtain their renewed importance no longer as general distributors of the second or third grade, but by specialisation of some definite type, as that of Northampton, or Portsmouth, or Brighton, or Swindon, or Oxford. It follows that they are not self-sufficing after the manner of the old market-towns, but must supplement one another, or depend on some vast neighbouring city. Thus a continuous organisation, with clearly articulated parts, is beginning to spread over groups of counties, binding them together into great loosely-knit urban federations. Of such groups there are at least three in Britain, one with a nucleus in London, a second in Manchester and Birmingham, a third in Glasgow and Edinburgh. In each, the unity tends to express itself by a community of amusements, of fashions, and of reading, so that, as has been seen in modern political contests, London, Birmingham-Manchester, and Edinburgh-Glasgow are so many foci of separate political and religious life.

Nor is it likely that the growth of a wider solidarity will cease at the point to which it has attained. The works of the engineer are now on a scale for which no smaller theatre than all Britain will suffice. The uplands of Wales and the North are becoming a national water estate. Already Manchester is served through a hundred miles of aqueduct from Thirlmere in the Lake district; Sheffield, Nottingham, and Derby have a joint water authority for the Peak valleys; and Liverpool has created Lake Vyrnwy in a valley of North Wales. Other moorlands further south are under tribute to Birmingham, and sooner or later London must inevitably obtain at least a supplementary stream from a group of valleys in the south of Wales, by an aqueduct on more than Roman scale. Moreover, we may see a third change in the methods of distributing mechanical power when electricity is used for the purpose of traction through cross-country and not merely suburban distances. Two generations ago men took the raw materials to be manufactured upon the coal-field ; one generation ago they began to carry coal to the deposits of the raw material, or to the cheapest residence for the workers. It now appears likely that they will distil power from coal at the pit mouth, possibly even at the foot of the pit, and convey it electrically whether for the driving of factories or the haulage of trains. Of course the time must come when the hidden reserves of coal, even beneath the later rocks of the plain, shall have been exhausted. It is not, however, quite impossible that Britain should even then retain if not pre-eminence, at least equality, in a world with more evenly diffused industrial activities. A vaster supply of energy .than can be had from the coal of the whole world is to be found in the rise and fall of the tide upon the submerged plateau which is the foundation of Britain. No one has yet devised a satisfactory method of harnessing the tides, but the electric conveyance of power has removed one at least of the impediments, and sooner or later, when the necessity is upon us, a way may be found of converting their rhythmical pulsation into electrical energy. Each of the great railway companies will then seek a terminus upon the ocean, and each inland municipality will have its agency for coastal power. In such a time it is probable that the economic causes amassing vast industrial populations will act with less compulsion than now, and that the distinction between even the continental angle of Britain and its oceanic border will have a diminished significance. But the greater the intricacy of the organism, and the more subtly its organs are correlated, the more essential becomes the control of the brain and subordinate ganglia, and we can hardly foresee any causes, apart from the decay of Britain itself, which shall lead to a failure of the few great nodal communities, and above all of London. Rather must we consider whether, with the more general distribution of industrial activity over all lands, the function of London as chief clearing-house for the adjustment of the world's exchanges will be lost or retained and magnified.

Note on Authorities.—The most generally useful of the annual statistical blue-books is the *Statistical Abstract for the United Kingdom.* The returns of the previous fifteen years are summarised in it, and the striking of averages is thus facilitated. Additional information must be sought in the *Agricultural*, the *Fisheries*, and the *Mines Returns.* Only the *Preliminary Reports* of the Census of 1901 have as yet been issued. On the water-supply, see *The Water-supply of England and Wales* by de Rance.

Note on Fig. 127.—This diagram has been constructed after a map in the *Agricultural Returns of Great Britain.* The acreages in the index refer to county areas. Although proportional statements would have been more satisfactory, yet the map suffices to give a fairly correct impression of the facts.

Note on Fig. 128.—The selection of county units in this as in other cases is necessitated by the form of the available statistics. But, in no small degree, it masks the real contrasts, as, for example, in Perthshire.

Section XII. includes the Counties Antrim, Armagh, Donegal, Down, Derry, and Tyrone. Section XIV. includes the Counties Carlow, Kildare, Kilkenny, King's, Queen's, Tipperary, Wexford, and Wicklow. In the table on p. 322 it has only been possible to make certain typical statements, as the Irish statistics are not published in a form similar to those of Great Britain.

CHAPTER XX

IMPERIAL BRITAIN

THE activities of the British people depend ultimately on the resources of Britain itself, on the fertility of its soil and the energy stored in its coal. But for more than a century past, owing in some degree to the security of insular position, the industries have been developed on a scale out of all proportion to the agriculture, and Britain is no longer a self-sufficing organism. It must exchange a portion of the products of its labour and coal for additional supplies of raw material and food. Such a system of trade is in a sense artificial; it can last only so long as circumstances render it worth the while of the workers to live in Britain rather than at the places where the food and raw material are produced. Fortunately there are causes always in action which counteract sudden change in any established system of trade and industry. For example, capital has of late become relatively cheap in Britain, owing to the long accumulation of savings, and the British capitalist can build factories, lay down machinery, and give credit more easily than he could a hundred years ago. In other words, the industrial organisation of Britain has acquired a great momentum.

A mere surplus of industrial activity would not, however, necessarily impel a nation to win the rights and incur the responsibilities of control over distant peoples. It is only when a state desires to secure or is driven to avert a monopoly of trade in any region, that the imperial motive becomes effective. When Britain was mainly an agricultural land, distant possessions were regarded chiefly from the point of view of the consumer. Territories were acquired in the East and West Indies as estates might be bought for an absentee landlord : they were valued only for their rent of precious metals or slave-grown tropical produce, and the colonists were thought of as merely factors. The monopoly of the East India Company, and the Navigation laws imposed on the North American plantations, were defensible only from this standpoint. But under the conditions obtaining in a modern industrial society, men talk chiefly of. winning and retaining markets where they may dispose of their manufactures, although the real end of their exertions is still, of course, to increase the wealth which is brought into the country. The import and export trades rest in different hands, and the balance-sheet of the nation as regarded by statesmen is a matter of relatively small concern for the individual merchant, or for the more or less organised groups which represent "interests" among the voters. It is, no doubt, true that the measure of our national gain from foreign trade is to be found in imports rather than exports, but the British manufacturer or artisan is more immediately concerned with the foreign markets for his particular textiles or machinery than with the import of wheat and tea. Britain might still be happy with a smaller population, a less import of food, and a less export of manufactured articles, but the process of reduction from the great to the small scale of trade would be painful alike to the employer, who would lose the use of his fixed capital, and to the artisan, who would lose the employment of his skill. Neither capital nor skill could be transported freely and immediately to foreign lands : hence the desire both of capitalists and workmen for foreign markets. This anxiety finds frequent expression in political contests, as in Lancashire in connection with the Indian cotton trade.

Under a condition of universal free trade, the dream of the sixties of the last century, industrial life and empire might be dissociated, but when competing countries seek to monopolise markets by means of customs tariffs, even democracies are compelled to annex empires. Of late, at any rate, the object of the vast British

annexations has been to support a trade open to all the
world. On the other hand, it is difficult to see how
foreign governments, concerned for the maintenance of
the nationality of poorer and continental peoples, can
resist the pressure put upon them for protection against
a trading nation which has insular security and a long
lead in the race. Under a condition of universal free
trade such a nation would almost inevitably increase
its lead, and might ultimately reduce the whole world to
economic subjection. Hence the most important facts of
contemporary political geography are the extent of the
red patches of British dominion upon the map of the
world, and the position of the hostile customs frontiers.
They are the cartographical expression of the eternal
struggle for existence as it stands at the opening of the
twentieth century. The free-trade zones established in
Africa by international agreement, and the idea of the
open door in China, are small indications of what may
prove to be a new trend in international politics, but the
future alone can show whether freedom of trade can be
secured without the assumption of imperial responsibilities.

Trade based merely on an industrial surplus, even if
secured by territorial rights, would tend to increase imports
and exports in somewhat like proportion. Yet the exports
of Britain are very far from balancing the imports. Perhaps
one half of the explanation lies in the fact that British
savings have been spent not merely in the betterment of
Britain itself, and in the increase of its productivity and
amenities, but have also been sent abroad, and the interest
on the capital so invested is annually received in the form
of a share of the harvests and minerals of the countries
improved at British cost. In such transactions, all that
the lender requires is security for the capital and sure
payment of the interest. These can be had wherever
government is stable and wherever honesty has been
recognised as the wisest policy. Lands blessed with such
government are, however, usually wealthy, and give a
return to invested capital at a rate little higher than can
be obtained in Britain itself. But since capital goes from

the lending to the borrowing country not in the shape of gold, which is comparatively useless in a new or barbaric land, but in the shape of steel rails, locomotives, and machinery, there is always on the part of a manufacturing community a motive for advancing loans. Much British capital has therefore been invested where government and morality were less favourable, in Egypt, in China, and in other similar regions. When order breaks down, or foreign interference is threatened in a land in which large British interests are at stake, Britain is often compelled to add to her possessions by assuming authority among an alien and distant population.

The career of annexation once commenced is for reasons of strategy difficult to check. Britain undertook the conquest of India in the course of trade-competition with France; she extended her Indian domain to prevent interference with her rule from without; she became mistress of Egypt and of the Cape because they command the roads to the Indies; she conquered the Sudan for the purpose of ensuring the water supply of Egypt; she has annexed Rhodesia and the Transvaal in order to protect her position at the Cape. Thus, and by similar processes, has Britain incurred vast Imperial responsibilities both in Asia and Africa. Internal and external peace and just administration are the returns made to India for freedom of trade and security of capital.

Not wholly dissimilar from annexed territory is the mercantile and naval shipping which flies the British flag on the high seas. The ocean, covering three-quarters of the globe, is a vast neutral territory controlled only by international law. Beyond the three-mile limit of coastal water, and for some purposes even within it, a ship is a moving island belonging to the state whose flag she bears. On account of the cheapness of capital, and of coal and iron, Britain has become the chief shipbuilder and shipowner of the world, and nearly half of the excess of imports over exports may be accounted for as the incoming profits of the British carrying trade. The mere fact of insular position would not suffice to produce this result. In the Middle Ages British commerce was conveyed in Venetian and Hanseatic vessels, and the profits of the carrying trade went to the alien communities. Before the American Civil War and the introduction of iron ships, the American flag was as frequent in the port of Liverpool as the British. Even at the present time British passengers show small preference for mail steamers of their own nationality if foreign lines happen to offer greater facilities. The vast predominance of the British mercantile marine is of very recent growth, and depends on a delicate balance of economic forces. The command of the sea, in the technical naval sense, would be just as necessary for the effective defence of Britain were her carrying trade smaller, but her fleet would be more difficult to maintain, for the national income would be less.

But the population of Britain has during the last three centuries produced not merely labour, to be embodied in exports, but also a surplus of men who have been driven by economic pressure to found new Britains across the ocean. These are now colonies in the old Greek meaning —independent nations tied to the mother country only by a sense of common ideals. It may be that in the presence of common dangers they are achieving a federal union for the protection of their liberties, but except in so far as she is likely long to remain the predominant partner in the federacy, Britain exercises little imperial control in these white men's lands. And yet, on the whole, over and above alliance in common defence, she derives profit from her daughter states. In Canada and Australia trade has undoubtedly tended to follow the flag, despite the protective tariffs established by practically independent governments. The colonists seek loans from the mother country, and spend the proceeds in the purchase of goods manufactured according to patterns familiar to them and to their fathers.

Thus Empire has for Britain two meanings: the federation, loose or close, of several British commonwealths, and the maintenance of British rule among alien races. The mercantile fleet and the savings ventured in foreign lands may also count among the imperial attributes. For all are ultimately held by naval power. The great creditor nation cannot afford to be weak.

The last of the long series of causes which have woven the complexity of British geography is to be found in the reaction of empire upon the condition of the motherland. It is a gift from the encompassing ocean. Metropolitan England would be poorer but for foreign investments and imperial rule. Industrial England would be less populous were not foreign markets open. Scotland has gained as well from investments as from markets. Even Ireland would find less custom for her agricultural produce were Great Britain more nearly self-sufficing. There are, in fact, in economic theory two mingled, inseparable populations now in these islands. The one is native and lives on the produce of Britain; the other is intrusive and does not depend on food grown at home. This adventitious population either manufactures for export from imported raw materials, or receives interest from foreign countries. The position is masked by the fact that the real owners of much of the imports—holders of foreign stocks and shares, for instance, and those dependent upon them—only touch their property through the intervention of bankers. Cleared from the confusion of ideas introduced by money, the fact is that a part of the British people is entitled to most of the imported food, and that it unconsciously barters a portion of this for some of the home-grown produce.

It would be impossible accurately to dissociate purely industrial from imperial gains; but some rough conclusions may perhaps be drawn from a statement in round figures of Britain's annual dealings with the world beyond the seas. On an average of ten recent years the value of the imports has amounted to four hundred and forty millions, and of the exports to three hundred and ten millions, showing an excess of imports to the extent of one hundred and thirty millions. Certain preliminary deductions may be made from both sides of the account. About sixty millions of colonial produce is re-exported without change, and an unknown sum, say fifty millions,[1] represents imported raw materials embodied in exported manufactures. Adjusted by these deductions, the imports would stand at three hundred and thirty millions and the exports at two hundred millions. Of the latter more than twenty millions represent exported coal, and nearly all the remainder manufactured articles. The excess of one hundred and thirty millions' worth of imports is to be reckoned as being payment of interest on foreign investments to the extent of about sixty millions ; freight earned by shipping, about another sixty millions ; and commissions obtained, chiefly by the city of London, for international banking, the remaining ten millions. Thus the ledger of Britain in account with the outer world would annually stand somewhat thus :—

Dr.			*Cr.*	
IMPORTS.		*£* Millions	PAYMENT FOR IMPORTS.	*£* Millions
For home consumption		330	By manufactures . . . 230	
For re-export—			Less embodied raw	
Unmanufactured .	60		materials 50	
In manufactures .	50			180
		110	By coal	20
				200
			By external credits—	
			Freight 60	
			Interest . . . 60	
			Commission . . . 10	
				130
			By re-exports—	
			As *per contra*	110
		440		440

Were any large repayment of capital included in the imports, this statement would be invalid, but the results obtained in a number of years do not give ground for the suspicion that British investments are being seriously

[1] See note at p. 352.

reduced. After making due allowance for the embodied value of raw material, about seventy out of the two hundred. millions' worth of exports are sent to the British possessions; and indicate the demand which arises either from India, under a condition of imposed free trade, or from white colonists, because of trust and predilection which naturally turn homeward. On the whole, then, it would not be unfair to credit the imperial connection with nearly half the exports, most of the freight and interest, and—in view of the sum of sixty millions for re-export of colonial produce—with no small share of the commissions. Therefore, of the three hundred and thirty millions of imports, perhaps three-fifths, or two hundred millions, would be a reasonable proportion to attribute to the Empire. It is obvious that the data upon which this result has been based are in several instances merely rough assumptions, and probably no two persons would agree as to the precise value of imperial support and protection in any given transaction. Yet some such calculation is the essential basis of any true judgment regarding British policy.

The effects of Empire are not, however, wholly economic; for good or for bad they are also moral. Most British families, whether rich or poor, have relatives in the colonies, and a widened outlook is the consequence. But in addition to colonists, properly so-called, and to mercantile agents within the tropics, there are in Asia and Africa at least ten thousand officers, civil and military, drawn largely from the middle classes, yet accustomed to the rule of subject races and to the thoughts of statesmen. They and those connected with them help to imbue British society with a tone of detachment which undoubtedly contributes to the morality of our rule and counteracts the lower impulse of commercial gain. At home, on the other hand, within the three seas, where a standing army has ever been regarded with suspicion, there is a sense of democratic equality before the law which is wholly antagonistic to the paternal attitude even of the nobler imperial rule. The clash of these two motives, the democratic and the imperial, has imparted a singular richness and resource to the modern British nation, and a basis for party struggle on a high plane. At the same time it has given fair ground for the foreign charge of hypocrisy, one-half of the nation seeming always to contradict the views of the other, so that uneasy compromise, the squaring of the national conscience, is often a necessary incident in the determination of policy. It is fortunate, however, that the struggle is never likely to end in the permanent victory of the imperial idea; for of all empires in the world's history, the British is probably the best calculated to preserve the dominant nation from the destruction of its own liberties. The intervening ocean holds wide apart the masses of the ruling and of the subject peoples.

The imperial tribute annually received by Britain is not a net income, since empire is costly. While the receipts on account of the Empire may, as we have seen, amount to some two hundred millions a year, the annual cost of the navy and army, in peace time, and of the debt incurred in winning and defending the Empire, exceeds seventy millions. Yet a portion of this expense may fairly be set down to the defence of the home land, owing to the peculiar nature of maritime empire. The British fleet in the Mediterranean, based on the diminutive territories of Malta and Gibraltar, is one of the most extraordinary instances of detached imperial power to be found in all history. The ships are there primarily, no doubt, for the defence of the road to India, but owing to the fact that both France and Russia have coasts on the Northern Seas and on the Mediterranean, the British Mediterranean fleet acts incidentally for the defence of London. Were Malta abandoned and the ships withdrawn to the English Channel, France and Russia would be free to concentrate a larger part of their naval strength in northern waters. Thus the Mediterranean fleet, while maintaining the imperial road, subserves also the purpose of the

defence of the island. Owing to the continuity of the
ocean and to the consequent mobility of sea power, the
same may be said of every British squadron, whether
in the Indian Ocean, at the Cape, in the China Seas, in
the Australian Seas, off the Pacific Coast of America, in
the West Indies, or at the Falkland Islands. The strength
of each is adjusted to the number of foreign ships in
the same waters, because each foreign ship in a distant
sea is absent from the neighbourhood of Britain itself.
Even the army in India, maintained always on a war
footing, is a school for the training of officers and men,
who, on their return to Britain, form reserves, whether
officially recognised or not, tending to reduce the risk
of invasion, and helping to avert the political dangers of
a great standing army at home.

In every empire there are elements of instability. No
state is so safe as that which rests wholly on the cultivation
of its own territory. Foreign markets may be lost, and
employment for British workmen reduced : capital may
be repaid by debtor countries, and the annual interest
may cease to be received : the carrying trade may dwindle,
and shipping be transferred to other flags : the preference
of later generations of colonists may grow weaker, and
they may buy more impartially from the competitors of
the mother country : finally, the coalfields at home may
be exhausted, and no fresh supply of energy be available.
Grown poorer, Britain may no longer have the means of
building and maintaining an adequate fleet, and may
lose command of the sea. Other empires have had their
day, and so may that of Britain. But there are facts in
the present condition of humanity which render such a
fate unlikely, provided always that the British race retain
its moral qualities. The world has lately seen a rapid
expansion of the theatre of international politics. The
European phase of history is passing away, as have passed
the Fluviatile and Mediterranean phases. A new balance
of power is being evolved, and already there are only five
great world-states, Britain, France, Germany, Russia, and

America. By their expansion they have all given hostages
for peace. France and Germany must maintain great
armies, and cannot afford supreme fleets, although possessed of vulnerable colonies. The United States has
sacrificed an impregnable isolation, and must see to the
defence of the ocean paths to her new possessions. Even
Russia has come down to the coast at points accessible to
sea power. One and all they have emerged from continental seclusion, and have made themselves neighbours
of the new Britains in the ocean. The North American
colonists did not revolt against England so long as
there were French rivals on the St. Lawrence and
Mississippi. In like manner foreign dominion in Africa
and the China Seas may prove to be the most effective
cement of the incipient British Federation. All the
Britains are threatened by the recent expansion of
Europe, and therefore all may be ready to share in the
support of the common fleet, as being the cheapest method
of ensuring peace and freedom to each. Thus the chief
danger of the Empire may be averted, and the old Britain,
when unable to maintain from her own resources a navy
equivalent to those of the United States and Russia, after
they shall have developed their vast natural potentialities,
may still find secure shelter behind the navy of the
Britains.

One ultimate consideration remains to be set against
the risks of the Empire. We must not exaggerate the
economic reaction of the outer possessions on the home
country itself. The total income of the British people
is estimated at from sixteen hundred to two thousand
millions a year. Of this sum not much more than three
hundred and thirty millions is due to net foreign imports.
The chief asset of Britain is still, therefore, the British
Isles, improved from prairie value by the vast toil of a
hundred generations, and capable with the advance of
knowledge and the investment of capital, of yet further
improvement and of a larger productivity. Even if
imperial ties were loosened, Britain would still be rich ;
perhaps, with the general growth of the resources of

humanity, actually, although not relatively, richer than to-day. But the aspect of national life and the distribution of the population would certainly be other than they are now, for Metropolitan England owes much of its governmental and financial activity, and no small part of its residential character, to the imperial rank of London, while Industrial England and Scotland have many trades adapted to the special demands of foreign markets.

Note on Authorities.—The subject of the excess of imports over exports has been dealt with more than once by Sir Robert Giffen, especially in a paper on " The Excess of Imports," published in the *Jour. Roy. Statistical Soc.*, vol. lxii., p. 1. The total income of the nation has been discussed by Giffen in his *Essays in Finance*, 2nd series, " The Growth of Capitalism."

CHAPTER XXI

SUMMARY AND CONCLUSION

"Britain is a world by itself."
—*Cymbeline*, iii. 1.

LET us now set together some of the typical results of this discussion of British geography, and inquire what broad conclusion may be drawn.

1. From two historic view-points the natural features of Britain are seen in two different perspectives. Approached overland from the south-east, from the great continent, the elements of the foreground are the Strait of Dover, the Kentish promontory, the Thames estuary, and the English plain. From these the landways radiate to the uplands of the oceanic border. Approached, however, from the south-west, over the seas, the significant features are the Channel Entries, whence divergent waterways penetrate between the lands.

2. This intersection of land and sea connections—of richest historical import—has a physical meaning, for the conformation of the neighbouring land of Scandinavia is analogous. There also, outer and higher Norway is in contrast with inner and lower Sweden, and the peninsulating Baltic is entered from the south-west. Northern Europe, in fact, has a raised broken rim, more or less detached from the mainland by seas branching from the ocean.

3. Such a description of the superficial outline is justified and reinforced by the shallowness of the Narrow and Baltic Seas, and by the continuity of the edge of the great shoal off Britain and Norway. Moreover, the fringe of headlands along the west coast of Scotland, and the lie of Glenmore and the Rift Valley, betoken a south-westerly

rock-graining, to be interpreted as the wreck of a Caledonian mountain range, which once crossed the site of the North Sea.

4. But the existing hills have not been shaped from the Caledonian peaks by uninterrupted erosion. The general equivalence of the higher summits, and the transverse, southerly trend of the consequent valleys, where they breach the ridges, can only be explained by the interpolation of an epoch during which the mountains were reduced to a basal plane. Thence followed a fresh cycle of denudation when this plane was raised to a grained plateau spreading back from the British uplands towards Iceland and Greenland.

5. By what process this plateau of Atlantis collapsed, and the uplands of its south-eastward face were transferred to developing Europe, may be imagined from the form of the ocean bed. Two abysmal pits, Atlantic and Arctic, gradually encroached upon the land until they merged across it, and the divide between them became the submarine isthmus known as the Scoto-Icelandic Rise. The southward belt of median uplands in Britain—Highland, Central, and Cambrian—is in prolongation of this rise, and no doubt due to the same terrestrial stresses.

6. Britain was differentiated from the rest of the slope of Atlantis by the formation of proto-Britain, in advance of the Caledonian shore line. Against the resistance of this salient block the Hercynian pressures crumpled the strata into northward and westward folds: these, together with the earlier south-westward features, have determined the triangular outline of Britain.

7. By their intersection the Hercynian axes also shaped the coal-basins of Great Britain. But Ireland, under the lee of proto-Britain, suffered less disturbance, and has therefore been stripped of most of its coal, unsheltered from denudation.

8. The posthumous Hercynian uplift, by raising the Wealden fold, produced an organic connection between the Kentish promontory and the Rhine-Seine divide. The English plain of softer rocks is, therefore, a segment of the

coastal plain of Atlantis, preserved and brought into European relations by subsequent events.

9. The broad north-eastward ocean-channel which has
replaced Atlantis, determines the climatic conditions of
Britain, by inducing in the atmosphere a corresponding
north-eastward gulf of winter warmth and moisture.
Therefore the iceless sea, and the cyclonic procession off
the open shores of Ireland and Scotland, may be regarded
as proceeding from the same events which cut short the
oceanic uplands and beheaded the consequent rivers of
Britain.

10. And as the northward belt of median uplands and
the Scoto-Icelandic Rise intersect the trend of the north-
eastward oceanic border, so the rain-shadow, extending
into Scotland under the eastern lee of the Highlands,
lies obliquely to the most frequented path of the cyclones.
Thus the climatic contrasts of Britain harmonise with its
structure.

11. The same is true of the anthropic aspects of
British geography. The east side of the Hercynian triangle
is opposed to the Baltic lands, and the south side—through
Gaul and the gap between the Pyrenees and the Alps—
to the Mediterranean lands. Upon these two sides are
based the northward spread of the darker men in Britain,
and the westward spread of the lighter.

12. But the contrasted radial advance of conquerors
from the Kentish angle to the oceanic border is illustrated
by the terminal remnants of Celtic speech.

13. The four parts of the realm are structural no less
than historic units. Wales is in some degree a remainder
of the proto-British land-block. The three kingdoms,
prior to the industrial revolution, were in essence three
lowlands, sundered by march-belts of barren upland and
sea-channel.

14. The English lowland consists of the soft, tilted,
overlapping strata characteristic of a coastal plain. It
was marginal to Atlantis, but was extended towards
Europe by the Wealden uplift. Beneath is a buried floor
with coal basins emergent along the north-western edge.

The European climatic system frequently overspreads it. Its chief properties are therefore breadth, arable fertility, and potentially of mechanical power—fit bases for the growth of the predominant partner in the union of kingdoms.

15. Ireland, on the other hand, has a pre-Hercynian plain, preserved by proto-Britain, consisting of almost undisturbed strata, which lap round emergent, ancient bosses of upland. The coal has been removed from above this plain by denudation. The soil has usually fewer constituents than in England ; and the climate is oceanic, hence the surface is generally of meadow and bog.

16. The Scottish plain is smallest of the three, merely the floor of a valley, rifted into the median belt of upland. But it has stored coal, and on the lee side rewards tillage.

17. The sites of the three capitals strikingly exhibit the effect of these contrasts. London, in the continental angle, but not far removed from the midst of the English lowland, is a focus of many ways radiating freely over the plain. The most important is that which enters through Kent, and leaves through the Cheshire gap, which is itself a legacy from the old Hebridean Gulf.

18. Dublin, opposite to Cheshire, is in the broad coastal entry of Meath, whence roads diverge northward, westward, and southward, through gaps among the isolated uplands.

19. Edinburgh is in the defile between the Pentlands and the coast, at the head of the sill-entry to the enwalled Rift Valley.

20. Finally, a vast imperial nodality has been accumulated in London during the centuries of oceanic mobility.

As the trend of this argument is surveyed, may we not conclude that on the whole the same geographical features are important whether measured by historical or by physical standards ? And are not the topographical monuments of geological revolution among the causes of analogous revolution in history ? The structural slope of

Britain inward towards Europe is an expression of growth from the northern Atlantis : the whole recent history of mankind would have been other than it has been, were the landward angle of England divided from the continent by a channel rifted through uplands. To the existence of proto-Britain, and to rock movements in the vast Hercynian crises, is due the triangular outline of Britain, resulting in that insulation without isolation which has made of the British state at once " a world by itself " and a great European Power. Moreover, the Industrial Revolution of English history could never have been accomplished unless preceded by the Hercynian Revolution, for the coal upon which the one change rested was preserved in the process of the other. By dividing the Seine and Rhine basins, and by accentuating the saliency of England towards the continent, the Wealden uplift has emphasised the contrast of the Romance and Teutonic influences which have interacted in British society. The great encroachment of the ocean behind the uplands of the north-west has determined the climate, and so permitted of the pastoral and maritime activities of Britain, notwithstanding the poleward latitude. Finally, the long brink of the submarine 'platform, by checking the advance of the oceanic tides, has originated the tidal currents of the Narrow Seas. It is not unlikely that the completion of British insularity by the broadening of Dover Strait was due to the scour of these currents when reinforcing wind-waves which had otherwise no great potency.

There is, however, a noteworthy, though inevitable and connected, inversion of the physical and historical relations of Britain. The British Isles have been built from a north-western foundation, but the British people and realm have grown in the main from south-eastern roots. By a progressive physical change, Britain has been transferred from Atlantis to Europe : by an inverse, but analogous, change the British community has passed from dependence upon continental Europe to be the outpost of the new Europe beyond the ocean. A constant recipient from the gifted races of the neighbouring continent, it has been the special function of the insular nation to convey to the outer lands what was best not merely in British but in European civilisation.

By virtue of her neighbourhood to the Continent, Britain is at the end of the Old World; by virtue of the ocean-arm which isolates her from the Continent, she is at the beginning of the New. Dover belongs to the New World, yet Liverpool is still of the Old. Geographical position has thus given to Britain a unique part in the world's drama. But the end of her history must depend on the ethical condition of her people, on their energy, knowledge, honesty, and faith. For the permanent facts of physical geography now bear a proportion to political organisation differing widely from that borne when England was making. In the presence of vast Powers, broad-based on the resources of half continents, Britain could not again become mistress of the seas. Much depends on the maintenance of a lead won under earlier conditions. Should the sources of wealth and vigour upon which the navy is founded run dry, the imperial security of Britain will be lost. From the early history of Britain herself it is evident that mere insularity gives no indefeasible title to marine sovereignty. In this respect the present situation is analogous to the condition which has here been described as of geographical inertia. It is the great opportunity of human initiative. The whole course of future history depends on whether the Old Britain beside the Narrow Seas have enough of virility and imagination to withstand all challenge of her naval supremacy, until such time as the daughter nations shall have grown to maturity, and the British Navy shall have expanded into the Navy of the Britains.

INDEX

THE END

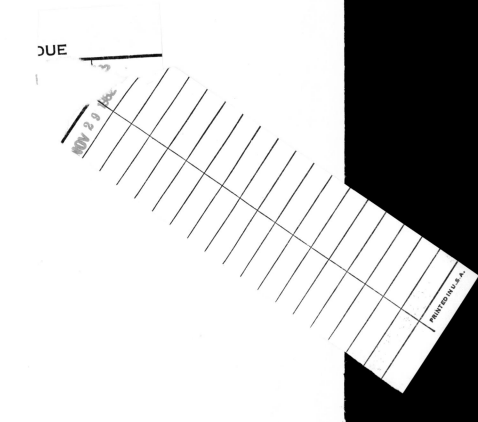